MW01287105

Mexico's Continental Divide Trail

THE OFFICIAL GUIDE

TEXT BY
BOB JULYAN

PHOTOGRAPHY BY
TOM TILL
AND **WILLIAM STONE**

The official guidebook of the
Continental Divide Trail Alliance.

www.westcliffepublishers.com

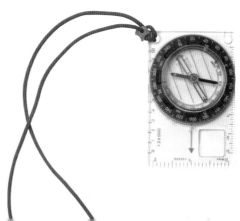

Table of Contents

For more information about other fine books and calendars from Westcliffe Publishers, please contact your local bookstore, call us at 1-800-523-3692, write for our free color catalog, or visit us on the Web at **www.westcliffepublishers.com**

PLEASE NOTE:
Risk is always a factor in backcountry and high-mountain travel. Many of the activities described in this book can be dangerous, especially when weather is adverse or unpredictable, and when unforeseen events or conditions create a hazardous situation. The author has done his best to provide the reader with accurate information about backcountry travel, as well as to point out some of its potential hazards. It is the responsibility of the users of this guide to learn the necessary skills for safe backcountry travel, and to exercise caution in potentially hazardous areas. The author and publisher disclaim any liability for injury or other damage caused by backcountry traveling, mountain biking, or performing any other activity described in this book.

COVER PHOTO:
Ghost Ranch buttes and badlands, Ghost Ranch.
Photo by Tom Till.

OPPOSITE: Chimney Rock, Ghost Ranch.
Photo by Tom Till.

INTERNATIONAL STANDARD BOOK NUMBER:
1-56579-331-5

TEXT COPYRIGHT:
Bob Julyan. 2001. All rights reserved.

PHOTOGRAPHY COPYRIGHT:
Tom Till. 2001. All rights reserved.
William Stone. 2001. All rights reserved.

EDITOR:
Jennifer Blakebrough-Raeburn

DESIGN AND PRODUCTION:
Rebecca Finkel, F + P Graphic Design, Inc.

PRODUCTION MANAGER:
Craig Keyzer

PUBLISHED BY:
Westcliffe Publishers, Inc.
P.O. Box 1261
Englewood, Colorado 80150
www.westcliffepublishers.com

Printed in China
through World Print

LIBRARY OF CONGRESS CATALOGING-IN-PUBLICATION DATA:
Julyan, Bob.
    New Mexico's Continental Divide Trail : the official guide / text by Bob Julyan ; photography by Tom Till & William Stone.
        p.   cm.
    Includes bibliographical references and index.
    ISBN: 1-56579-331-5
        1. Hiking—New Mexico—Guidebooks. 2. Hiking—Continental Divide National Scenic Trail—Guidebooks. 3. New Mexico—Guidebooks. 4. Continental Divide National Scenic Trail—Guidebooks. I. Title.

GV199.42.N6 J83 2000
917.8904'54—dc21   00-023499

Preface   by Bob Julyan

First, I must tell you that in doing the fieldwork for this book, I didn't tackle the
Continental Divide Trail in New Mexico as a thru-hiker. I say that with a certain
sense of regret—but not much, really. Whenever I considered doing a thru-hike,
life always seemed to shout in my ear, "Are you kidding? Get real, you dreamer."

Eventually, I had to abandon the idea of a thru-hike, at least at this stage in
my life; and to my surprise, the letting go was far easier than I'd expected. For one thing,
I recognized and accepted that I don't have the temperament of a thru-hiker. With time,
my hiking has changed; I'm now more of a dawdler. I like to linger, arrive in camp early,
leave late, poke around. For most thru-hikers, such luxuries steal too much time from
the hike.

Not basing this guide upon my personal thru-hike allowed me to sample the
multiplicity of CDT routes in New Mexico and to gain the perspective of other hikers,
as well as that of land managers. I have based this guide on these premises:

- The CDT accommodates many users—hikers, equestrians, mountain-bikers.
  And even within these groups, considerable diversity exists. Some hikers, for
  example, will embark upon the full 3,100 miles from Mexico to Canada; others
  will attempt only the New Mexico section; still others will tackle two- or three-
  day backpack trips in selected portions, such as the San Pedro Wilderness, the
  Continental Divide Wilderness Study Area, or the crest of the Black Range in
  the Aldo Leopold Wilderness. Some will enjoy day hikes along such stretches
  as the Ojitos Trail in the Chama River Canyon Wilderness, the Zuni-Acoma
  Trail in El Malpais National Monument, on the Jacks Peak Trail in the Burro
  Mountains, and the Gila National Forest. And some users may not travel on it
  at all but prefer to picnic beside it or even simply read about it at home.

- Throughout its length, and certainly in New Mexico, the CDT is a work in
  progress, with changes taking place even as this book goes to press—and the
  changes will continue. Thus, it remains the responsibility of hikers to contact
  land-management agencies for the most current information.

- As a corollary of the above, the CDT for the foreseeable future will present a
  menu of alternative routes rather than being a single route. Some users will
  travel in leisurely fashion on a cross-country trail, while others, pressed for time,
  will push forward on a more direct, primitive road.

*Castle of the Chama ruins at sunset above confluence of Rio Chama and Rio Gallinas,
Santa Fe National Forest. Photo by William Stone.*

- Despite a seemingly chaotic, anarchic situation, a core route nonetheless exists; this route has been identified by the federal land-management agencies (mandated by Congress) to create and maintain the CDT. Although other visions of the CDT exist, this book focuses on and reflects the most recent status of the routes currently identified and endorsed by the agencies charged with administering the CDT.

- The CDT is as much a process as a product. Sure, hiking the CDT is exciting and satisfying, but so is working on the trail—identifying routes, building cairns, creating tread, etc. I've hiked large stretches of the CDT in New Mexico over the years and enjoyed it, but I hold among my fondest memories the time I spent with a group of young AmeriCorps volunteers as we scraped out tread in the Black Range for two cold November days. That and the time I joined some fellow New Mexico Mountain Club members erecting cairns on a stretch of the Bureau of Land Management's (BLM) Rio Puerco lands. Satisfying, rewarding —and just plain fun. I know what Paula Ward of the Continental Divide Trail Alliance (CDTA) was feeling when she said, "Nothing touches my heart more than when people show up to work on the CDT."

- Because hiking is more than just putting one foot in front of the other to reach a destination or attain a mileage quota, I've included information about the history, human and natural, that you'll encounter along the trail. I like to know as much as possible about the terrain through which I'm hiking, and I expect most of you do, too.

I like to think that by staying fit yet not turning into an ironman; by enjoying hiking and camping yet not doing them for months at a time; and by appreciating the grandeur of the Continental Divide yet not hesitating to pause and watch the tarantula sharing the Divide with me, I probably typify the majority of people who, along with the thru-hikers, share the CDT.

Rio de las Vacas and meadow fog in early morning, San Pedro Parks Wilderness.
Photo by William Stone.

This book is for Virginia, my sister, with fond memories of love, loyalty, and laughter.

—BOB JULYAN

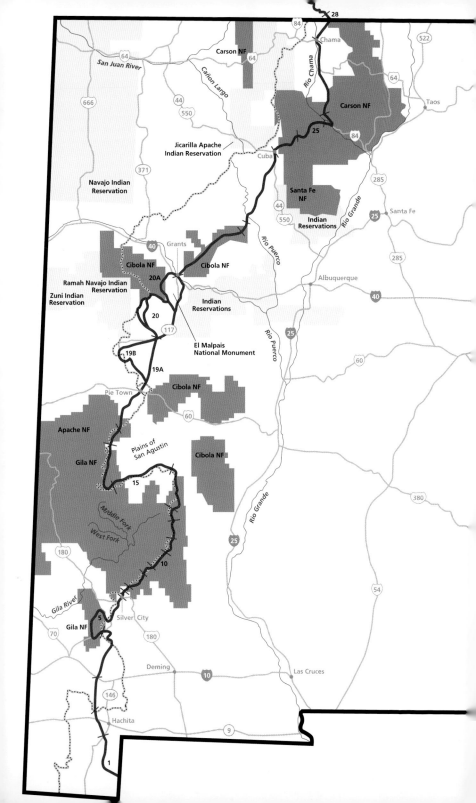

CONTINENTAL DIVIDE TRAIL
SEGMENTS 1–28

Continental Divide Trail
(segments)

Continental Divide

River

Road

City or Town

National Forest

Indian Reservation

Segments Chart

SEGMENT	STARTING POINT	ENDING POINT	DIFFICULTY
1	Mexican Border	NM 81	strenuous
2	NM 81	NM 9	moderate
3	NM 9	Separ	easy
4	Separ	NM 90	easy
5	NM 90	Silver City	moderate to strenuous
6	Silver City	Forest Road 506 (Little Walnut Road)	easy
7	Forest Road 506 (Little Walnut Road)	NM 15	easy to moderate
8	NM 15	NM 35	strenuous
9	NM 35	Forest Road 150	moderate to strenuous
10	Forest Road 150	Reeds Peak	strenuous
11	Reeds Peak	Diamond Peak	strenuous
12	Diamond Peak	Lookout Mountain	strenuous
13	Lookout Mountain	NM 59	moderate
14	NM 59	NM 163	moderate
15	NM 163	Coyote Peak Stock Tank	strenuous
16	Coyote Peak Stock Tank	NM 12	strenuous
17	NM 12	Valle Tio Vences Campground	easy
18	Valle Tio Vences Campground	Pie Town	moderate to strenuous
19A	Pie Town	NM 117	moderate
19B	Pie Town	NM 117	moderate
20	NM 117	Grants	varies
20A	NM 53	Grants	easy
21	Grants	Forest Road 239A	strenuous
22	BLM 1103 (Forest Road 239A)	Mesa Chivato Escarpment	easy
23	Mesa Chivato Escarpment	Cuba	strenuous
24	Cuba	NM 96	moderate
25	NM 96	Skull Bridge	moderate to strenuous
26	Skull Bridge	US 84	easy
27	US 84	Chama	moderate
28	Chama	Cumbres Pass	easy

MILEAGE	TOTAL ELEV. GAIN (FEET)	TRAILHEAD ACCESS	MTN. BIKE DIFFICULTY	PAGE	SEGMENT
28	2,342	rough road	non-technical/ prohibited	50	1
18.6	1,053	paved road	technical	62	2
20.25	171	paved road	technical	70	3
35.2	1,400	paved road	non-technical	78	4
24.25	2,655	paved road	technical	86	5
12.4	978	paved road	non-technical	94	6
8.2	1,569	graded or paved road	technical	98	7
21.3	5,113	paved road	non-technical	104	8
13.5	2,297	graded or paved road	prohibited/ non-technical	112	9
14.5	4,041	graded or rough road and hiking	non-technical	120	10
9.5	2,639	hiking or rough road	prohibited	130	11
15.8	2,946	hiking or horseback	technical	136	12
12.25	1,222	graded or paved road	non-technical	144	13
25.8	2,127	graded or paved road	not ridable	150	14
32.5	3,399	graded road	prohibited	156	15
52.25	7,802	graded road	not ridable/ non-technical	166	16
11.2	1,513	graded or paved road	non-technical	178	17
28.8	2,125	graded road	non-technical	184	18
31.6	321	paved road	non-technical	194	19A
48.3	984	paved road	non-technical	204	19B
0.7 (varies)	varies	paved road	technical/ non-technical	208	20
25.75	973	paved road	non-technical	224	20A
48.2	4,273	paved road	technical/ non-technical	230	21
8.9	979	graded road	non-technical	244	22
46.1	2,736	graded or paved road and hiking	non-technical	250	23
26	3,904	paved road	prohibited	262	24
20.2	1,730	graded or paved road	non-technical	274	25
10.7	506	graded or paved road	non-technical	284	26
44	5,471	paved road	non-technical	290	27
11.25	1,250	paved road	non-technical	300	28

Introduction

The Continental Divide has been called the Western Hemisphere's dominant feature. Running from Alaska's Bering Strait approximately 8,000 miles south to the tip of Patagonia in South America, the Continental Divide, with the authority of an absolute monarch, parts the waters of two continents, dictating into which ocean even the mightiest rivers shall flow. No other divide on earth holds such sovereignty over so vast a realm.

Few divides anywhere are so capricious and complex in their wanderings. For example, the popular notion that the Divide separates the waters of North and South America into either the Atlantic or Pacific Ocean isn't quite accurate. Sure, that's true for South America and for most of North America, but where the Continental Divide begins at Wales at the tip of Alaska's Seward Peninsula, it runs east-west, along the Brooks Range, and the separation lies between the Pacific Ocean and the frozen Arctic Ocean. Indeed, not until Yukon Territory in Canada does the Continental Divide end its northwest course and begin the generally north-south orientation that it will keep all the way to Patagonia.

The key word is "generally," for the Continental Divide, like a tourist with lots of time, follows a meandering course as it heads south and crosses valleys winding from mountain range to mountain range. It even splits twice—one of those splits in New Mexico. As the National Geographic Society writer Michael Robbins observed: "The flat zone southeast of Silver City is one of only two known places along the Divide where the water doesn't divide but instead goes into a kind of hydrologic 'black hole.' It simply disappears underground."

Native Americans surely knew of the line that divided watersheds, and they surely knew this line did not end abruptly but that it continued. And perhaps, despite their parochial knowledge of New World geography, they even sensed its continental significance: The Blackfoot Indians of northern Montana called the Continental Divide the "Center of the World."

The American explorers, trappers, gold-seekers, and settlers who headed west in the 1800s spoke of this continent-cleaving height-of-land. They called it the Great Divide and regarded it as a momentous milestone on their treks. But the Spaniards—the Europeans who preceded the Americans in the West by 200 years—had little or no awareness of the Continental Divide. For one thing, their explorations had a north-south orientation. Their main route into the Southwest was along the Rio Grande, a north-south-flowing river. When they left the Rio Grande to head west, they encountered an arid landscape in which a continental watershed divide was anything but conspicuous. The streams that existed tended to flow southeast or southwest—and many streams never made it to any ocean; they simply sank into the desert.

THE CONTINENTAL DIVIDE IN NEW MEXICO

Even today, the Continental Divide in New Mexico presents an underwhelming physical presence. Sure, with a length of approximately 700 miles, it is by far the state's longest linear feature. But travelers on Interstate 10 in the south, Interstate 40 in the central part of

Aerial view of rugged mesas near Acoma Pueblo, Acoma Reservation. Photo by Tom Till.

the state, and NM 44/US 550 in the north must rely upon highway signs to inform them that they've crossed the Divide.

Michael Robbins wrote: "The Continental Divide is a matter of water. It is also an idea, at once a geographer's abstract concept and a solid reality. It is a dashed line on maps of the West, and a place high in the mountains where you can stand and watch waters part at your feet." That certainly is true, but I doubt Robbins had New Mexico in mind when he wrote that. In few other places does the Continental Divide less fit the stereotype of a continent-splitting mountain crest than in New Mexico; here the Divide resembles that image only in the remote, all-but-inaccessible Animas Mountains and the equally remote Black Range. Indeed, at least one book about the Continental Divide didn't even include New Mexico but stopped at the Colorado border! That was unfortunate, because it's the *Continental* Divide; as such, it includes the continent's rich ecological diversity. And diversity—ecological, cultural, historical—is New Mexico's greatest asset.

State boosters proudly point out that New Mexico has six of North America's seven life zones, lacking only the tropical zone (during the state's "monsoon season" some hikers might even include that!). From torrid, arid deserts of cactus and mesquite, the home of Gila monsters and javelinas, to high conifer forests inhabited by beaver and elk, the Continental Divide Trail in New Mexico winds through them all.

The highest point on the Continental Divide and the CDT is 14,270-foot Grays Peak in central Colorado's Front Range. In New Mexico, the highest point on the Continental Divide is 10,244-foot Alegres Mountain in southwestern New Mexico, but the CDT runs elsewhere. The New Mexico CDT's highest point is either 11,301-foot Mount Taylor or, if you accept the Forest Service's proposed detour around Mount Taylor, 10,015-foot Reeds Peak at the crest of the Black Range.

The lowest point on the Continental Divide in the United States occurs in the Playas Valley south of Lordsburg, where the Continental Divide descends to 4,460 feet. The lowest point on the CDT, however, occurs almost 200 feet lower, at 4,280 feet, where the CDT begins at Tierra Común on the U.S.–Mexican border.

"WHY ISN'T THE CONTINENTAL DIVIDE TRAIL ON THE CONTINENTAL DIVIDE?"
That's the most common question hikers and non-hikers alike ask about the CDT in New Mexico—and it's a legitimate question. After all, how can it be the "Continental Divide Trail" when any congruence between the trail and the actual Continental Divide seems purely coincidental?

Well, it's not quite that bad, but the inescapable reality is that the CDT in New Mexico rarely follows the actual physical Divide, the line that parts the waters. Indeed, if you were thru-hiking the CDT in New Mexico from north to south along the official route, you wouldn't set foot on the physical Divide until you crossed it on NM 53, west of El Malpais National Monument and south of Grants—halfway down the state!

In New Mexico, land ownership governs the route of the CDT. In the south, for example, soon after crossing the Mexican border, the Divide runs north over the crest of the Animas Mountains. These mountains lie within the former Gray Ranch, now managed for long-term ecological research by the Animas Foundation. For a variety of reasons, the Foundation resolutely forbids hiking on its lands. Thus, in southern New Mexico, CDT hikers must depart from the Divide itself right from the get-go.

Most people express curiosity about this lack of congruence, but are not overly bothered by it. After all, the Divide in most of New Mexico is hardly a dramatic knife-edge ridge as it is in, say, parts of Colorado. In New Mexico, you can stand on the Divide and not have any sense of being on a divide at all; the terrain for miles on either side looks the same as that on the Divide itself. In departing from the Divide in New Mexico, the CDT is not giving up high alpine ridges; more often, it's giving up monotonous scrubland.

Actually, it's better than that. Because the route designated by land-management agencies runs primarily through public lands—five National Forests and three Bureau of Land Management districts, as well as lands administered by the National Park Service and the U.S. Bureau of Reclamation—the CDT includes some of New Mexico's most spectacular and interesting natural landscapes: the Big Hatchet Mountains Wilderness Study Area, the Gila and Aldo Leopold Wildernesses, El Malpais National Monument, Mount Taylor, the wild lands of the Rio Puerco, the San Pedro Parks Wilderness, and the Chama River Canyon Wilderness.

Moreover, departing from the physical Divide allows land-management agencies (and they were mandated by Congress to create the CDT in the first place) to manage the CDT responsibly. Thus, these agencies, when designing the route, paid attention to such issues as water availability, hiker access, avoidance of conflicts with other uses, and so forth. These agencies also mark the route and provide information to hikers.

This is not to argue against the CDT's following the physical Divide wherever practical, and CDT users should remember that the CDT is, and will remain, a work in progress. Land-management agencies constantly negotiate land exchanges and recreational easements, and attitudes constantly evolve. Ranchers, tribal authorities, and rural Hispanics who today don't welcome the trail and its hikers on their lands may feel quite differently in the future; this is one of many reasons it's so important that CDT users be goodwill ambassadors to the local people they meet.

RESPECT LAND OWNERSHIP Each hiker who flouts land ownership jeopardizes the reception subsequent hikers will receive when they hike through the state. New Mexico enjoys a long, proud history, but for more than four hundred years that history has included intense, sometimes violent struggles for territory among peoples and cultures. Land ownership has been and continues to be a sensitive issue here. Today, the state includes nineteen Indian pueblos, each considering itself a separate tribe, as well as three Navajo reservations and two Apache reservations. This is in addition to numerous Spanish and Mexican land grants, still owned in common by the descendants of the original grantees. In much of New Mexico, Spanish is the first language in many homes and villages not because the people haven't learned English but because Spanish symbolizes their roots and culture. And finally, New Mexico has a community of ranchers of all ethnicities, also trying to preserve their traditions in the face of a changing world.

While you're hiking in New Mexico, you *will* meet members of all these groups. The CDT here isn't like the CDT in, for example, Colorado, where it stays primarily among the high unpopulated peaks of the Rockies, insulated from most local people by miles of National Forests. In New Mexico, even on public land, in the National Forests, you're never far from local people; in the San Pedro Parks Wilderness, you'll likely meet Hispanics whose ancestors grazed cattle there long before the National Forest was created. Similarly, on the Forest Roads around Mount Taylor, you might meet Acoma and Laguna Indians gathering piñon nuts or hunting deer; they've considered the mountain theirs since long before Europeans even suspected North America existed. And in southern New Mexico, land owned by ranchers whose windmills and stock tanks are all but essential for CDT travelers flanks many CDT routes. (If possible, always ask permission.)

The overwhelming majority of local people will greet you warmly, inquire about your trek, offer valuable advice, and welcome you to share their land, their water, and sometimes even their homes. But if the previous hikers they've met have trespassed and willfully ignored fences and signs, you'll be considered one of them—and treated accordingly.

I can't overemphasize how important it is to build good relations with local people in New Mexico. The CDT is new here; we haven't had time to screw things up. How wonderful if the CDT could become a bridge linking the many traditions and cultures along it. *Please* respect land ownership.

NATIVES, LOCALS, AND WHATEVER   In this book, I refer several times to the potential suspicions and hostility of local people, especially prevalent in Hispanic northern New Mexico, but also elsewhere, for example, among Anglo ranchers in southwestern New Mexico. These attitudes spring from deep historical and cultural roots, which in no way excuses the theft, vandalism, and boorishness that sometimes result from them. Indeed, such people, like xenophobes anywhere, victimize themselves by isolating themselves from the diversity and richness of life. Still, this hostility exists, and I'd be remiss if I didn't advise you of it.

Having mentioned the reality of these attitudes in northern New Mexico (and elsewhere), I also would be negligent if I didn't add that there, as everywhere, people are individuals and should be judged as such. I lived for a year in northern New Mexico when I moved to the state, and I count among my fondest memories the wonderful local people I met there. What's more, not only were they fine people generally, their knowledge of and roots in the local area greatly enhanced my stay.

So although it's important not to leave yourself vulnerable to misguided hostility from people with closed minds, neither should you close your own mind. The local people have so much to share, and their history goes so far back and is so rich with history and tradition, that meeting them as friends can yield memories you'll treasure.

How to Use This Guide

This book is intended to serve not just thru-hikers but also day hikers, campers, mountain bikers, and equestrians, as well as those who just like exploring New Mexico via the Continental Divide Trail. (*Note:* The official name is the Continental Divide National Scenic Trail, but most people call it simply the Continental Divide Trail, which I've abbreviated to CDT.) The book's core is divided into chapters corresponding to the 28 segments of the CDT in New Mexico, although I've treated two significant alternative routes as separate segments.

The segments chart on pages 12–13 lists each segment's difficulty, mileage, total elevation gain, trailhead access, and suitability for mountain bikes, as well as starting point and ending point. Consulting this chart will help you in your planning, whether you're a thru-hiker or a day hiker. You'll also find a map of the entire trail on pages 10–11.

SEGMENT INTRODUCTION

Each segment makes up a chapter in this book. Information at the beginning of each segment summarizes the important features of that segment. First, you will see the segment's distance in miles and difficulty rating: easy, moderate, and strenuous. The background color of each segment's introductory page also corresponds to difficulty: green for easy, blue for moderate, and red for strenuous. These ratings, of necessity, reflect a highly subjective judgment. I tend to be conservative when rating difficulty; many hikers will find hikes that I have labeled as moderate to be easy. Hikers not accustomed to the elevation or other conditions, however, might find some hikes more difficult than they'd expected. Use the ratings as general guidelines only.

The introductory page also includes an elevation profile of the segment. This profile illustrates elevation gain and loss and notes the total elevation differential over the entire segment. The profile box indicates the trail's mileage from Mexico and to Colorado. These figures are calculated from the segment's starting point.

You will find information about other trail uses next to each profile box, ranging from foot-travel-only to automobiles.

TRAIL OVERVIEW

After the elevation profile, several paragraphs describe the segment generally; they include information about water, camping, highlights and hazards, unique features, and natural and human history.

MOUNTAIN BIKE NOTES tells you whether the segment is suitable for mountain biking and what you might expect. (Similarly, **EQUESTRIAN NOTES** gives useful general information to horseback riders.) The following mountain bike symbols accompany that paragraph and provide a quick visual reference:

Most of the terrain is non-technical, but you may encounter some elevation gain. Check the segment's elevation profile.

You will find steep or technical riding on most of the segment, and you may have to carry your bike in spots. These segments are not recommended for novice cyclists.

 Some or all of the terrain on the segment is not ridable due to rocks, steepness, lack of a trail, environmental sensitivity, or general unsuitability for mountain biking (such as uninteresting terrain).

 The segment passes through a designated wilderness area, national park, or other area where bikes are prohibited.

Because the segments are in geographical order from south to north, the trail description flows naturally from one segment to the next, allowing a thru-hiker to use the book from start to finish. I chose this south to north orientation not only to stay consistent with the other Westcliffe CDT guides in this series but also because north-bound hikers have a better chance of finding water in the spring than do southbound hikers in the fall, especially in the southern portions of the route. Important information about water is marked throughout the text with this symbol:

But many hikers have good reasons for hiking north to south, and let's face it, hikers who've traveled all the way from Canada can certainly deal with scarce water when less than a hundred miles from journey's end. Therefore, southbound hikers will find important information throughout the book, marked with this symbol: **S**

MAPS Each segment includes a list of the maps covering that segment. Hikers most commonly use the U.S. Geological Survey (USGS) 7.5-minute topographic quadrangles; at a scale of 1:24,000, they show the greatest detail and also illustrate relief and elevation.

As valuable as these maps are, they have limitations. For example, many New Mexico quads have not been updated for many years and don't show current conditions; none of the quads currently include the CDT; and they don't always label Forest Roads or land ownership. For this reason, I've also listed other helpful maps; these include Forest Service maps, which are especially useful in showing Forest Roads in National Forests, as well as BLM maps, which show land ownership.

See Appendix C for a list of map sources, and Appendix D for lists of the maps required for the entire trail in New Mexico.

A FEW NOTES ABOUT THE MAPS Because the USGS quadrangles are so important in hiking the CDT, it's worth running through a quick checklist of things to notice about each map you use:

• **Contour interval.** On standard USGS quads, the contour interval is labeled beneath the map in the center. The most common contour intervals USGS uses for its New Mexico maps are 20 feet and 40 feet—a big difference. If the hill you're hiking spans 10 contour lines, it's either 200 feet high—or 400!

- **Edition date.** Maps start to go out of date almost as soon they're printed, so when you buy a map, look in the bottom right corner (on USGS maps) to see its date of preparation. Some maps in New Mexico haven't been revised for 40 years! The mountains and valleys won't have changed much, but roads and other human-made features might have.

- **Declination.** Because the geographic North Pole doesn't sit quite squarely over the magnetic North Pole, the north our compass needle points toward isn't quite the same as the north shown on maps. The difference between the two norths is declination, and on USGS maps this is indicated near the bottom edge, along with the scale. In central New Mexico, magnetic north is shifted about 10° east of map north. See "A Few Compass Facts," page 23.

- **Caring for maps.** Even the best map becomes useless if it turns into a soggy wad of pulp. Most outdoor stores carry inexpensive map cases featuring see-through plastic panels. You can often hang these cases around your neck so that your map is instantly accessible—invaluable in difficult terrain.

LAND-MANAGEMENT AGENCIES

The last item you will find here are the names of various land-management jurisdictions through which the route passes, including those governed by the U.S. Forest Service and the Bureau of Land Management. Because the agencies employ different administrative units within the state, I list the specific division for that segment. Appendix A lists complete addresses and phone numbers for these agencies.

ACCESS TO TRAILHEADS

Detailed directions for driving to the segment's starting and ending points, including information about trailheads, enable you to reach the access points as easily as possible and on good roads whenever possible. Because the CDT traverses some of the most inaccessible land in New Mexico, many segments may require driving on dirt roads or four-wheel-drive roads to reach the trailheads. To give you a quick visual reference of what terrain to expect, the following symbols precede each set of driving directions:

 The trailhead is accessible with a normal passenger car. The road is either paved or well-graded dirt.

 A normal passenger car can get to the trailhead, but the road is not paved and may be rough. Adverse weather conditions could make these routes impassable.

 You will need a high-clearance, four-wheel-drive vehicle for these roads.

 A hike is required to reach the CDT.

 Mileage is given where these symbols are used in combinations. In this example, you would drive 14.4 miles over bumpy or rough roads and hike an additional 2.7 miles to reach the CDT.

Note: You should keep in mind that in New Mexico, the CDT and roads often coincide; sometimes the CDT here *is* the road.

SUPPLIES, SERVICES, AND ACCOMMODATIONS

Thru-hikers as well as segment hikers will find the information here useful for itinerary planning. You will find the names of towns on or near the CDT, as well as information about important businesses, such as grocery stores, motels, and post offices. This section also lists information for local medical and emergency services. If you plan to send supply boxes ahead to post offices along the route before you depart, you should give the post office a call to confirm current hours of operation and whether and for how long they will hold general delivery parcels.

TRAIL DESCRIPTION

This section, which makes up most of each chapter, details the segment's route and includes pertinent information on water sources and navigation.

TRAIL MARKERS

 This CDT trail marker is a regular feature along the route, and the book refers to it frequently. But remember: Not all portions of the CDT have been signed with this marker.

 In sections where a distinct tread does not exist, rock cairns sometimes mark the route.

OTHER HIKES AND RIDES
After the detailed segment description, you will find information about hikes and mountain-bike rides on or near the trail segment. These range from short day hikes in the vicinity of the CDT to extended multiday adventures. Each of these hikes or rides includes the distance, a difficulty rating, and a brief description. Because these descriptions are not as detailed as the regular segment descriptions, you should supplement the information with a good map.

NAVIGATION AND THIS BOOK

DIRECTIONS AND THE COMPASS

People understand directions primarily in two ways: one, using the cardinal directions (north, south, east, and west), along with compass bearings (145°); and two, using directions such as up, down, left, and right, along with cues such as landmarks, trail markers, and terrain features and variations. To make directions in this book as clear as possible for everyone, I have used both methods. Particularly obscure areas are marked in the text with this symbol:

Owning a good compass and knowing how to use it are *essential* for traveling the CDT. Remember, the place to learn about your compass is *not* on the CDT itself. Nor is a GPS (Global Positioning System) unit a substitute for a compass: Batteries sometimes die and satellites sometimes shut down, but Earth's magnetism never fails. When shopping for a compass, look for one with a rotating dial and the degrees ticked off around it. A see-through plastic straight edge and a mirror add precision to your calculations.

Lest I sound too smugly self-righteous, I recall scouting the CDT in the Big Hatchet Mountains in southwestern New Mexico. Our party of five had good, detailed maps, more than one serious orienteering compass, a GPS unit, and experience in using all of them. Despite this, we still had a very difficult time route-finding, and we were scouting in an environment where getting lost could turn into disaster. Hikers more experienced than I could tell similar stories.

A FEW COMPASS FACTS The compass dial is divided into 360 equal units called degrees. Degrees, which are numbered, start with 0 at due north and increase clockwise on the dial. Due east is at 90°, south is at 180°, and west is at 270°. Degrees are subdivided into 60 minutes, abbreviated with the superscript ', as in 35°25'. Minutes, in turn, are divided into 60 seconds, abbreviated with the superscript ", as in 35°25'43" latitude; longitude would appear as 107°43'20". You should become familiar with this system; it is the basis for precise locations on USGS 7.5-minute quads.

The compass needle always points toward magnetic north, but maps are based upon "true north." The difference between the two, which varies with location, is listed in degrees at the bottom of most maps under the label "declination." If magnetic north is 10° (the average declination for central New Mexico) east of true north from your location, any direction you wish to find will lie 10° to the left, or counterclockwise, of the direction indicated by the compass needle.

Note: All USGS quads show declination, but, deplorably, other maps sometimes omit it. Declination doesn't vary so much that you need to recalibrate whenever you move from one quadrangle to the next, but you should have a general idea. Bearings in this book are based on true north.

ABOUT GPS RECEIVERS AND THIS BOOK

GPS technology uses signals received from orbiting space satellites to provide accurate locational positions on Earth. Until recently, the units were accurate to approximately 300 feet or less. This changed dramatically when the U.S. Departments of Defense, which originally placed the satellites into orbit to provide guidance for missiles and other military uses, removed the accuracy degradation program installed to prevent the system's use by hostile powers. Now the units are accurate to within 30 feet—and actual readings may be even closer.

GPS technology continues to evolve rapidly and you can now buy a lightweight handheld GPS receiver at an affordable price. Each year, more outdoor recreationists use GPS, a trend that will only continue. For one thing, a GPS unit is a *great* gadget for gadget-addicted hikers (guys—and gals too—you know who you are).

More important, though, GPS units confer some real advantages. When we enter coordinates of important features (water sources, trail junctions, campgrounds, etc.), we can use GPS units to take us unerringly to those features. When we aren't sure where we are, GPS receivers will tell us—assuming, of course, that we know how to transfer the coordinates onto a map. A GPS receiver is *not* a replacement for map and compass; it is a complement to them.

Because of the increasing use and importance of GPS receivers, I've included latitude-longitude coordinates, in North America Datum 27, for important features. I obtained these coordinates from two sources: (1) directly from the USGS quadrangles using a simple but essential plastic map ruler (no GPS user should be without one); and (2) the USGS Geographic Names Information System (GNIS) database. This database includes, among other things, latitude-longitude coordinates for all named features on 7.5-minute USGS quadrangles (and many other features as well). This database is available online at http://mapping.usgs.gov/. All coordinates are North American Datum 27. Also, the coordinates appear in degrees-minutes-seconds, rather than in decimal degrees, because the locations are listed in GNIS in degrees-minutes-seconds; coordinates are also obtained in the field by using the ruler and the tick marks on the USGS quadrangles. I've tried to be as accurate as possible when recording these coordinates, but human errors do occur, especially when transcribing strings of numbers, so use these coordinates with appropriate caution and always check them.

Note: Waypoints provided do not constitute a route; they are not intended to guide you around obstacles and dangers, such as cliffs. Rather, they are intended to provide coordinates for specific features whose location you might otherwise miss.

Afternoon storm clouds above Red Mesa, south end of Sierra Nacimiento near San Ysidro.
Photo by William Stone.

History of the Continental Divide National Scenic Trail

The Continental Divide National Scenic Trail (CDNST) began in 1966 as the dream of Benton MacKaye, an 87-year-old man who had already devoted much of his life to seeing the Appalachian Trail come to fruition. MacKaye's idea was to create a trail that would connect a series of wilderness areas along the Divide from Montana's border with Canada to New Mexico's border with Mexico.

MacKaye (rhymes with "deny") proposed his idea to Congress, which soon authorized a study of the trail under the National Trails System Act of 1968. At around the same time, a Baltimore attorney by the name of Jim Wolf was hiking the 2,000-mile-long Appalachian Trail, which he completed in 1971. Inspired to seek out a new hiking challenge further afield, Wolf walked the Divide Trail from the Canadian border to Rogers Pass, Montana, in 1973. He soon published a guidebook covering that section of the trail and devoted much of his time to advocating its official designation. After a 1976 study by the Bureau of Outdoor Recreation found the scenic quality of the trail to surpass anything available anywhere else in the country, the Congressional Oversight Committee of the National Trail System held hearings on the trail in 1978, at which Wolf testified. The CDNST received official recognition from Congress later that year under the National Parks and Recreation Act.

In that same year, Wolf founded the Continental Divide Trail Society (CDTS) to garner publicity for the trail and involve the public in work surrounding its construction, particularly its route selection. Wolf continued to hike portions of the trail each summer, and by the mid-'80s he had completed all of its 3,100 miles. The CDTS has grown to a membership of 250 from 46 states and several foreign countries.

The United States Forest Service is responsible for managing most of the land through which the trail passes. In the 1980s, its work on the trail progressed at different rates in different areas, but it suffered in general from a lack of public involvement. In 1994, two trail advocates began working under the auspices of a group called the Fausel Foundation to raise funds and build support for the trail. By 1995, their efforts evolved into the Continental Divide Trail Alliance (CDTA), a nonprofit organization devoted to fund-raising, publicity, education about the trail, and grassroots volunteer coordination. The CDTA founders were Bruce Ward, formerly the president of the American Hiking Society, and his wife, Paula, a landscape architect. The CDTA is based in Pine, Colorado.

In its first year, the CDTA grew to include 425 individuals or families, 20 corporate sponsors, and a budget of $400,000. Estimates suggest the Alliance coordinated volunteer work worth $70,000 in that first year. However, trail advocates are quick to point out that there is much work yet to be done. Completion and maintenance of the trail will require funding and volunteer coordination throughout the 21st century. For more information about joining the CDTA, see page 314.

Generously contributed by Tom Lorang Jones
Revised from *Colorado's Continental Divide Trail: The Official Guide*

History of New Mexico's Continental Divide Trail

The Continental Divide belongs to the land, but the Continental Divide Trail belongs to the people who build it, maintain it, administer it, use it, and dream about it. And for those of us now involved in the CDT, including you, dear reader, we are blessed by being here in New Mexico for the birth of the CDT. The CDT may last a thousand years (or longer), but it can be born only once, and we're here to witness it and be a part of it. Sure, the Continental Divide itself has been here a long time, but it has never had as much of a presence here in New Mexico as it has in the states to the north. Explorers and settlers here didn't rhapsodize about crossing the Great Divide; more likely, they weren't even aware of it.

Certainly the idea of a Continental Divide Trail is modern. In the 1930s, Rufe and Rita Hotchkiss worked as volunteer trailmakers from their ranch near Silver City. "Back in the 1930s the Civilian Conservation Corps had a camp near here and laid out a trail along the Divide from Pinos Altos to Mimbres," Rita recalled 50 years later. "In 50 years, though, a lot of brush grows up. The old ax marks get grown over. Trees with blazes die or get burned. Rufe found the old trails and worked it out, and we've been clearing now for about eight years."

To be sure, Jim Wolf and his Continental Divide Trail Society have, since the 1970s, included New Mexico in their vision of a Mexico-to-Canada trail. But until the 1990s, the CDT in New Mexico remained lines on maps, words in reports, dreams in people's heads.

Now, routes have been designated, trail markers put up, cairns erected, tread laid down, and a guidebook written. The Continental Divide Trail in New Mexico has become a reality.

It's been a long time coming. In 1966, Appalachian Trail founder Benton MacKaye proposed another long-distance trail—this one connecting wilderness areas from the Mexican to the Canadian borders. In 1968, the U.S. Congress passed the National Trails System Act, which authorized study of such a trail. A decade later, Congress, in its National Parks and Recreation Act, recognized the Continental Divide National Scenic Trail.

But proclamations aren't pulaskis and reports aren't actual routes. Years passed, advisory councils were formed, plans were made, reports were issued, and though some actual trail work occurred in the northern states and a few hikers remained committed in New Mexico, not much happened on the ground here.

That began to change dramatically in 1996, when the CDTA included New Mexico in its series of CDT State Summits. Formed the year before, to partner with federal agencies and to mobilize public and corporate involvement, the CDTA called upon all interested parties to meet in Albuquerque to discuss the trail. The turnout was far greater than anyone had expected. It included not only representatives of federal agencies but also people from groups such as the New Mexico Mountain Club, Backcountry Horsemen of New Mexico, New Mexico Volunteers for the Outdoors, Recreational

Equipment Inc. (REI), and, most important, many individuals (including this writer) who simply liked the idea of the CDT being in New Mexico.

Suddenly, things began to happen.

Since then, the federal agencies and the CDTA, working separately and together, have continued the impetus toward actually putting the trail on the ground. In 1997, the CDTA organized Uniting Along the Divide, the first end-to-end volunteer survey of the CDT, as well as national CDT conferences. In 1998, the CDT initiated the Adopt-a-Trail program. In the meantime, federal agencies began including CDT trail-building in their district budgets, and some offices, such as the Gila National Forest Black Range Ranger District and the BLM's Albuquerque Field Office, showed great skill in recruiting volunteers to build trails and become involved.

This citizen involvement, perhaps more than anything else, bodes well for the CDT's future in New Mexico. Mountain Clubbers, Backcountry Horsemen, Boy Scouts, college students on spring break, Volunteers for the Outdoors, retirees, and families—all these and many more have gotten their hands dirty building trail.

For me personally, the realization that the New Mexico CDT would succeed and survive came on a snowy day one November in the remote Black Range, when I helped a group of AmeriCorps volunteers build new tread. They were great young people—friendly, enthusiastic, and hardworking. And, though many of them had never heard of the CDT when they arrived in New Mexico, most wanted to return to hike it because it was, after all, now their trail.

It's yours, too.

Sunflowers and sandstone cliffs, Red Rock State Park. Photo by Tom Till.

The Natural Environment Along New Mexico's Continental Divide Trail

New Mexico is characterized by extraordinary diversity, and that certainly is part of the state's appeal among hikers. Not only can they hike somewhere in the state at any time of year, they can explore ecosystems ranging from Lower Sonoran to tundra; in the same week they can hear pikas barking above timberline in the Rocky Mountains and look for Gila monsters in the Chihuahuan Desert.

The major determining factors behind this diversity are latitude and elevation. The Continental Divide Trail here begins at the Mexican border, in the Chihuahuan Desert, but ends at the Colorado border, in the Rocky Mountains. Furthermore, elevations along the CDT extend from 4,280 feet at the Mexican border to 11,301 feet atop Mount Taylor, a vertical relief of more than 7,000 feet. Moisture, temperature, habitat, and so forth, influence the occurrence of specific plants and animals within this enormous range. Thousands of micro-ecosystems thrive throughout the state.

Still, New Mexico can be divided into several major life zones based mostly on dominant vegetation; hikers should be familiar with these zones because an awareness of them not only enhances the hike but also enables the hiker to recognize each one's characteristics and challenges. Because classification systems and labels vary widely among naturalists, the situation is more complex than that presented here. The following classification is nevertheless in general use and is easy to understand.

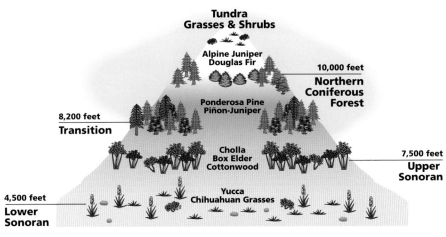

New Mexico's Life Zones

NEW MEXICO'S LIFE ZONES

LOWER SONORAN

This life zone occurs below 4,500 feet in New Mexico, and, despite its name, features the plants of the Chihuahuan Desert, not those of the Sonoran Desert (which is not in New Mexico). Temperatures and evaporation are high for most of the year. Characteristic plants include mesquite, creosote bush, yucca, agave, four-wing saltbush, and Chihuahuan grasses. Animals are desert-adapted and include coatimundi, javelina, ringtails, desert bighorn sheep, coyotes, mountain lions, and rattlesnakes (as well as numerous other reptiles). Bird life is surprisingly diverse and abundant.

UPPER SONORAN

Within this zone, generally occurring up to 7,500 feet, summers are hot, winters somewhat mild. Precipitation is modest and evaporation is high. This is the zone of the piñon-juniper forest, New Mexico's most widespread vegetation type. Other characteristic plants include alligator juniper, Chihuahua pine, chamisa, cholla, Apache plume, Gambel oak, and, near water, box elder, tamarisk, and, of course, cottonwood. Considerable species overlap exists between this zone and the Lower Sonoran, but here whitetail and mule deer become more common, along with black bears, prairie dogs, rabbits, and pronghorns.

TRANSITION

Within this zone, 7,500 to 8,200 feet, summers are mild, winters cold, often with substantial snowfall. Ponderosa pines replace piñons and junipers, and native pines such as the limber pine and Apache pine also occur here. Other typical plants are Rocky Mountain maple, New Mexico locust, and riparian willows. Here, elk join deer, bears, and lions as dominant large mammal species, and beavers, bobcats, foxes, and tufted-eared squirrels represent smaller mammals; rattlesnakes are less common in this zone.

NORTHERN CONIFEROUS FOREST

From 8,200 feet to timberline (10,000 to 11,500 feet), Douglas fir, white fir, subalpine fir, Engelmann spruce, blue spruce, alpine juniper, limber pine, and, occasionally in the north, bristlecone pine dominate the vegetation. Aspens are common in disturbed or transitional areas. Summers here are cool, winters cold, and mountains with these elevations receive lots of rain and snow. Elk are the dominant mammal, and gray jays frequent camps.

TUNDRA

Here above timberline, the dominant vegetation becomes a tough, windswept mat of low, hardy grasses, sedges, and shrubs. Temperatures are cool to cold, even in summer, and evaporation is high because of wind, elevation, and exposure; although considerable snow falls, high winds sweep most of it away. Hikers should be prepared for severe weather at all times of the year. The CDT in New Mexico doesn't cross any true tundra.

The above classification is oversimplified, and the elevation cut-offs vary enormously by latitude and slope aspect.

GEOLOGY

The CDT takes hikers through some of New Mexico's most scenic and interesting geology. Because New Mexico is an arid state, the formations are not hidden by dense vegetation but are readily visible (geology in the nude, if you will). Learning a little about the geology will enhance your appreciation of the landscape, as well as help explain why surface water exists in some places and not in others and why knobby black rocks keep tripping you as you hike in certain areas.

Geologists group rocks into three types according to how they formed: igneous, sedimentary, and metamorphic. Igneous rocks originate from molten rock. Molten rock that cools beneath the earth's surface, as does granite, is called intrusive igneous rock; molten rock such as basalt, which cools above the surface, is called extrusive igneous rock. Sedimentary rocks, such as sandstone, limestone, and shale, result from the compression of layers of rock or sediment deposited by water, wind, or marine accumulation, and often represent ancient beaches, sand dunes, and coral deposits. Metamorphic rocks, such as gneiss and schist, result from great pressures and temperatures altering existing igneous or sedimentary rocks.

Of the rocks you will see on the CDT in New Mexico, sedimentary sandstone and extrusive igneous rocks resulting from volcanism are the most common, their land forms the most striking. Sandstone formations include the scenic sandstone bluffs at the western edge of the Cebolla Wilderness, the badlands in the Rio Puerco area, and the dramatic multicolored cliffs forming the canyon walls in the Chama River Canyon Wilderness.

Volcanic formations along the CDT include the vast Gila Wilderness, which is the remains of a gigantic caldera (the subsidence basin created when a volcano collapses into its empty magma chamber). Volcanic rocks make up the Black Range and the Aldo Leopold Wilderness. Isolated volcanic formations appear as you head north, but El Malpais National Monument and associated public lands are New Mexico's volcanic showcases. Small but conspicuous cinder cones dot the landscape in the Chain of Craters Wilderness Study Area; a portion of the CDT follows the Zuni-Acoma Trail over several lava flows, including a very recent one that ancestral Acoma Indians beheld as a river of fire. To the north, the CDT passes 11,301-foot Mount Taylor, New Mexico's largest volcanic mountain; Mount Taylor spewed the lava that created the sprawling Mesa Chivato volcanic plateau. The CDT traverses Mesa Chivato before plunging into the valley of the Rio Puerco, where numerous volcanic plugs create an almost surreal landscape.

The CDT in New Mexico takes you on an interesting journey through geological time, a span of as much as 2 billion years. In the Zuni Mountains and the Sierra Nacimiento of the San Pedro Parks Wilderness, you find outcrops of pink and gray granites, formed during the Precambrian era before life existed on Earth; the pink and gray outcrops make a pleasing contrast with the surrounding green meadows and forests.

Erosion has devoured most rocks laid down during the Paleozoic era, 600 to 230 million years ago, but a few fossil-bearing limestones from the Mississippian period, 345 to 310 million years ago, remain around the western base of the Sierra Nacimiento uplift.

The Mesozoic era, 230 to 70 million years ago, saw the time of the dinosaurs, and paleontologists search for fossils in the sedimentary deposits of the Rio Puerco area, through which the CDT passes. Indeed, the bones of *Seismosaurus* were found in the Ojito Wilderness Study Area, not far from the CDT. At the time of its discovery in the 1980s by local hikers, *Seismosaurus* was the world's largest dinosaur.

During the Cenozoic era, things began to explode—literally. The Tertiary period, 70 to 2 million years ago, witnessed the Laramide Revolution, the mountain-building that produced the Rocky Mountains and that is ongoing. Then, beginning about 40 million years ago, volcanoes erupted throughout the state's southwestern quadrant; these were cataclysmic eruptions that have few, if any, equals in human history. This vast region, called the Datil–Mogollon Volcanic Plateau, includes the Black Range, the Kelly, Jerky, and Diablo Mountains, and the high peaks of the Gila country, as well as portions of the Burro and Peloncillo Mountains.

In the Quaternary period, 2 million years ago to the present, more volcanic eruptions occurred. Mount Taylor erupted, and so did the gigantic volcano whose caldera and compacted ash deposits formed the Jemez Mountains and the Pajarito Plateau. From volcanic fissures south of Grants, lava flowed to produce the recent lava flows known by the Spanish term *malpais,* literally "bad land." These volcanic processes continue today. Indeed, geologists have predicted where New Mexico's next volcano will occur—near Socorro, where a magma chamber is rising toward the surface—but they don't say when!

La Ventana Arch in El Malpais National Conservation Area. Photo by Tom Till.

Leave No Trace

As ever more people use America's wild lands, they have learned to minimize their impact by adopting an ethic known as Leave No Trace. Leave No Trace requires even more vigilance in New Mexico, where scant rainfall, sparse vegetation, and thin topsoil mean that recovery from damage can take a long time. Your experience on the Continental Divide Trail in New Mexico will range from areas that are conspicuously fragile and pristine to areas trampled by cows and rutted by vehicles. No matter; practice Leave No Trace in all situations, if for no other reason than it's simply the right thing to do. Leave No Trace really isn't difficult. It just means adopting some fairly simple habits and practices:

PLAN AND PREPARE   Repackage and store food in reusable containers, and always have on hand bags in which to pack out garbage and trash. Planning ahead also means learning about the local ecology and selecting appropriate equipment.

TRAILS   Stay on designated trails and walk single-file in the middle. Don't take shortcuts on switchbacks. When traveling off-trail, as the CDT often requires in New Mexico, try to stay on durable surfaces. Use map and compass or Global Positioning System units to eliminate the need for cairns or blazes.

CAMP   Where possible, choose established camps, preferably those where the soil is bare already. Avoid places where impact is just beginning; desert soils can take many years to recover from compaction. Avoid camping 200 feet (about 70 adult steps) from lakes and streams. Control pets. Take everything you bring into the wilderness out with you— and take out at least some of other people's trash.

FIRES   Best of all, don't build a fire; use a portable stove. If you do build a fire, use established fire rings only. Don't scar the landscape by snapping off branches from trees or shrubs, living or dead. Completely extinguish your fire and make sure it's cold before departing; remove all unburned trash from the fire ring and scatter the cold ashes over a large area. If you want to build a fire in an area where no fire ring exists, build a "mound fire." Find a source of mineral soil, such as a low stream bed or hollow beneath an over-turned tree. Pile mineral soil on a tarp, making a flat-topped mound from 6 to 8 inches high. Build a small fire on this. When you break camp, scatter the cold ashes over a wide area, then return the soil to its source.

Many people enjoy a campfire for the warmth, the light, and the camaraderie. I carry a small Ultralite oil lantern, and I've found to my surprise that its tiny flame, while short on warmth, provides much of the psychological comfort of a campfire.

HUMAN WASTE   The recommended method of disposing of human wastes is the "cat hole," dug 6 to 8 inches deep at least 200 feet away from water sources. Cover and disguise the cat hole when you're finished. Toilet paper should be used sparingly and packed out (sealed double plastic bags)—or use a natural alternative.

GARBAGE AND FOOD: PACK IT IN, PACK IT OUT

All trash, including food scraps, should be packed out. Most trash, including paper, doesn't burn well and ends up scattered by wind or animals. Long-distance hikers should not use food caches in their planning. A food cache, not allowed in some areas, is a stash of food the hiker deposits somewhere along the route before a hike begins; but animals often dig them up and hikers leave them behind when their plans change. Careful planning will eliminate the need to cache food.

WILD ANIMALS   Don't attract them. Don't feed them. Don't approach them or touch them. Not only do these actions disrupt wildlife ecology and encourage animals to become dependent on humans, but they expose humans to the possibility of bites and infection by animal-borne diseases, such as plague (that's right, Black Death). Hang your food supplies from tree limbs, out of reach, and prepare food and clean up away and downwind from your camp. Most of New Mexico's wilderness areas don't have the problems with bum animals that other areas do, and we should try to keep it that way.

TREAD SOFTLY   In arid regions, the soil often acquires a protective "crust" that, once disturbed, leaves the soil vulnerable to erosion. In areas of sandy soil, a living community of bacteria, fungi, and lichens forms a cryptobiotic crust, or cryptogamic soil. This living soil has a distinctive dark, lumpy appearance, and although it may resemble mere soil, it is a complex living community. It takes 100 to 200 years for even a thin layer of cryptobiotic crust to develop. Avoid stepping on or making camps on this inconspicuous but important part of desert ecology.

DOMESTIC ANIMALS   Although a dog can be a welcome companion in the wilderness, you'll have a more successful, more responsible trip if you don't take the dog. On the trail, the dog must be under control at all times so that it won't threaten or hinder other hikers. (Even friendly dogs that just run up and sniff can terrify some people, especially those who may have been attacked in the past.) At camp, the dog must also be under control so that it won't bother other campers, whether by visiting their campsites or by chronic barking. And because dogs are predators, they can harass and kill wild birds and animals. What's more, domestic animals often behave unpredictably when suddenly placed in wild nature and may run away. I've known more than one hiker whose trip was ruined because the family pet didn't return with them. My advice is leave the dog at home; that way, you'll make everything much simpler and, besides, in many areas dogs are not allowed. A final caveat: Dogs are fond of catching rodents and snuffing around dead ones. In New Mexico, those rodents can carry fleas, which jump onto the dog; the fleas sometimes harbor plague bacteria.

MOUNTAIN BIKING   Mountain bikes are permitted on many parts of the CDT, except where the route passes through designated Wilderness or Wilderness Study Areas; but bikers should still consult the appropriate land-management agency indicated for a segment. Also, some sections of the CDT are unsuitable for mountain biking, for a variety of reasons. Mountain bikers are reminded that it is their

responsibility to ride in control, yield to all other users, and conscientiously minimize their impact on the land.

The Adventure Cycling Association in Missoula, Montana, is currently working to create a Great Divide Mountain Bike Route. Contact them at (406) 721-1776, or contact the International Mountain Bike Association in Boulder, Colorado, at (303) 545-9011.

CULTURAL ARTIFACTS   New Mexico has a *very* long history. Indeed, until recently, the oldest evidence of human presence in the New World came from New Mexico, where sites such as Blackwater Draw near Clovis gave evidence that Native Americans lived here at least 13,500 years ago. On a relative scale, Europeans' presence here is also old. The Spanish conquistador Francisco Vasquez de Coronado led an expedition here in 1540; in 1598, Don Juan de Oñate founded a colony here, nine years before Jamestown was founded.

Thus, New Mexico abounds with cultural artifacts. You simply cannot hike in New Mexico without finding artifacts, whether pieces of worked flint, pottery sherds, or old bottles and horseshoes. You'll also likely come across remains of abandoned structures, from prehistoric cliff dwellings and pit houses to log cabins and adobe dwellings built by homesteaders and ranchers.

Resist the temptation to acquire souvenirs. I can relate from personal experience that you'll say to yourself, "But no one will miss this little piece of pottery." Perhaps not. But I can also promise that as time goes by, and despite your best intentions, your memory of where you got that little piece of pottery will fade, it will lose its significance to you, and eventually you'll wonder where—and why—you picked it up.

Let artifacts be. Take photographs of them, write about them in your journal, and revel in the satisfaction of having done the right thing.

For a more in-depth discussion of the concept of Leave No Trace, as well as more information, call the Leave No Trace office (see Appendix E).

Ice-encrusted ponderosa pine on rim of Cebollita Mesa overlooking snow-covered lava flow, El Malpais National Monument and Conservation Area. Photo by William Stone.

Planning a Thru-hike

Tom Lorang Jones, writing about the Continental Divide Trail in *Colorado's Continental Divide Trail: The Official Guide,* put it well: "Planning a long hike is a little like trying to plan the course of a marriage, even before you know who your spouse will be. To illustrate the metaphor, all you know about your future mate (the CDT) is what you've seen in photos (maps), hearing through the rumor mill (trail descriptions from various sources), and gathered about character flaws (hazards like lightning storms, snow, etc.). Not much to go on!" So here are some tips to minimize the chances of your relationship with the CDT ending in an unpleasant divorce:

TAKE TIME TO PLAN THOROUGHLY

A thru-hike requires enormous preparation. Exhaustive planning won't eliminate every obstacle you'll encounter—but it may eliminate the critical ones and make the others easier.

CHECK WITH THE APPROPRIATE LAND-MANAGEMENT AGENCY

Get information about permits and closures before entering a particular area. At present, the only permits required to hike or camp along any portion of the CDT in New Mexico are the State Land Office recreation permits for Segments 3 and 4, and even those are of marginal necessity because the route stays primarily on County Roads. You should be aware, however, that during periods of extreme drought, not exactly unheard of here, some National Forests may be closed to visitors, and certainly to campers, because of extreme fire hazard.

TALK TO HIKERS WHO HAVE GONE BEFORE

They'll advise, warn, educate, encourage, enlighten, and inspire you. They might even hike with you!

GET ON-LINE

Among the easiest ways to find information about the CDT is on the Internet. To contact other hikers, I strongly recommend the site of ALDHAW (American Long Distance Hikers Association West) at gorp.com/nonprof/aldhaw/. ALDHAW is a clearinghouse for long-distance hikers, and at its site you'll find hikers' journals, tips and techniques, contacts with other hikers, and much, much more. (ALDHAW is not to be confused with ALDHA, the Appalachian Long Distance Hikers Association, another great organization but focused primarily on the Appalachian Trail.)

Another valuable information source is the alt.rec.backcountry newsgroup. The hundreds of people who regularly surf here represent a deep, rich mine of information. "Views from the Top" at Lexicomm.com provides easy newsgroup access.

Both the Continental Divide Trail Alliance (cdtrail.org) and the Continental Divide Trail Society (gorp.com/cdts/) maintain websites, as do local Forest Service, Bureau of Land Management, and National Park Service offices that administer trail segments.

General backpacking and hiking sites also publish articles and information about the CDT, as well as places to post messages and ask questions. GORP, *Backpacker* magazine (bpbasecamp.com), and the backpacking section of About.com are among many. I also have a special fondness for the website of Walking Jim Stoltz: walkinjim.com.

I couldn't begin to list all the potential sources of on-line CDT information, so I recommend that you use your favorite search engine to locate useful websites. If nothing else, it'll be good practice for navigating an often bewildering landscape!

MAKE LISTS

As Karl Diederich said so well in GORP: "A list can do more than just provide a set of choices. It can help you realize the accomplishment of worthwhile pursuits. Studies have clearly shown that if goals are written down (as in long-distance hiking or otherwise), the chances of achieving them are greatly increased. Without a good idea of what you want to do, what are your chances of getting it done?"

So make lists, including checklists of things to do (contacting people to handle resupply, contacting land-management agencies, etc.), equipment, food, clothing, useful phone numbers, etc. One of the most experienced thru-hikers I know spends much of her tent-time just making lists. The books in the bibliography in Appendix F, as well as CDT websites, provide checklists from which to begin.

GET FIT

Running, cycling, swimming, and, of course, hiking and backpacking all are good for building the aerobic capacity you'll need for a thru-hike. Weight training builds strength and stretching promotes flexibility. No, you don't have to do the Ironman triathlon, but every hour spent getting fit is money in the bank, and you'll also earn important I-can-do-it dividends.

BE REALISTIC ABOUT HOW FAR YOU CAN HIKE PER DAY

Even if you're fit, long-distance backpacking is physically demanding—carrying up to 50 pounds, over rough terrain, perhaps climbing a thousand feet or more, in all weather conditions, up to 12 hours a day, day after day. You'll enjoy your hike more if you don't abuse yourself by trying to reach unrealistic goals. Naturally, you'll find it easier to hike longer distances later in the trip, after you've acclimated and gotten your "trail legs." But in the beginning, listen to your body and keep your expectations modest. And above all, ignore those writers and hikers who talk about their distance and speed records!

PLAN FOR REST DAYS

Even people in great shape find that a long hike wears them down. A day of rest is surprisingly rejuvenating after several days of hiking. One day off for every four to six days of hiking is not unrealistic.

CONSIDER WATER WHEN PLANNING YOUR ITINERARY

Ideally, water sources should be spaced no more than 8 miles apart—closer in hot, dry weather. Use maps to organize your hiking around water sources to minimize the amount of water you'll have to carry. Because you'll be perspiring heavily, you should consider adding an electrolyte replacement to your fluid regimen.

LEARN ABOUT FOOD REQUIREMENTS

On long-distance hikes your daily calorie requirements can more than double. *Backpacker* magazine estimated that a 200-pound man who in normal life requires 3,600 calories will require an additional 3,000 calories when hiking all day with a heavy pack at high altitude. The source of those calories is important and should include a reasonable balance of carbohydrates, protein, and fat. (Hikers endlessly debate the exact percentages.)

You will also need to ensure that you're getting adequate vitamins and minerals on your hike. Fresh fruits and vegetables are heavy and impractical, but dehydrated or freeze-dried fruits and vegetables weigh very little. GORP (Good Old Raisins and Peanuts), supplemented with such things as M&Ms, carob chips, or sunflower seeds, is standard high-energy food. Jerky provides a good lightweight source of protein and other nutrients. Grains and pastas are staples. Powdered milk is handy, as is cooking oil. Spices help make it all palatable.

If you've never shown interest in nutrition before, now is a good time to begin. Forget the fads; just search out what good-tasting lightweight foods will give you the basics—and then stock up with lots of them.

UNDERTAKE A SHAKEDOWN HIKE

Do a multiday backpack using the equipment you'll be using on your thru-hike. And be sure you use and examine all the equipment, including tent, pack, stove, water filter, and cookset. Check for frayed straps, loose pins, broken zippers, uncomfortable adjustments, and so forth.

BREAK IN YOUR BOOTS

Especially if they're new. And don't assume that because they were comfortable on a day hike they'll be equally comfortable on a multiday trek with a heavy pack. Many hikers hedge their bets by carrying lightweight shoes to wear around camp and give their feet a break. Be sure to include in your planning ample items to prevent or treat blisters, such as moleskin, duct tape, gauze, and the like.

PLAN TO HIKE LIGHT

Although experienced hikers vary enormously as to what compromises they feel are justified to keep pack weight down, they agree that the goal should be to carry as little weight as possible. You'll travel farther, faster, and have a better experience. Weight is of special concern in New Mexico, because on some segments you can expect to carry a gallon or more of water. Each hiker has his or her own list of which items are expendable, which are nonnegotiable, but do remember that if you're not to be a miserable beast of burden on your hike, you will have to make some hard choices. The best way to learn what you can live without is to take preliminary backpack trips and then make lists: what you used; what you wished you had; what you didn't use; and what you could forgo.

Safety Concerns on New Mexico's Continental Divide Trail

Hiking in the American Southwest presents some unique challenges, even to experienced hikers. In this section, I'll share with you some observations and experiences that will help you avoid most of the hazards you might encounter along the Continental Divide Trail in New Mexico. I've listed them in approximate order of importance:

DEHYDRATION

While writing this book, I got tired of saying, again and again, "Water is sparse in this segment." But there's no avoiding that this is indeed an arid region; 90 percent of the state receives less than 20 inches of moisture annually, and from 20 to 30 percent receives less than 10 inches. Ecologists formally classify much of southern New Mexico as part of the Chihuahuan Desert. What's more, the low humidity and high temperatures greatly increase your fluid requirements while hiking here. "Dehydration exhaustion" results from failing to replace water losses over several days, resulting in weight loss and excessive fatigue. Here are some heat-management tips I've picked up over the years:

- Don't wait until you're thirsty to begin drinking; by then you probably are already suffering some dehydration.

- Don't underestimate dehydration; a 2 percent loss of body fluids can result in a 20 percent decline in performance.

- Be aware that rapid evaporation in dry air can lead you to believe that you're sweating far less than you actually are.

- Soaking a bandanna or similar cloth and wearing it over your head, preferably dangling from a hat, can help cool your head, which is very important. You can gauge how well hydrated you are by the color of your urine; clear urine is a good sign, increasingly yellow urine means you need to drink more water.

- And finally, one of the best heat-management techniques is that adopted by many desert animals: Don't go out during midday; hike early in the morning or late in the afternoon, and hole up and rest during the heat of the day.

The importance of staying well hydrated in an arid environment means that hikers, especially thru-hikers, must pay special attention to planning for and locating water sources, and, quite frankly, they often cannot be too picky about the water they drink. (When I was hiking a stretch of the CDT on the far backside of Mount Taylor, I discovered just how low I was willing to go for water. No, the bottom wasn't the rain water in the tire tracks; that was great compared to the gray, gooey sludge churned up by cows' hooves in a stock pond named Ned Tank.)

In addition to low standards of water quality, hikers must also depend upon local people, especially ranchers. At least four CDT segments in southern and central New Mexico have no natural surface water. No lakes, streams, or even springs. None! All water along these routes must be carried, cached, or obtained from stock tanks.

The term "tank" in New Mexico can refer to a large metal container, but just as often it refers to a small earthen dam that catches runoff. Moss and crud often accompany water from the metal tanks—though not always—and if the windmill is working, it's advisable to take the water directly from the pipe before it enters the tank. The metal tanks are vastly preferable to the pond tanks; here cattle and other animals wade in and out of the water, muddying and fouling it. Also, pond-tanks, dependent upon runoff, are notoriously unreliable, especially during dry times—when they're needed most!

Tanks, of course, weren't intended for humans; they were created for cattle—and are usually found on private land. In this book, I've pointed out these tanks and, where possible, given their latitude-longitude coordinates, because not to do so would be irresponsible. But I urge you, when feasible, to seek the landowner's permission, and at the very least don't damage fences or harass livestock. Without the goodwill of New Mexico's ranching community, and without the water facilities they've created, hiking the CDT in New Mexico would be all but impossible.

In the strongest terms, I recommend treating *all* water along the CDT. All water. Period. Cattle are ubiquitous in New Mexico, even in wilderness areas, and even where they're absent, other pollutants exist. Sure, you might get away with not treating some water, but why risk ruining your trip?

As for methods of treatment, that's up to you. Iodine, filtration, boiling: whatever suits your hiking style and constraints.

THE SUN

Skin cancer kills more New Mexicans each year than all the rattlesnakes, scorpions, spiders, flash floods, plague, and hantavirus combined; yet many hikers who dutifully pack a snakebite kit routinely go out without sun protection.

Three factors make the sun especially searing here. One is latitude: New Mexico is closer to the equator than more northern states, the sun more directly overhead. Another is aridity; the dry air doesn't contain much moisture to block harmful rays. But most important is elevation. Most of the state is around 5,000 feet, and many areas are much higher. Thus, harmful ultraviolet rays more easily penetrate the less-dense atmosphere here than they can at lower elevations.

Protecting yourself against the sun involves avoiding the outdoors when the sun moves directly overhead, wearing long-sleeved shirts, wearing hats (there was a reason cowboys in the Old West wore broad-brimmed hats), and wearing sunscreen that's rated at least 15. In New Mexico, even a tan doesn't prevent eventual skin damage; the darkest tan provides less protection than sunscreen rated 15.

The sun also causes heat-related disorders. Here's a summary of those, their symptoms, and their treatment:

HEAT CRAMPS

Loss of electrolytes, such as salt, through sweating causes heat cramps. Drink fluids that replace electrolytes, such as lightly salted water, lemonade, or sport drink, and stretch the cramped muscle.

HEAT EXHAUSTION

Again, if you fail to replace water and salts lost through sweating, you could suffer heat exhaustion. Symptoms include weakness, instability, or extreme fatigue; wet, clammy skin; headache, nausea, and collapse. To treat heat exhaustion, rest in the shade and drink salt-replacing fluids.

HEATSTROKE

Heatstroke is a very serious condition in which the body's temperature-regulating mechanisms collapse. Symptoms include hot, dry skin; high body temperature (as much as 106° F); mental confusion; delirium; loss of consciousness; and convulsions. This is a true medical emergency, and treatment must begin immediately. Cool the victim as rapidly as possible, either by immersing in cold water or soaking his or her clothing and fanning to promote evaporative cooling. Treat for shock, if necessary, when the victim's temperature lowers. If medical help is available, seek it at once.

HUMANS

Regrettably, the hazard I fear most while hiking in New Mexico is other people. No, I don't feel on the trails the way joggers do in New York's Central park after dark—I actually feel very safe in the wilderness—but my car at the trailhead . . . Vandalism of vehicles and theft are real and serious problems for New Mexico's hikers, especially in the northern part of the state, where villagers often regard outsiders with suspicion and a few see them as fair game. Here are some suggestions for protecting your vehicle:

• Don't leave anything of value in your vehicle.

• Don't leave valuables in plain view; cover or conceal them.

• Check with the local rangers or public lands managers to see which areas have been safe and which have not.

• Ask someone at the trailhead—a campground host, a camper—to watch your vehicle, or, better yet, to allow you to park it nearby.

LIGHTNING

Lightning is a serious hazard, most common during New Mexico's summer thunder-shower, or monsoon, season. The dark clouds presaging these storms can move fast and should inspire hikers to consider escape from ridges and other exposed areas. Because lightning tends to follow the shortest distance between the ground and the sky, you should avoid high points or lone trees. Experts recommend seeking a low, treeless area in the terrain and squatting there until the storm passes. For those concerned about getting drenched, taking shelter in a low-exposure stand of trees, preferably of uniform height, is the best alternative. Hiding in shallow caves or overhangs is not recommended, as ground currents from nearby strikes flow through them.

FLASH FLOOD

Until you've seen one, the suddenness and ferocity of a flash flood are difficult to imagine, especially on the sunny days when only sand fills the arroyos. Be mindful of weather conditions as you hike, especially during the summer thundershower season, and not just overhead but also in the distance. When you hike in narrow canyons, ask yourself whether you could climb to higher ground if you had to. And don't camp in drainages. Many times I've hiked in dry watercourses and noticed weathered water-borne debris tangled in tree branches higher than my head.

STICKERS AND PRICKERS
New Mexico has a wonderfully diverse array of cacti, as well as other spiny plants such as mesquite. That's one reason my utility knife must include a pair of tweezers.

POISON IVY
This plant is locally common, especially around moist areas. Your only protection is learning to recognize it, even when its shiny green leaves, in groups of three, are absent. Some studies suggest that washing with soap and water immediately after contact removes at least some of the noxious oil, *urushiol.*

STINGING NETTLE
This plant occurs occasionally along streams, and all outdoors people should learn to recognize it, just as with poison ivy. Contact with stinging nettle results in mild to moderate skin pain that typically disappears in an hour or less.

PLAGUE, HANTAVIRUS
Regrettably, New Mexico is among the North American reservoirs for *Yersinia pestis,* the bacterium that causes plague, and each year a few cases, and even a few deaths, occur. Similarly, hantavirus, a serious disease, first surfaced in New Mexico, and it has since been discovered elsewhere.

Your chances of being infected by one of these diseases are minuscule, and the strategy for protecting yourself is simple: Avoid *all* contact with rodents—their droppings, their holes and dens, their dead carcasses, everything. Actually, avoiding all contact with all wild animals is a good idea.

RATTLESNAKES
Several species of rattlesnakes (the western diamondback is the most common) are found throughout New Mexico, though above 8,000 feet they're increasingly rare. My home in the southern Sandia Mountains is in rattlesnake habitat, and I go trail running or walking in the Sandia foothills almost every day, not to mention the numerous hikes and outings I take elsewhere in New Mexico. Over the years, I've averaged about two rattlesnake sightings a year, and I've never been bitten or even struck at. I am convinced that rattlesnakes want to avoid a confrontation and thus are reluctant to strike. I'm alert to news accounts of rattlesnake bites in New Mexico; they're uncommon, and almost invariably result when someone has attempted to handle or provoke the snake. I hope you find all this reassuring.

If you are still terrified of rattlesnakes, that's okay; I understand. They scare the hell out of me when I encounter them, and I all but refuse to walk outdoors on warm nights without a flashlight. The rules for avoiding unpleasant rattlesnake encounters are simple:

- Watch where you put your hands and feet; don't reach up to grab ledges without looking first.
- Check around tents, sleeping bags, packs—anything left on the ground.
- Be aware that rattlesnakes are most active at night; use a flashlight.
- Be aware that you cannot rely on rattlesnakes to rattle and alert you to their presence; fewer than half the snakes I've encountered have ever rattled.
- *Never* attempt to touch, move, annoy, or capture a rattlesnake.
- *Never* touch or handle a dead rattlesnake; amazing how many bites occur from so-called dead snakes.

What if you or a member of your party, against all odds, is bitten? The recommended responses vary widely and are controversial. About the only thing everyone agrees upon is this: Seek medical help *immediately.*

SPIDERS

Two dangerous spider species live in New Mexico: black widows and brown recluses. Both are retiring and nonaggressive, and most bites occur when a spider has found its way into clothing or bedding. Symptoms of a bite include pain centered on a red area. If you suspect a bite has occurred, do not wait for symptoms—seek medical help immediately; countermeasures are available. Fortunately, both species of spider are more often found around human dwellings than in wild nature. I have never seen either species on a hiking trip in New Mexico. I have, however, encountered tarantulas—and count myself fortunate when I do. These gentle giants are interesting to watch, but don't attempt to handle them. Although the tarantula's bite is not dangerous, it can still be painful and can become infected.

SCORPIONS

These exist in the state's warmer regions, but they're rare and retiring; the lethal species is not found in New Mexico. Most stings occur when people lift stones or logs because scorpions hide beneath them. When camping, don't leave clothing, shoes, and bedding out, and inspect and shake these before using them. In all hiking in New Mexico, I've found only one scorpion, a dormant one my daughter dug out of a dirt bank in winter.

Climate and Seasons on New Mexico's Continental Divide Trail

Weather patterns in New Mexico differ in important ways from those in other states. For example, many hikers assume that because the state has an arid climate, rain isn't a consideration. Not only does it rain, but it often does so with a ferocity seldom experienced elsewhere. The wettest months are July, August, and early September—New Mexico's so-called "Monsoon Season"—when moisture-laden tropical air triggers frequent, and sometimes violent, afternoon thunderstorms. Lightning associated with these makes summits and ridges especially dangerous, and flash flooding makes camping in dry watercourses unwise. In the high mountains, monsoon thunderstorms—and associated lightning—can occur every day, so hikers hoping to climb peaks or ridges during the monsoon season should plan to be off them by noon. By mid-September, the monsoon pattern usually has weakened substantially; by late September and October, the weather is glorious —bright, sunny days with clear turquoise skies, and cool (but not bone-chilling) nights.

By November, higher elevations and the state's northern sections become vulnerable to winter storms. Barring storms, winter can offer some surprisingly good hiking, especially in the state's southern part. Snow rarely lingers, and because the general humidity is low, chilly nights soon meld into bright, warm days.

April, May, June, and early July typically are dry. As I write this on June 21, however, I am watching thunderclouds gather over the Sandia Mountains; it has rained for most days this particular June.

I tell you this as a reminder that New Mexico experiences great variation in precipitation—and not just from season to season but also from year to year. The winter of 1998–1999 was one of New Mexico's driest ever, with almost no precipitation after November. Dry winters mean that some high-elevation areas, normally snowbound, are open for hiking much earlier than usual. But severe drought also means that marginal water sources—springs and intermittent streams—will eventually run dry. Even worse, summer thunderstorms ignite forest fires throughout the state, and tinderbox conditions force forest managers to restrict public access. Your CDT route runs through the Gila National Forest? Sorry, try again next year.

Yet the winter of 1997–1998 in New Mexico was one of the wettest on record; deep snowpack made high mountain areas impassable far later than usual, water was everywhere, and the state burst into a verdant garden. The year before that—another drought. In planning your hike, then, it's essential that you contact local land managers for current conditions.

New Mexico also has a windy season, typically from late March to early April, when strong westerlies scour the state with dust and grit. Not pleasant hiking, especially in open, exposed areas. One springtime thru-hiker in southern New Mexico had to lash his hat onto his head!

Here is some climatological information for four New Mexico towns on or near the CDT, south to north:

	Elevation	April average high/low	October average high/low	Annual precipitation
Deming	4,335 feet	77º/42º	78º/46º	8.5 inches
Silver City	5,895 feet	67º/37º	70º/41º	15.6 inches
Grants	6,462 feet	67º/27º	70º/41º	9.8 inches
Taos	6,950 feet	64º/29º	67º/32º	12.1 inches

Snow-laden cholla above Rio Chama near Abiquiu, Santa Fe National Forest. Photo by Tom Till.

Horses on New Mexico's Continental Divide Trail

Horses have been part of New Mexico since, well, the Ice Ages, although the popular image of horses in New Mexico has less to do with the Pleistocene than with the cowboy scene. Reintroduced by the Spaniards in 1540, horses have formed an inseparable bond with New Mexico's history and culture—and continue to do so. In the state's backcountry and wild lands, horses have constituted the traditional mode of travel. Aldo Leopold rode a horse when he explored what became the Gila Wilderness and the Aldo Leopold Wilderness, the latter named for him because his vision led to their creation.

Boulders in a meadow at sunset, Rio de las Vacas and Rito Anastacio confluence. Photo by William Stone.

New Mexico's great conservationist, Elliott Barker, born and raised in the Pecos country, rode horses throughout his long life as an outdoorsman. Senator Clinton P. Anderson, wilderness advocate and chair of the committee responsible for the watershed Wilderness Act of 1964, acquired his love of wilderness while riding horses. Indeed, when a couple of young men in the 1950s undertook to spend a week in the Pecos Wilderness on foot, carrying their gear on their backs, the idea was so novel it was featured in *New Mexico Magazine.*

It is appropriate then that when Congress authorized the Continental Divide Trail in 1978, they mandated that horse travel be among the nonmotorized uses allowed; this mandate has benefited everyone. Many New Mexico CDT segments were laid out, marked, and maintained by equestrians, especially those belonging to Backcountry Horsemen of New Mexico. These equestrians have improved springs and built corrals and formed part of every central New Mexico CDT work party. When CDT volunteers arrive to build trail in the remote Black Range, the Forest Service gets them and their supplies there—by horse. Indeed, when Forest Rangers reconnoiter and maintain the CDT, they usually do so by horse.

Equestrians also provide an important link to New Mexico's ranching community. One horse person talking to another is probably the best way to promote understanding of the CDT among ranchers, whose water facilities are so important to CDT users.

Not all sections of the CDT are suitable for equestrians. Water is a critical issue for hikers, but it is even more so for horses, each of which can drink up to 30 gallons at a stop. Terrain is also an issue; no one would take a horse across a lava field. Cliffs, steep side slopes, sharp rocks—humans will hike many places they wouldn't in conscience take a horse. Also, trailheads must be accessible to vehicles with horse trailers.

But some segments, such as the San Pedro Parks, the Zuni Mountains, and the Mangas Mountain area, are excellent for horseback riding. Furthermore, many CDT sections hold historical significance for equestrians. The Separ Road segment intersects the old Pony Express route. Along segments near Pie Town some of the West's largest cattle drives passed. In the Mount Taylor and Rio Puerco areas are remnants of the stagecoach and military route connecting Santa Fe and Fort Wingate, as well as points in Arizona.

In some parts of the West, animosity has arisen between hikers and equestrians. That's regrettable for everyone. Fortunately, that situation really hasn't emerged in New Mexico. I want to believe that hikers and equestrians here recognize they share common goals, and will gain far more by cooperating than by competing.

GUIDELINES FOR HIKERS

Horses can be dangerous, to their riders and to bystanders. Equestrians request that hikers observe the following behaviors:

If you're wearing a pack when you approach a horse—talk. Horses sometimes misinterpret the large shape as a bear.

If you have dogs with you, put them under leash control.

Segment 1
Mexican Border to NM 81: Big Hatchet Mountains

Animas Mountains in New Mexico's Bootheel, seen from Animas Valley grasslands near Cloverdale. Photo by Tom Till.

28 miles
Difficulty: Strenuous

You may encounter: ranch vehicles and livestock

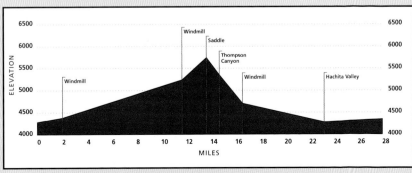

Segment 1   **Total Elevation Gain:** 2,342 feet
From Mexico 0 miles
To Colorado 699 miles

CONTINENTAL DIVIDE
TRAIL ALLIANCE

TRAIL OVERVIEW The first segment covers the southern beginning—or end—of the 3,100-mile-long Continental Divide National Scenic Trail. It's a rather inauspicious beginning and a challenging one. As occurs so often in New Mexico, the Continental Divide Trail at its outset is less a single marked trail than a network of alternative routes. This network occurs at least partly because the CDT here cannot follow the physical divide along the crest of the Animas Mountains, where the Continental Divide enters New Mexico from Mexico. The Animas Foundation, which owns the mountains and manages the land for long-term ecological research, resolutely forbids hiking. Thus, CDT hikers begin their journeys elsewhere, to the east. Of the three alternative routes hikers have followed, two follow paved roads. Although this guide discusses these routes, it focuses primarily on the more primitive route, sanctioned by the Bureau of Land Management, through the Big Hatchet Mountains and along associated dirt roads. The wild and rugged Big Hatchet Mountains include the 48,720-acre Big Hatchet Mountains BLM Wilderness Study Area (WSA), as well as the Big Hatchet State Game Refuge, established primarily to protect a herd of desert bighorn sheep. The terrain is complex, and often very steep; the vegetation, although interesting, is conspicuously hostile to hikers—thorny, prickly, spiny, jagged, sharp, serrated, stabbing—you get the idea. I hiked here with two thru-hikers who wore shorts; blood soon ran down their legs. Except for a faint, unmarked path leading to Big Hatchet Peak, and a primitive road up South Sheridan Canyon now reverting to wilderness trail, trailheads and trails are completely absent; the CDT will be marked by stakes and cairns. Your chances of encountering other humans in the Big Hatchet Mountains are small; your chances of meeting other hikers minuscule. Most New Mexicans have never heard of the Big Hatchet Mountains, much less visited them.

So this is indeed a difficult, perhaps even daunting (after all, it's wilderness) CDT segment, fraught with challenges and obstacles. Approached with preparation and an awareness of these challenges, however, it can also be a beautiful, exciting, and satisfying beginning—or end—to a beautiful, exciting, and satisfying journey.

WATER NOTES

No water drops are necessary in this segment—if you hit the windmills and stock tanks right. The average distance between sources is about 8 miles, and they are well-spaced. But these sources are by no means guaranteed, and, as for the water quality, well, Sheridan Tank has been reported to be a giant algae culture. At any source, stock up enough to get you not just to the next source but to the one beyond as well.

MOUNTAIN BIKE NOTES

The severe climate, exposed and arid terrain, and vast distances over endless treeless plains argue against this section as a desirable mountain bike destination, though many of the primitive tracks comprising the CDT, especially from NM 81 to Thompson Canyon, are ideal terrain for mountain biking. On the other hand, this area is open for mountain biking throughout the winter, and the scenery and vegetation, especially mountains and

wildflowers, can be spectacular in the spring (about March). Note that because the Big Hatchet area is a BLM WSA and State Game Refuge, some parts are forbidden to mountain biking.

EQUESTRIAN NOTES

Lack of trails, steep and rocky terrain, and paucity of water make this segment unlikely for horse travel.

SOUTHBOUND HIKERS

S You have all but arrived at your long-desired goal. The final miles to the Mexican border will be challenging, and even if your journey began no farther north than the Colorado border, its end will differ dramatically from its beginning. This is the Chihuahuan Desert, and though you've been traversing this habitat since the Separ Road segment, not until here, in the Big Hatchet Mountains WSA, do you finally experience its pristine richness.

Of course, if you're sick of the desert, or sick of hiking, you can skip the Big Hatchets and simply walk the BLM roads to the border. You'll still experience great views of the Big Hatchets.

The CDT's end, or beginning, will be, well, unassuming, at best. Underwhelming, perhaps anticlimactic. A wire fence, a dirt road, and miles of scrub and brush. But that's okay. After all, on journeys such as these, the inner landscape is what's really important, the pride and satisfaction you feel inside. So revel in your accomplishment.And then go about returning to civilization. You should not have begun this segment without making some arrangements to return, at least to Hachita or perhaps to Interstate 10.

MAPS

USGS QUADRANGLES: Cabin Wells, Sheridan Canyon, U Bar Ridge, Big Hatchet Peak, Hatchet Ranch

OTHER MAPS: BLM 1:100K Animas.

LAND-MANAGEMENT AGENCIES

BLM/Las Cruces Field Office

BEGINNING ACCESS POINT

Smooth road to Trailhead 15.5 miles + Bumpy road to Trailhead 23 miles

MEXICAN BORDER: The first major challenge CDT hikers face in this segment is simply getting to its beginning; this is less difficult—but still problematic—for hikers starting out either in Antelope Wells or in Columbus, reached by paved roads. Beginning the "scenic route" through the Big Hatchet Mountains requires a long drive over rough dirt roads. The simplest way to start is to contract with someone in Hachita to drop you off. Pat Harris, who, with his wife, runs the restaurant and gift shop called the Egg Nest in Hachita, strongly supports the CDT and for a reasonable fee, which you negotiate with him, will take CDT hikers either to the Antelope Wells or to the Big Hatchet starting point. Otherwise, from Hachita, take paved NM 81 south about 15.5 miles to Hatchet Gap, a low divide between some small but steep and well-defined hills. Just northwest of the hill south of the highway, a dirt road heads south, runs through an area of corrals and pens, then about a mile south of the highway heads east, just south of the hill. The large mountains looming farther south are the Big Hatchet Mountains.

All the maps show a maze of unmarked BLM and ranch roads, but the recently upgraded road you're following is the main road. *Note:* The BLM is planning to develop new public access routes to the Big Hatchets. You'll stay on this road as it parallels the Big Hatchets' eastern escarpment, gradually swinging from east to southeast to south. After about 23 miles from NM 81, you will reach an abandoned and decaying adobe building with a windmill and large stock tank nearby (N31°30'07", W108°14'30", elevation 4,380 feet). Walk or drive past the stock tank and proceed 2 miles due east to where the road ends unceremoniously at a wire fence and the border (elevation about 4,280 feet).

ENDING ACCESS POINT

 NM 81: Paved NM 81 runs south 12 miles from NM 9 at Hachita to reach this segment's end, the Granite Gap Road. Traffic along this highway is light; near the windmill just south of the highway you'll find space for parking.

SUPPLIES, SERVICES, AND ACCOMMODATIONS

HACHITA, population 100, is the community nearest this segment. No overnight accommodations exist in Hachita. The Egg Nest has a restaurant and basic supplies, as does the Hachita Café and Store. You'll find the nearest larger towns along Interstate 10, 19 miles north of Hachita. To the west along Interstate 10 is Lordsburg with grocery stores, restaurants, banks, motels, and a post office (88045), but larger and closer is Deming, about 33 miles to the east. Deming has supermarkets, restaurants, banks, numerous motels, and post offices; see Segment 3, page 73).

Distance from Trail	12 miles	
Zip Code	88040	
Bank	None	
Bus	None	
Dining	The Egg Nest	(505) 436-2666
	E-mail: theeggnest@vtc.net	
	Hachita Café and Store	436-2682
Emergency	911; non-emergency, Grant County Sheriff	538-2555 or 538-3797
Gear	None	
Groceries	The Hachita Café and Store and The Egg Nest	
Information	The Egg Nest and the Hachita Café and Store	
Laundry	None	
Lodging	None	
Medical	None	
Post Office	(88040)	436-2220
Showers	None	

TRAIL DESCRIPTION If you expected something striking to photograph to commemorate your journey's beginning or end, you'll be sorely disappointed. Rather, you'll find a wire fence with the United States on this side, Mexico on that, and lots of flat scrubland all around. You will find a commemorative plaque at the site, but this has nothing to do with the CDT: A cracked concrete block commemorates the murder of one Frank Evans, born June 12, 1865, and "killed by a crazy cook with an ax" on May 11, 1907. Or you can follow the fence 1.0 mile south to a border monument. For any inaugural festivities, you're on your own—but then, some of the best journeys see the most prosaic beginnings. And it's in that spirit that Joseph Gendron, who identified this beginning, used his prerogative as pioneer to name it Tierra Común, "Common Ground," in the hope that the CDT here could be a link of greater peace and understanding between the United States and Mexico. After all, the Divide ignores borders, and the terrain does not suddenly change at the boundary.

Once you've reached the fence and taken your photos (consider using the scenic Big Hatchet Mountains to the west as a background), turn around and retrace your route west back to the stock tank. Fill your gut and all your water bottles here because your next water is about 8 hot, dry miles away. Hike past the abandoned building and you'll soon leave the road you came in on for a more primitive dirt two-track heading northwest into the BLM's Big Hatchet Mountains WSA. This road gradually goes uphill through open scrubland, affording spectacular views to the south of the dramatic formations of the Alamo Hueco Mountains.

After about 3 miles the road supposedly ends, near the mouth of South Sheridan Canyon, but a faint 4WD track continues northwest into the broad canyon. It continues approximately 2.25 miles following the drainage until it climbs out to a divide (N31°34'35", W108°19'40", elevation 5,280—one mile!). From the divide, the 4WD road follows another drainage downhill about 1.25 miles before leaving the drainage and heading northwest to the windmill (N31°35'50", W108°20'10", elevation 5,038 feet), your next—and only—source of water. If you find yourself hiking about due east in Sheridan Canyon, you've missed the windmill and need to backtrack up Sheridan Canyon to find it. *Note:* This windmill is said to pump dry by late afternoon, but the water tank for cows usually has water.

At the Sheridan Canyon windmill, all roads and trails end, so again, fill your gut and water bottles here. From now on you hike cross-country and use map, compass, and Global Positioning System to make your way into Thompson Canyon. The topography here is complex. Your goal is the windmill near the mouth of Thompson Canyon. From the Sheridan Canyon windmill, head northwest out of the broad wash to cross a small drainage and climb onto a ridge trending northwest. Many small ridges and drainages enter the wash here, and it's not a large problem if you choose a less direct one, as long as you get to N31°36'22", W108°20'37", or the point just above the lettering for the 5,239-foot elevation notation on the Sheridan Canyon quadrangle, about 0.7 mile from the windmill.

Having reached this point, you now climb steeply about 0.8 mile northwest along this ridge as it trends toward a 6,123-foot summit (N31°36'50", W108°21'07"; elevation labeled on map). The CDT actually runs just south of this summit to a saddle southwest of the summit. From here the CDT descends along the west side of the canyon running north, crossing to the east side after about 0.5 mile, to the junction with Thompson Canyon about a mile from the saddle. The junction's coordinates are N31°37'29", W108° 21'40," elevation 5,360 feet.

 SOUTHBOUND HIKERS: This is the crux of the Big Hatchet Mountains segment. Use your GPS and map and compass to find where the CDT leaves Thompson Canyon. No tread exists here, but you may find CDT markers. Your goal is to cross from Thompson Canyon over the mountains into Sheridan Canyon.

From here, route-finding is simpler. Pause a moment to admire the rugged limestone cliffs forming the canyon's northern wall. Then follow the Thompson Canyon road/trail northeast as it runs gently downhill, out of the canyon and the mountains. The canyon broadens, and the trail becomes a two-track. You'll pass through a gated fence, then continue down the two-track to the windmill, N31°38'39", W108°20'01", elevation 4,705 feet. Here as you emerge onto the Hachita Valley plains the terrain is gentle, open, and exposed. The vegetation is classic Chihuahuan Desert: creosote bush, mesquite, several species of yucca and cacti, and intermittent grasslands.

SOUTHBOUND HIKERS: The road—just a very rough two-track, actually —leading into Thompson Canyon isn't marked, so either set your GPS unit for the windmill above or use your map and compass to guide you into Thompson Canyon. The canyon, with its dramatic limestone cliffs, is a major feature.

From the windmill and tank to the junction with the Hatchet Ranch road is 0.7 mile. At this junction, the Hatchet Ranch road runs northeast just about 100 yards before swinging north-northwest. It runs north-northwest about 2.7 miles before jogging west-northwest. To the north you'll see the Hatchet Ranch, slightly less than a mile away. Some CDT hikers have taken the road leading past the ranch to continue north to NM 81, but because this traverses private land the official route continues west-northwest 2.5 miles to N31°42'10", W108°22'35". Here a dirt road runs southwest 0.2 mile to a windmill-fed stock tank, a reliable water source. Also here a dirt track marked with CDT signs on carsonite posts branches northeast and runs 2.7 miles to a fenceline, which it then follows north 2.1 miles to yet another reliable windmill-fed-stock tank, surrounded by cottonwoods at N31°45'58", W108°23'00". From here it's just 0.33 mile to NM 81.

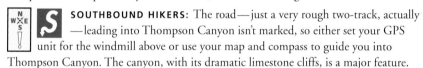 **ALTERNATIVE ROUTES: NM 81 AND NM 11** Before Joseph Gendron and the BLM pioneered the routes through the Big Hatchet Mountains, most CDT hikers began their journeys by walking NM 81 between Antelope Wells and Hachita, approximately 47 miles, all paved. The highway is uncomplicated, the few gradients long and gentle, and traffic light. Water is available primarily from windmill-fed stock tanks. Antelope Wells is a border crossing, not a settlement, with no services on either side of the border.

Other thru-hikers have begun their treks by starting at the Mexican border just south of Columbus and hiking paved NM 11, 37 miles to Deming. Traffic along this highway is much heavier than NM 81, and likely to be fast. Again, water is found primarily in stock tanks. Just across the border lies the Mexican town of Palomas, with 8,000 people. The church of Nuestra Señora de Guadalupe is worth a visit. The border crossing is open 24 hours a day. Columbus, with 1,700 people (fewer in summer), has basic supplies and services. Deming, the seat of Luna County, has 14,000 residents and a full array of services. As you approach Deming from the south you see to the east the dramatic peaks of the Florida Mountains, where in the 1950s a herd of Persian ibex was introduced by New Mexico archaeologist and big-game hunter Frank Hibben. He'd noticed in his travels that the habitat here seemed identical to that of the ibex in the Iranian mountains, and he believed an ecological niche here was unfilled. Apparently he was right, for the ibex have flourished, so much so that hunters are allowed to take a few each year.

OTHER HIKES AND RIDES: BIG HATCHET PEAK

APPROXIMATE ONE-WAY DISTANCE: 4 miles
MODE OF TRAVEL: Hiking
DIFFICULTY: Strenuous

The only hiking trail in the Big Hatchet Mountains leads to the summit of the range's highest peak, 8,366-foot Big Hatchet Peak. This trail, unmarked at the trailhead and elsewhere, begins near the mouth of Thompson Canyon, on the range's east side. Drive the dirt BLM road from Hatchet Gap to where a rougher dirt road heads west toward Thompson Canyon. You'll pass a windmill and stock tank, likely the only water you'll encounter.

Approximately 0.5 mile west of the windmill you reach a gated fence. Park here and begin walking the two-track west into the canyon. To the north stand some impressive limestone cliffs. The two-track continues along the canyon's bottom, getting rougher and narrower until it's no longer a road but a trail. As the canyon begins to bend to the northwest, the trail leaves the canyon to begin slabbing up the steep slopes, eventually to reach the summit, N31°38'08", W108°23'53". This is a challenging hike, especially in hot weather, so take plenty of water. The views from the summit make it all worthwhile.

HISTORICAL NOTES

About the Bootheel. This CDT segment traverses the Bootheel (a glance at a state map will explain the name); it's arguably the state's most remote, least populated region, although New Mexico has several competitors for that title. Three thousand of Hidalgo County's 6,270 residents live in Lordsburg, its county seat and largest town. As one goes farther south, the land progressively becomes even less populated: The Bootheel lies deeply embedded within the hot, dry Chihuahuan Desert. In 1910, the locality of Hermanas, just to the east of the Bootheel, captured the state's aridity record when just one inch of precipitation was recorded for the year. Such desert plants as mesquite, sotol, creosote bush, century plant, agave, and numerous species of cacti thrive in these mountains and broad valleys.

To ecologists, this part of the great Chihuahuan Desert, North America's largest, is exceptionally interesting because it's a transition zone between more tropical ecosystems to the south and more temperate ones to the north. The endangered night-blooming cereus grows here, as well as at least two species of pincushion cacti. Among the animals found here are javelina, coatimundi, pygmy mouse, thick-billed kingbird, golden eagles, giant spotted whiptail lizard, and Sonoran mountain king snake. The Big Hatchet Mountains are home to one of New Mexico's last indigenous populations of desert bighorn sheep, and it was to protect them that the Big Hatchet State Game Refuge, through which the CDT passes, was established.

Because seemingly rich grasslands exist elsewhere in the Bootheel, geography alone doesn't explain this region's isolation; the Chiricahua and Gila Apaches also had much to do with it. The Bootheel was their territory, and their fierce warfare against Mexicans and Americans persisted here into the 1880s. In September 1886, in Skeleton Canyon in the Peloncillo Mountains on the Bootheel's western edge, Geronimo finally surrendered. As one historian summarized, during those fearful years it was almost impossible for would-be stockmen to maintain their herds in Apache country. When ranches were finally established, the sparse desert and lack of water dictated that they be very large. The conservationist Animas Foundation now owns and manages the 321,000-acre Gray Ranch here; the pattern of relatively few individuals and interests controlling very large ranches continues to this day.

Without wanting to prejudge individual Bootheel ranchers, I must note that in the Bootheel, suspicion of outsiders often subsumes Western hospitality. This tendency stems in part from the region's traditional isolation and also from occasional incidents involving illegal migrants and drug smugglers from Mexico. The U.S. Border Patrol will likely scrutinize anyone on foot in the Bootheel outside the Big Hatchet Mountains WSA. Even as the Bootheel is a daunting, difficult land, it's also one of sublime beauty and peace. Here legends of the Old West thrived, and here legends of the New West are born.

Hiking the Bootheel. The Bootheel is arid; there are no permanent streams, no permanent lakes, and few springs. Often the only reliable water sources are those ranchers have created for cows: stock tanks, usually fed by windmills. In the Bootheel's heat and low humidity, you will need a lot of water, but long distances frequently separate water sources. These conditions mean that you'll have to carry substantial amounts of water, and your pack weight will increase accordingly.

More bad news: The Bootheel is exposed. The Chihuahuan Desert's vegetation is low and sparse. The Bootheel lies within the Basin and Range Physiographic Province and thereby is characterized by expansive valleys with only distant mountains to break the prevailing winds. One CDT thru-hiker wrote in his journal: "Two days of 50 mph winds from the west. Had to rope my hat on."

These conditions mean that timing is everything when hiking the Bootheel. March is not too early; indeed, you'll find desert plants greening and blooming as if to say that it's spring as far as they're concerned. If the winter has been a wet one (relatively speaking), the desert wildflowers will bloom as in a garden. If winter has been dry, flowers will be less likely to bloom, springs will be less likely to flow. April is considerably warmer than March, but still not oppressive. In May, temperatures will soar. No one would hike here in summer, except in the very early morning, late evening, or by the light of a full moon. September is still hot. In October, the heat wanes, and November is quite pleasant, although the midday sun can still beat down intensely. No one should assume that, because this is desert, winter holds no dominion here; savage storms sometimes rake the desert, though the snow never stays for long. To gauge weather and water conditions in any given year, contact the BLM's Las Cruces Field Office (see Appendix A), which has extensive holdings in the Bootheel, including much of the CDT.

Remoteness, difficult access, forbidding terrain, and paucity of trails make the Big Hatchet Mountains seldom visited by hikers, and these few hike primarily to Big Hatchet Peak (described on page 56). Despite all this, the Big Hatchets are scenic, and the desert vegetation and wildlife are interesting; hikers accepting the mountains' challenges will be well-rewarded.

Mimbres Culture petroglyphs on exposed rock south of Cookes Peak, Luna County. Photo by William Stone.

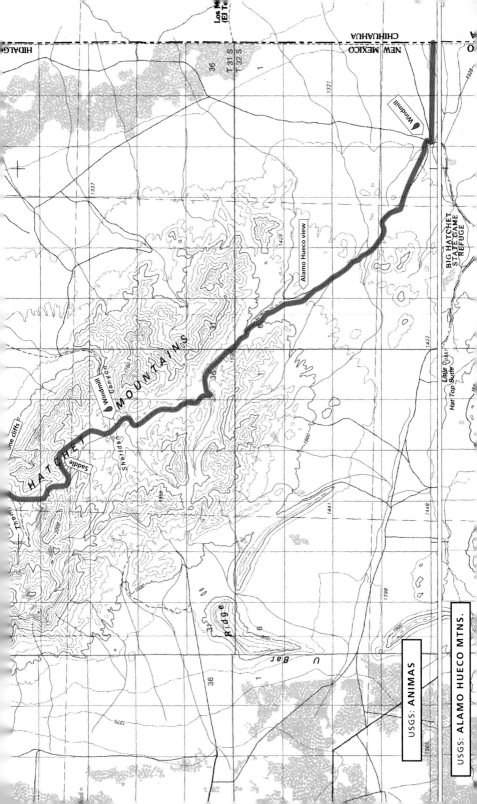

USGS: ANIMAS

USGS: ALAMO HUECO MTNS.

Segment 2
NM 81 to NM 9: Little Hatchet Mountains

Animas Mountains and evening storm
clouds in New Mexico's Bootheel region.
Photo by William Stone.

18.6 miles
Difficulty: Moderate
You may encounter: motorized vehicles

Segment 2   **Total Elevation Gain:** 1,053 feet
From Mexico 28 miles
To Colorado 671 miles

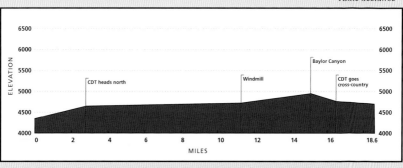

TRAIL OVERVIEW For an hour I'd sat gripping the door tightly as Bureau of Land Management/Continental Divide Trail volunteer Jim Scanlon prodded the Ford three-quarter-ton 4WD pickup over a gut-churning, boulder-studded road whose steep descents and clogged washouts pummeled even this heavily muscled vehicle. Finally, as we neared the ribbon of pavement to the south that was our destination, we met an older man in a weathered cowboy hat riding a shiny red dirt buggy to which a shotgun was strapped. According to the West's unwritten code, we stopped to talk.

He was quail hunting, hadn't seen any, though some "damned pig hunters" had killed a javelina the day before in the draw just to the west. He was bitching eloquently about how crowded with other hunters the area was; we'd seen no one but him since we'd passed two small hunting camps 10 miles north. Thinking I'd toss something positive into the conversation, I remarked, "But it's nice country."

"Like hell it is!" he snapped. "It's goddamned desolate!"

He was so obviously right that I could only laugh. "Goddamned desolate" pretty much summarizes this stretch of the CDT running between NM 81 on the south and NM 9 on the north. The vistas are pleasant enough, and in fortuitous light would even be spectacular. To the east, across the broad treeless flats of the Hachita Valley, the bare Sierra Rica summits present their profile. To the north the valley continues. To the south rise the Big Hatchet Mountains, culminating in 8,366-foot Big Hatchet Peak. And to the west the limestone eminences and ridges of the Little Hatchet Mountains snake north-south. It's up close that the land sprawls in desolation.

Dry. (This is the Chihuahuan Desert, after all.) Bone-dry. The exposed soil is as rough as the dirt road, both studded with white limestone cobbles that brutally reflect the intense sunlight. No trees. None. Not even New Mexico's normally ubiquitous piñons and junipers. No shade. No relief from the relentless sun. Except during the cooler seasons, it's the kind of terrain best traversed early in the morning, late in the afternoon, or at night by the light of a full moon. In the approximately 12 miles between NM 81 and Old Hachita, you should carry enough water to make it all the way between windmills in one day.

Although the pronouncement "goddamned desolate" seems self-evident, this segment holds a certain appeal. Hike it in the early morning, when the day is fresh. Or hike it at evening, when the air turns soft and the declining sun enriches the light. Or late in the fall or early in the spring. You'll be surrounded by long vistas, a depth of open space unknown in many parts of the country. It's the kind of place that inspired Marjorie Hope Nicholson, in *Mountain Gloom and Mountain Glory: The Development of the Aesthetics of the Infinite,* to talk about "the attraction of the vast." If you hike at these times, avoiding the blank glare of midday, you'll likely discover that this desolation is home to a surprising array of wildlife—deer, javelina, wild turkeys, Gambel quail, rabbits (desert cottontails and antelope jackrabbits—but not jackalopes!), coyotes, reptiles, and many more. One CDT hiker saw a coatimundi and described it moving "in a sort of funny hunched-up run, not unlike the sea otters on the coast back home."

Approach this segment with good planning and a positive attitude; be open to serendipity. Joseph Gendron hiked this route in late spring of 1999, a year singularly dry. He said that he had no trouble making it between stock tanks—and he had a great time.

From NM 9 to Old Hachita makes for a good day hike. It even crosses the Continental Divide.

WATER NOTES

 The caveats for Segment 1 apply here. Water is available just across the road from the beginning of the segment—and not again until a similar stock tank 12 miles away. After that, the next water is in Hachita, at least 6 miles away. Carry more water than you expect to need.

MOUNTAIN BIKE NOTES

 NM9 to Old Hachita makes for a good mountain bike excursion. Most of the CDT, although on dirt road, is too rough for pleasurable travel.

EQUESTRIAN NOTES

Paucity of water, lack of facilities for horses, rocky soil, and fences without gates argue for this being an unlikely equestrian destination. This could change, however, given gates, corrals, and access to water.

SOUTHBOUND HIKERS

  The route south is fairly uncomplicated, except at the northern end, though this could be bypassed by simply walking the dirt road from NM 9 west of Hachita (see Trail Description, page 65). Your biggest concern will be water. If you're starting from Hachita, fill up there. Water is available at a stock tank toward the segment's northern end, but its reliability—and certainly its quality—are problematic. A good water source is at the segment's end.

MAPS

USGS QUADRANGLES: Hachita Peak, Playas Peak
OTHER MAPS: BLM 1:100K Animas, Lordsburg

LAND-MANAGEMENT AGENCIES

BLM/Las Cruces Field Office

BEGINNING ACCESS POINT

  NM 81: This paved road goes south 12 miles from NM 9 at Hachita to reach this segment's beginning. Traffic along this highway is light; near the windmill just south of the highway is space for parking.

ENDING ACCESS POINT

NM 9: A paved but lightly traveled road connecting the farming communities of Animas and Hachita, a village 10 miles east of the CDT.

SUPPLIES, SERVICES, AND ACCOMMODATIONS

HACHITA, once known as New Hachita, was born soon after 1900 when a railroad line was built through here. The cowboys, ranchers, miners, prospectors, and others in this vast, arid land must have seen Hachita and its saloons as a welcome oasis. Most of the cowboys and miners are gone now, but there's still a bar, which William Least Heat Moon wrote about in *Blue Highways.* For CDT hikers, Hachita is still an oasis, the first town (albeit a small one) above the Mexican border; see Segment 1, page 53.

TRAIL DESCRIPTION   With a water tank fortuitously nearby, this segment begins at N31°46'16", W108°23'06", elevation 4,360 feet, where a well-graded dirt road branches west-northwest from NM 81, 4.4 miles northeast of Hatchet Gap. Visible just 0.33 mile south of this junction is a windmill-fed stock tank, called Twelve-mile Tank, surrounded by cottonwoods. Take advantage of this reliable water source to fill your stomach and your water bottles, because you have many long, dry miles ahead of you.

The CDT route from NM 81 is marked with CDT signs. Walk the graded road 2.8 miles toward Granite Gap to N31°46'49", W108°25'42", where a much rougher dirt road branches right to head north. From this junction you can see the remains of a windmill in the draw to the northwest, but you'll find no water there. Continue following the rough dirt road north; constructed by miners, this road does not appear on the Hachita Peak quad until it junctions at an east-west dirt road just southeast of Howells Ridge at the north end of the map. It does appear on the Animas 1:100K. The junction and the road are marked with CDT signs.

This road is very rough as it climbs and descends the steep flanks of innumerable arroyos and washes. Don't even think about finding water in them. Indeed, you won't have to worry about missing water sources because there aren't any. The Animas 1:100K map indicates these drainages with blue lines, which is perversely inappropriate as many of these drainages go years without flowing water. Local lore says that springs once flowed in the Big and Little Hatchet Mountains, but most vanished when windmills began tapping the water table. A few springs still exist on the Little Hatchets' western slopes.

Now the only water sources on the east are two stock tanks, 12 miles apart— another good argument for doing this stretch at the coolest time of day, in the coolest season. The vegetation is Chihuahuan Desert: creosote bush, mesquite, several species of yucca and cacti, and sparse desert grass. To the west the limestone ridges and summits of the Little Hatchet Mountains parallel your journey north. At

6,585 feet, Hachita Peak is the highest point in the range, but most summits are lower, giving the range an average relief of 1,500 feet from the eastern foothills. The mountains are as devoid of trees as the surrounding plains.

You'll follow this dirt road north for about 10 rough, dry, exposed miles until at N31°53'33", W108°25'22" the CDT route, marked by signs, briefly leaves the road to cross a creosote bush–filled wash and traverse an easy slope and then rejoin the road after 0.6 mile; this detour, marked with CDT signs, allows you to avoid some private land. Back on the road you can look due east and see 0.3 mile away a windmill structure, N31°53'55", W108°24'19", elevation 4,725 feet. At the windmill's base you'll find a stock pond fed by an electric well pump, the first reliable water you've encountered since NM 81, 12 miles away. The banks of this pond will have been trampled by cattle, and the water will be muddy and grungy, but it is plentiful—and it is there. Treat it and be grateful.

Just before you reached the private land detour you noticed some ruined buildings to the northwest. Though not labeled on either the Playas Peak or Animas USGS quadrangles, this is the ghost town of Old Hachita, a little mining camp that sprang up after 1875 to house miners working nearby claims for silver, lead, copper, and turquoise. By 1884 the village had 300 residents, but by 1890 it had begun its decline, and then in 1900 the El Paso and Southwestern Railroad (EP&SW RR) laid tracks 9 miles north and east, creating the community of New Hachita, 6 miles east; Old Hachita's days were numbered. A few hollow, weathered masonry structures remain— one even retains its roof—and the pockmarks of mines and prospect holes litter the area, reminders of when people found something of intense interest here. But those days are long past; now the Little Hatchet Mountains are ignored by everyone but a few ghost town and mine buffs, a few ranchers, a few quail and javelina hunters, and a few CDT hikers, all of whom are likely to echo the opinion of the man from Silver City: "It's goddamned desolate!"

From where the CDT rejoins the road after the private land detour, the dirt road heads north-northeast for 0.5 mile before making a 0.25-mile jog northwest to join the dirt road heading west past the old Copper King Mine toward an arroyo at the base of Turquoise Mountain, 1.25 miles. After Turquoise Mountain, the CDT heads north, following a dirt road climbing over some low hills to drop after 1 mile into Baylor Canyon. The dirt road crosses the drainage heading north until after 1.25 miles it ends at an east-west dirt road, N31°56'42", W108°26'57". From here the CDT heads north cross-country, intersecting the Divide after 0.4 mile at N31°57'11", W108°26'29", elevation 4,780 feet, en route to NM 9, 1 mile north, N31°58'02", W108°26'15", elevation 4,702 feet. Hachita lies 8.5 miles east along NM 9, paved but with very light traffic.

Should you choose to walk to or from Hachita to where the CDT intersects NM 9, this segment's end point, an alternative to walking along the highway is to walk on the old EP&SW RR, later the Southern Pacific, grade. The tracks were laid after 1900 but have long since been removed. The grade is readily visible just north of the highway, except for where just east of this segment's start it departs from the highway for the same distance you'd walk along the highway; the grade rejoins the highway west of Hachita.

Should you choose to go directly to Hachita after the private land detour, you will continue on the dirt road north-northeast for 3 miles to its intersection with NM 9, at N31°56'03", W108°24'06", not heading northwest towards Turquoise Mountain. From there it's 5 miles east along the highway to Hachita. Most hikers will take a break in the village of Hachita. Hachita, population 100, is the first settlement encountered north of the Mexican border, and after the previous day's traveling, it will seem like New York City.

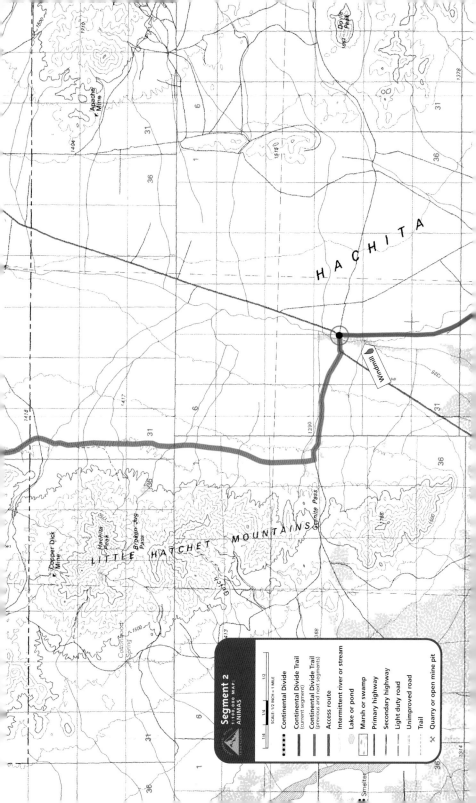

HACHITA

Do b
Peak

Apache
Mine

LITTLE HATCHET MOUNTAINS

Hachita
Peak

Copper Dick
Mine

Broker-Jug
Pass

Granite Pass

Cottonwood
Spring

Windmill

Smelter

Segment 3
NM 9 to Separ: Desert Flats

Mexican gold poppies.
Photo by Tom Till.

20.25 miles
Difficulty: Easy
You may encounter: ranch vehicles and livestock

TRAIL OVERVIEW Getting to Separ is this segment's primary goal. The route is relatively straightforward, the walking relatively easy, though the terrain is exposed and the scenery not exactly Bierstadt material. Gradients are gentle. You'll find the segment's highest point at the beginning, and the two maps covering most of this segment show contour intervals of only 10 feet (with supplemental contours of 5 feet!). The vegetation consists of creosote bush, grading into yuccas, grasses, and other plants of the Lower Sonoran life zone. Water is scarce to nonexistent along the route, except for windmills and stock tanks.

Despite all this, wildlife is rather common here—coyotes, pronghorn, jackrabbit Cedar Mountains Wilderness Study Area, just to the east, has large populations of hunter-attracting deer, wild turkey, and quail.

The terrain is not suitable for day hikes.

WATER NOTES

 The water closest to the beginning of the segment is in Hachita. Information from Segments 1 and 2 apply. From NM 9 it's 10 miles to the next water source, which is a windmill that may not be accessible or functioning. After that, the next windmill is 7 miles farther, with the same caveats. Then there's no water until Separ. If the cattle water is available and potable, this segment should pose no problems. But hedge your bets.

MOUNTAIN BIKE NOTES

Flat terrain, paucity of features, and exposure to wind and sun make this segment unappealing to mountain bike travelers.

EQUESTRIAN NOTES

Unsuitable for horse travel.

SOUTHBOUND HIKERS

Although this segment has a trashy beginning as it goes over crumbling pavement past the deteriorating remains of failed businesses, once you head south on a dirt road, the ambiance improves.

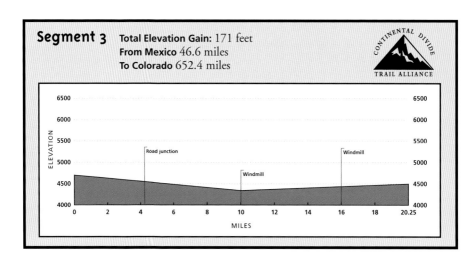

This segment is very dry, with two windmill-fed stock tanks the only probable water sources. There is no water waiting for you when you reach the end at NM 9, either, so be sure to stock up before starting out. You probably will want to hitchhike into Hachita at the end.

MAPS

USGS QUADRANGLES: Playas Peak, Brockman, Separ
OTHER MAPS: BLM 1:100K Animas, Lordsburg

LAND-MANAGEMENT AGENCIES   BLM/Las Cruces Field Office

BEGINNING ACCESS POINT

 NM 9: This segment begins on NM 9, 8.5 miles west of Hachita, just 0.25 mile east of where the Continental Divide crosses the highway. (The Continental Divide crosses the highway again about 1.2 miles southeast.) Should you choose to walk to or from Hachita to this segment's beginning, an alternative to walking along paved but lightly traveled NM 9 is to walk on the old El Paso and Southwestern Railroad grade. The tracks were laid after 1900 but have long since disappeared. The grade is readily visible just north of the highway, except for where, just east of this segment's start, it departs from the highway for 6.5 miles, the same distance you'd walk along the highway to where the grade rejoins the highway west of Hachita.

ALTERNATE ACCESS

 NM 9 FROM ANIMAS: From the west, this segment can be accessed from southwest of Lordsburg by taking NM 338 south from Interstate 10 to NM 9, which heads east toward the Continental Divide Trail from the little farming community of Animas, 30 miles to Hachita, 21.5 to the CDT. NM 9 also can be accessed by taking NM 113 south 20 miles from Interstate 10.

ENDING ACCESS POINT

SEPAR: The segment ends at the interstate locality of Separ, at Exit 42 on Interstate 10. Separ is accessed from the north via the so-called Separ Road, a graded and maintained road that connects with NM 90 after approximately 30 miles.

TRAIL DESCRIPTION   Beginning where the last segment ended on NM 9, 8.5 miles west of Hachita, at N31°58'03", W108°26'15", elevation 4,702 feet, this segment heads due north. Be sure to undertake this segment with plenty of water. The Continental Divide Trail goes cross-country from NM 9, following the 4,700-foot contour past the eastern foothills of the low Coyote Hills, along whose crest the Continental Divide runs. After 0.6 mile you cross a shallow drainage, then another 0.5 mile farther north, then yet another after 0.5 mile. The CDT follows this third drainage as it runs gently downhill to the north-northwest.

SUPPLIES, SERVICES, AND ACCOMMODATIONS

HACHITA, 8.5 miles southeast on NM 9 and described in Segment 1, page 53, has the nearest supplies and services at this segment's southern end.

SEPAR, the segment's northern end, consists essentially of the Continental Divide Trading Post, (505) 546-3635, which specializes in tourist curios and aside from soda and snacks has no other supplies or services. The nearest campground is the Butterfield RV Park, (505) 546-8511, 20 miles east at the Gage exit. (For that distance, you might as well go another 19 miles to Deming.)

LORDSBURG, 25 miles northwest on Interstate 10, with a population of 3,000, is the nearest community offering more extensive services and supplies, having motels, restaurants, grocery stores, and pharmacies. Lordsburg lacks comprehensive medical facilities, however. For these, you should travel east on I-10 to Deming.

Distance from Trail	25 miles	
Zip Code	88045	
Bank	Western Bank, 140 East Motel Drive	(505) 542-3521
Bus	(TNMO line) 112 Wabash Street (behind McDonald's)	542-3412
Dining	Several options	
Emergency	Hidalgo County Sheriff	542-8828
Gear	None, except for limited hunting, fishing, and car camping items at hardware and discount stores	
Groceries	Several options	
Information	Lordsburg–Hidalgo County Chamber of Commerce 208 E. Motel Drive	542-9684
Laundry	Several options	
Lodging	Several options	
Medical	See below (Deming)	
Post Office	(88045) 401 Shakespeare Street	542-9601

DEMING is a major stop on I-10 and with a population of 14,200 has facilities far exceeding those of Lordsburg, including medical facilities. The outdoor stores, however, cater more to fishermen and hunters than to hikers and backpackers.

Distance from Trail	39 miles	
Zip Code	88030	
Bank	First New Mexico, 300 South Gold Avenue	546-2691
	First Savings Bank, 520 South Gold Avenue	546-2707
	Wells Fargo Bank, 223 South Gold Avenue Mon–Thur 9–3, Fri 9–5	546-8871
Bus	(TNMO line) 300 East Spruce Street	546-3412
Dining	Several options	
Emergency	911; Police/Sheriff (non-emergency): 116 East Poplar Street	546-3011 or 546-2655
Gear	D&M Sporting Goods, 616 West Pine Street	542-3505
	Mostly hunting and fishing items; hardware and discount stores.	

continued next page

SUPPLIES, SERVICES, AND ACCOMMODATIONS   *continued from previous page*

DEMING (continued)

Groceries	Several options	
Information	Deming Luna Chamber of Commerce	
	800 East Pine Street (88030-3533)	
Laundry	Several options	
Lodging	Several options	
Medical	Mimbres Memorial Hospital and Nursing Home,	(505) 546-2761
	900 West Ash Street	
Post Office	(88030) 209 West Spruce Street	546-9461

The goal is to reach a three-way road junction 4.3 miles north of NM 9. Follow the drainage downhill. You'll cross a dirt road, then by continuing another mile, going slightly east of the drainage, you'll reach the junction, N32°01'11", W108°25'43", elevation 4,550 feet. Creosote bush, a signature plant of the Chihuahuan Desert, dominates the vegetation thus far. Creosote bush secretes a substance that inhibits plant growth beneath its canopy, causing the regular, if monotonous, spacing of the plants.

At the junction, the CDT follows the dirt road heading east and gently downhill for 1 mile, then again runs cross-country approximately north. In the first mile it crosses the snout of a low ridge, then continues downhill, keeping to the east of a hill to the north-northeast. As it leaves the hill behind, at approximately 3 miles from the dirt road, the CDT crosses the bed of the old Arizona–New Mexico Railroad, which connected Lordsburg and Hachita. Continuing north cross-country 1.2 miles from the railroad bed brings you to a dirt road running southeast-northwest. The approximate coordinates at this point are N32°04'30", W108°24'50". The CDT doesn't follow this road, but if you were to follow it 0.5 mile to a pipeline and continue on the dirt road northwest another 0.5 mile, you'd arrive at a windmill and tank, N32°05'13", W108°25'30", the first water you've encountered.

From the dirt road, the CDT again heads cross-country. The terrain here is all but flat; the dominant vegetation is grass and yucca. In about 0.5 mile you cross a pipeline route running east-northeast–west-southwest. From the pipeline, head north-northwest for 2.6 miles to a road junction. If you go too far east, you hit a north-running dirt road, which also leads to the junction, whose coordinates are N32°07'10", W108°25'00", elevation 4,379 feet.

From here the route is simple. Follow the dirt road north for 6 miles to Interstate 10. At 3.5 miles from the junction, a dirt road branches west to lead after 0.5 mile to a windmill, N32°10'00", W108°25'03".

At Interstate 10, follow a frontage road northwest 0.5 mile to the locality of Separ.

HISTORICAL NOTES

Separ. This segment ends at Separ, today a service point for truck and car traffic on Interstate 10, but 200 years ago this point saw travelers of a different sort: New Mexicans on horses and in wagons on the Janos Trail, which connected the copper mines at Santa Rita with the town of Janos in northern Mexico. According to *The Place Names of New Mexico:* "With the coming of the RR Separ became a cattle-loading station for nearby ranches. Folklore says it took its name from a RR construction camp called Camp Separation, but in fact, the station here originally was called Sepas, not Separ, possibly from the Spanish *cepas,* 'tree stumps, shoots from the base of a tree.' Little remains today of the settlement."

SCALE 1/2 INCH = 1 MILE

1/4   1/4   1/4   1/2

········· Continental Divide

———— Continental Divide Trail
         (current segment)

———— Continental Divide Trail
         (previous and next segments)

———— Access route

 ～～ Intermittent river or stream

        Lake or pond

        Marsh or swamp

———— Primary highway

———— Secondary highway

———— Light duty road

- - - - Unimproved road

········· Trail

×   Quarry or open mine pit

Windmill

Windmill

Black

Mountain

Brockman

The Saltys

Burro

Ninetysix

Pigeon Hill

RAILROAD

DODGE

Draw

Draw

Draw

Valley

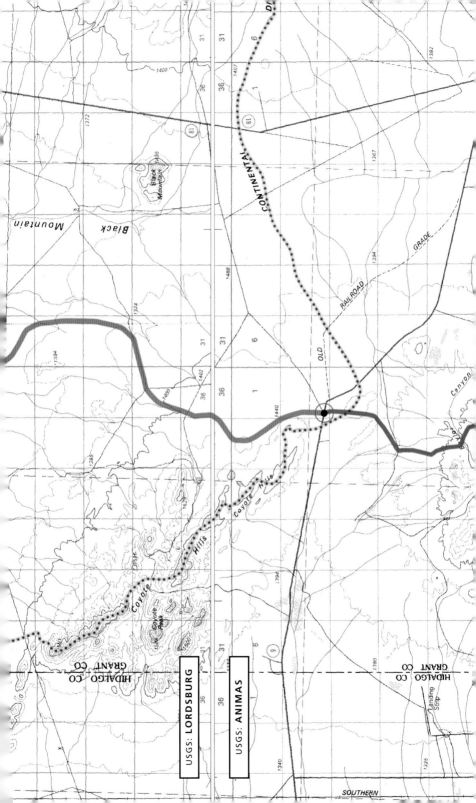

USGS: LORDSBURG

USGS: ANIMAS

Segment 4
Separ to NM 90: Separ Road

From left, JPB Mountain, Soldiers Farewell Hill, and Bessie Rhoads Mountain near the Butterfield Trail. Photo by William Stone.

35.2 miles
Difficulty: Easy

You may encounter: motorized vehicles and livestock

Segment 4
Total Elevation Gain: 1,400 feet
From Mexico 66.85 miles
To Colorado 632.15 miles

CONTINENTAL DIVIDE
TRAIL ALLIANCE

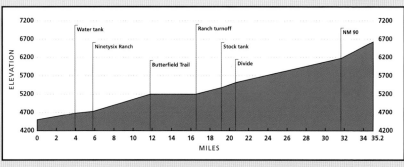

TRAIL OVERVIEW A strong imagination, a fondness for history, and a taste for desert vistas reveal subtleties along this segment that will make the long miles of exposed road go more easily. For example, on this route you'll intersect the historic Butterfield Trail and Soldiers Farewell Hill (see Historical Notes, page 83)—a reminder of when, not much more than 100 years ago, people traveling by foot here did so at peril of their lives, as Apaches ambushed and attacked any Americans or Mexicans they encountered. Geronimo, Cochise, Mangas Coloradas—the Apache leaders who have become part of the iconography of the Old West—knew this territory well.

As you hike, you'll see to the north and northwest the Big Burro Mountains. To the south rise the Big and Little Hatchet ranges. To the west look for Pyramid Peak. From the Separ Road the landscape looks not much different than it would have to the people who passed here before you. Perhaps you imagine you're a woman of the prehistoric Mogollon culture, responsible for gathering edible plants as your little family band migrates north toward the Gila country; along the way you'd gather yucca leaves, the fruit of prickly pear cactus, and seeds from the abundant grasses. Or perhaps you're a trader from pre-Columbian Mexico, following an ancient route, bringing parrot and macaw feathers to the ancestral Puebloan peoples living here and to the north, hoping to return with precious turquoise mined in the nearby Burro and Little Hatchet Mountains.

Perhaps you're a member of one of the Spanish expeditions through this territory, maybe the one led by Governor Juan Ignacio de Flores Mogollón in the 1700s; or maybe the one led by Governor Juan Bautista de Anza around 1780. Perhaps you are one of the many American soldiers who patrolled this region during the conflicts with the Apaches. Maybe you see yourself as an Apache, possessed of an extraordinary knowledge of the land and an ability to live off it. Perhaps you're the wife of a homesteader, who came here after 1900 to begin a new life because land, although tough and arid, was abundant and cheap. All along this segment linger thousands of ghosts, just waiting to be remembered.

Walking a ridge along the Divide in this segment's northern part, you have the sensation of being on an actual divide, one of the few places in New Mexico where this happens. The open country, allowing views far into the distance, reinforces this feeling. No campgrounds, formal or otherwise, exist along the route, though you can find pleasant, sheltered sites along drainages. Either state or private ownership holds most land along the Separ Road, with small parcels owned by the Bureau of Land Management. Private land should be respected.

The terrain and preponderance of private land don't lend themselves to day hikes.

WATER NOTES

 No natural water sources exist along this segment, once again making Continental Divide Trail users dependent upon the livestock industry's windmills and stock ponds for water. Fortunately, this segment contains an adequate number of these, fairly well spaced. Obtain water wherever you can.

MOUNTAIN BIKE NOTES

 Although most mountain-bikers will prefer smaller roads and more forested terrain, those with a taste for desert vistas will enjoy the Separ Road.

EQUESTRIAN NOTES

Paucity of water, absence of trails, and lack of facilities for horses, coupled with more attractive alternatives nearby in the Burro Mountains, make the Separ Road unappealing to equestrians.

SOUTHBOUND HIKERS

 Beginning on NM 90, you face a long but straightforward walk over well-graded dirt roads. Water is available along the route but mostly from stock tanks, so be sure to carry enough to get you beyond the next source if it proves unavailable or unacceptable.

MAPS

USGS QUADRANGLES: Separ, Ninetysix Ranch, Werney Hill, C Bar Ranch, Burro Peak
OTHER MAPS: BLM 1:100K Lordsburg, Silver City

LAND-MANAGEMENT AGENCIES

BLM/Las Cruces Field Office

BEGINNING ACCESS POINT

 SEPAR: The Separ exit, Exit 42 on Interstate 10's, is 39 miles west of Deming, 21 miles east of Lordsburg. The Separ Road begins at this exit.

ENDING ACCESS POINT

 NM 90: This segment ends at the CDT campground on NM 90, 10 miles southwest of Silver City.

TRAIL DESCRIPTION

The Separ Road begins at Interstate 10's Exit 42 at the highway locality of Separ, elevation 4,505 feet. The well-maintained dirt road, marked by a sign, heads north at the concrete underpasses beneath the highway. For the first few miles the road traverses flat rangeland; grass, yuccas, and the shrub with erect, dark-green, leafless stalks called Mormon Tea, a member of the genus *Ephedra,* comprises the vegetation. (Mormon Tea does not contain the stimulant properties of Chinese ephedra.) At

 3.9 miles from Interstate 10 you'll see a water tank beside the road to the east, N32°14'55", W108°23'17", elevation 4,680 feet. At 4.3 miles the road forks; the Separ Road heads left, or northwest. At 5.8 miles, where the Separ Road crosses Ninetysix Creek (don't expect water), you'll see a substantial ranch beside the road.

At 7.3 miles the Separ Road intersects the El Paso Natural Gas pipeline, running southeast-northwest. Should easements be obtained, this pipeline would

SUPPLIES, SERVICES, AND ACCOMMODATIONS

SEPAR, at the segment's southern end, consists essentially of the Continental Divide Trading Post, HC 1, Lordsburg, NM 88045 (505) 546-3635. This store specializes in tourist curios and, aside from soda and snacks, provides no other supplies or services.

SILVER CITY, with a population of 5,902, is southwest New Mexico's second largest town. It originally owed its existence to mining, especially of copper, but it has since diversified its economy and is enjoying a renaissance as a regional cultural center. Western New Mexico University is located here, and for CDT hikers the town has a diverse array of facilities.

Distance from Trail	On the CDT	
Zip Code	88061	
Banks	AmBank, 610 Silver Heights Boulevard	(505) 534-0550
	Mon–Thur 9–5, Fri 9–6, Sat 9–1	(800) 440-8751
	First New Mexico, 1928 Highway 180	388-3121
	First Savings Bank, 1221 North Hudson Street	388-1531
	Wells Fargo, 12th and Pope Street	538-5302
	Mon–Fri 9–5, Sat 9–1	
Bus	Las Cruces shuttle and charter services run buses daily	800-288-1784
	connecting El Paso, Las Cruces, Deming, and Silver City	
Dining	Several options	
Emergency	911; non-emergency, Grant County Sheriff	538-2555
		or 538-3797
Gear	Gila Bike and Hike, 103 East College Street	388-3222
Groceries	Several options	
Information	Silver City–Grant Chamber of Commerce,	538-3785
	1103 North Hudson Street	(800) 548-9378
Laundry	Several options	
Lodging	Several options	
Medical	Gila Regional Medical Center, 1313 32nd Street	538-4000
Post Office	(88061) 500 North Hudson Street	538-2831
Showers	Several options	

become part of an alternative CDT route and include the southern Burro Mountains. At present, however, locked gates block this pipeline and the one 0.2 mile to the north; "No Trespassing" signs appear at both sites.

By about 8 miles, the terrain changes, becoming more rolling; mesquite appears in the vegetation. Soon, by 9.5 miles, you'll have good views of the three landmark mountains just to the east: Bessie Rhoads Mountain, the southernmost, has a distinctive conical shape. Just to the north rises Soldiers Farewell Hill (see Historical Notes, page 83), larger and much more rocky and rugged than Bessie Rhoads Mountain. North of Soldiers Farewell Hill, you'll spot JPB Mountain. To the north, the Burro Mountains appear in the distance, and to the west rise the low but rugged Langford Mountains, a small sub-range of the southern Burro Mountains.

At 10.6 miles, you'll see a ranch just west of the road. At 11.2 miles the road forks, the Separ Road forking right, or northeast, toward JPB Mountain. Somewhere in the next mile, N32°21'07", W108°23'49", elevation 5,200 feet, near where the Separ Road crosses a broad gravelly wash (at 12.4 miles), you'll intersect the old Butterfield Trail (see Historical Notes to right). You won't be able to see anything on the ground, but portions of the route are supposedly visible from the air, and ruins of the horse-exchange stations still exist in southern New Mexico. Indeed, about a mile east of the Separ Road lies the site of the Soldiers Farewell Stage Station.

Drainages (all dry) now dissect the terrain, much more interesting than the flats. At 14.1 miles you cross JPB Draw, then at 16.5 miles a turnoff leads to another ranch nearby. At 18.1 miles you encounter a steel stock tank about 0.3 mile west of the road, at N32°24'53", W108°19'54". Also at about 18 miles, the drainages and ridges become broader, the terrain more open. At 19.2 miles you'll find another stock tank, beside the road on the east, N32°25'20", W108°19'09".

At 20 miles appears yet another fork. Southbound hikers should take the road heading southwest. Just beyond here, the Separ Road crosses a shallow valley, then climbs the ridge to the north to join the Continental Divide, N32°24'36", W108°15'53", elevation 5,520 feet. The ridge, the Divide, and the CDT now all swing northwest, climbing gently to a cattle guard at about 5,500 feet elevation before leveling out. From this ridge stretch expansive views of the plains of southwestern New Mexico. The vegetation here consists of grass, yucca, and beargrass, which you can recognize from the long, linear evergreen leaves growing in a large tuft at ground level; it takes its name from bears' fondness for its edible tubers.

Southbound hikers will note that at about 5.9 miles from NM 90, the Prevost Road heads downhill and south toward a water tank in the distance. The Separ Road, however, heads southeast, and you'll find water much closer to the road.

At 20.6 miles, after following the ridge for about 6 miles, the Separ Road descends to cross a shallow valley, in which you'll see a windmill and metal stock tank, N32°26'50", W108°19'23". Far to the east juts the distinctive fang of 8,408-foot Cookes Peak, southwestern New Mexico's most distinctive landmark. The Butterfield Trail ran through Cookes Canyon at the peak's base, as did a stage route, but the area was exceptionally vulnerable to Apache ambushes; stage passengers once complained about the disturbing effect of the numerous skeletons along the road! The situation improved after Fort Cummings was established there in 1863.

At 29.9 miles, still another fork in the trail; the Separ Road goes right. Then finally, at 31.7 miles, the Separ Road ends at NM 90, N32°32'56", W107°23'38", elevation 6,180 feet. From here it's 3.5 miles west and gradually uphill along the highway to the Gila National Forest's CDT campground—no water—and the beginning of the next segment.

HISTORICAL NOTES

Soldiers Farewell Hill, 6,173 feet, is the largest and most rugged of three hills dominating the landscape just east of this segment's central section. As *The Place Names of New Mexico* explains: "At least three legends—all dating from the late 1800s and all apocryphal-explain this romantic name. One is that soldiers manning a signal station here—mirrors by day, flares at night—were trapped by Apaches and, tormented by thirst, signaled a farewell, saying they were going down to battle the Indians; all were killed. Another story says a soldier from the East, despondent over separation from his sweetheart, killed himself here. The most widely accepted story says soldiers, escorting wagon trains and travelers en route to California, were ordered to go no farther than here, where they were forced to say 'farewell.'"

The Butterfield Trail is the route over which Pony Express riders with the Butterfield Overland Mail carried mail from St. Louis, Missouri, to Stockton, California, a distance of 2,701.5 miles. When John Butterfield and his associates received the contract for the mail route, they purchased 1,000 horses, 700 mules, 800 harnesses, and 250 coaches and Celerity wagons. Butterfield's instructions to his drivers were, "Remember, boys, nothing on God's earth must stop the United States mail." The mail route lasted only from 1857 to 1869, yet in those brief 12 years, the Pony Express riders became permanently established in the mythology of the Old West.

The Butterfield Trail continued to be a major route west until 1881, when the southern-route transcontinental railroad was completed.

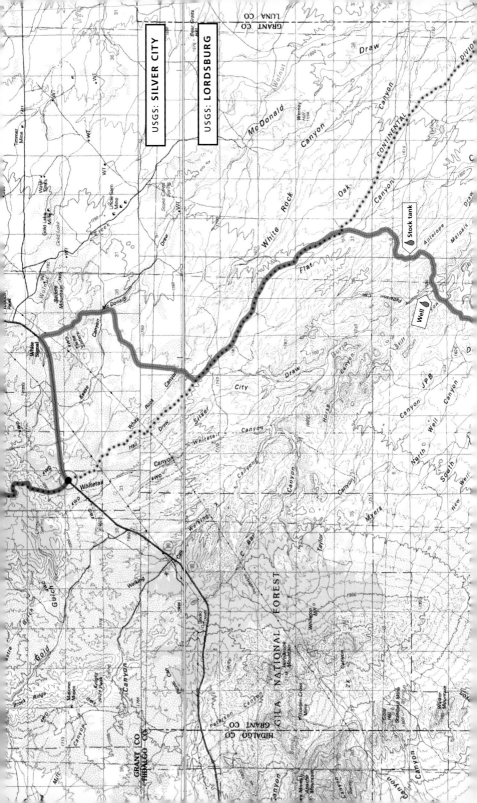

USGS: SILVER CITY

USGS: LORDSBURG

Stock tank

Well

Butterfield Trail

Historic mountains to east

Ninetysix Ranch

Water tank

Canyon

Smith

Draw

Prairie Rhoads Mountain

Soldiers Farewell Hill

Cienega

Creek

Jones

Canyon

Crawford Draw

Mesquite Draw

Borrow Pit

Borrow Pits

Borrow Pits

Borrow Pit

Separ

Borrow Pits

Ninetysix

PACIFIC

10

70 80

W Pit

Wells

Segment 4
T:I BLOOD MAPS:
LORDSBURG and
SILVER CITY

7/16   7/16

SCALE 7/16 INCH = 1 MILE

7/16   7/16

• • • • • •   Continental Divide

————— Continental Divide Trail
            (current segment)

————— Continental Divide Trail
            (previous and next segments)

− − − −   Access route

〜〜〜   Intermittent river or stream

           Lake or pond

           Marsh or swamp

————— Primary highway

————— Secondary highway

————— Light duty road

- - - - -   Unimproved road

·········   Trail

✕   Quarry or open mine pit

Segment 5
NM 90 to Silver City

*View to south from flank of
Jacks Peak, USFS Continental
Divide Trail Campground,
Gila National Forest.
Photo by William Stone.*

24.25 miles
Difficulty: Moderate to Strenuous
You may encounter: motorized vehicles

Segment 5   **Total Elevation Gain:** 2,655 feet
From Mexico 102 miles
To Colorado 597 miles

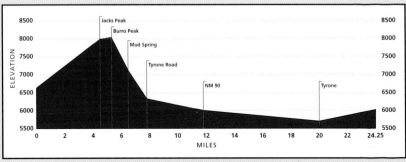

TRAIL OVERVIEW As unsung as their namesake, the Burro Mountains occupy a minor place in most people's consciousness in the state. Once, minerals gave them an ephemeral fame, but today their main cachet is the presence of the Continental Divide and the Continental Divide Trail.

Maps and geography texts tell you the Burro Mountains are subdivided into the Little Burros and the Big Burros. But as you hike along NM 90 southwest of Silver City, you'll pass through the Little Burro Mountains—and likely not notice them. A mere 8 miles long, with relief of only 650 feet, the Little Burros are more hills than mountains. They're separated from the Big Burros by the valley of Mangas Creek, and with little public access they're all but an afterthought of the larger group nearby.

Not that the Big Burros are exactly famous (see Historical Notes, page 90). True, they're sure-enough mountains, but except for local ranchers, hunters, 4WD drivers—and CDT hikers—the Big Burros are largely ignored by the public. The Burros have their charms, to be sure, but who would go to the dry, undistinguished Burros when the vast Gila Wilderness, with 600 miles of trails, as well as hot springs, beautiful rivers, and magnificent peaks, is nearby?

Actually, only about a third of this segment runs through the mountains; the rest takes to the roads. After the Big Burro Mountains, the Continental Divide goes past the huge pit mine operations of Tyrone, then through the Little Burro Mountains, in state or private ownership. Alternatives to a road CDT route are being explored, but for now …

Few people go to the Big Burro Mountains to hike; the nearest town is modest Silver City, and in its backyard stretches the vast Gila Wilderness, many of its trails among the finest in the Southwest. Indeed, about the only trail of note in the Big Burros is the CDT, but its southern end here coincides with a quite pleasant day hike, described on page 90.

WATER NOTES

 In this segment, northbound hikers reach a milestone—the first naturally occurring surface water in the entire journey from Mexico. (I can think of no more defining statement of the CDT in southwestern New Mexico.) What's more, this landmark water is a small spring, not actually on the CDT but close, named Mud Spring. It's better than the name suggests. The next permanent surface water outside Silver City is a spring in Webb Gulch, in Segment 7, or Bear Creek, at the end of that segment. Neither is a sure thing, so plan to carry enough for long, dry stretches.

MOUNTAIN BIKE NOTES

 The trails and Forest Roads of the Big Burro Mountains offer excellent mountain biking, of various lengths and difficulties.

EQUESTRIAN NOTES

The Burro Mountains aren't likely to lure many equestrians from the nearby Gila Wilderness, though riders interested in mining history will enjoy riding the many dirt roads here to look for the sites of old mining camps. The CDT to Jacks Peak is suitable for horses, but, except at Mud Spring, water is scarce.

SOUTHBOUND HIKERS

  This segment begins with a 16-mile, not very interesting walk along NM 90. Nor is water readily available along the highway. Try to fill up before turning onto dirt Tyrone Road, because your next water is at Mud Spring or, failing that, perhaps the tank atop Jacks Peak. Wherever you find water, fill up. The hike from Jacks Peak down to the CDT campground on NM 90 is pleasant, but there is no water at the campground.

MAPS

USGS QUADRANGLES: Burro Peak, Wind Mountain, Tyrone, Silver City
OTHER MAPS: Gila National Forest

LAND-MANAGEMENT AGENCIES

Gila National Forest/Silver City Ranger District

BEGINNING ACCESS POINT

 NM 90: This paved highway provides easy access to the Gila National Forest's CDT campground, 19.75 miles southwest of Silver City.

ENDING ACCESS POINT

 SILVER CITY: This segment ends in Silver City, located at the junction of NM 90, NM 15, and US 180.

SUPPLIES, SERVICES, AND ACCOMMODATIONS

SILVER CITY. See Segment 4, page 81.

TRAIL DESCRIPTION The Gila National Forest–Silver City Ranger District has done an excellent job with the trail that begins this segment, N32°32'45", W108°25'31", elevation 6,630 feet. The CDT trailhead is well-marked, there's ample parking and space to camp, and the CDT itself is well-maintained and well-signed. Now, if only there was water . . . . So begin this segment with full water bottles and a full stomach, especially as the route to Jacks Peak faces south and is exposed.

The CDT, which coincides with Trail 74, leaves the parking area and winds over sandy soil through dense vegetation before ascending gradually. With elevation, the views expand, especially toward the south and east. The vegetation here is typical of the Lower Sonoran Desert life zone: juniper, evergreen oak, mesquite, yucca, and mountain mahogany.

The trail climbs persistently, but nowhere steeply. After 1.25 miles, at elevation 6,800 feet, the trail heads north along a ridge, climbing gradually. After about a mile, the CDT enters a pleasant ponderosa pine forest benefiting from the higher elevation and increased moisture. At 3.5 miles from the trailhead, the CDT intersects a dirt road, which it follows beneath cool pines 0.3 mile north-northeast to a junction. From here, a dirt maintenance road leads 0.25 mile to the cluster of electronic towers atop Jacks Peak. The views from the summit—and the possibility of water in a cistern—make the side trip worthwhile.

From the junction, the CDT follows the Divide north, descending a northern ridge 0.25 mile to a saddle, then climbing another ridge 300 feet in 0.4 mile to reach the summit of Burro Peak, at 8,035 feet the range's highest point, about 4.5 miles from the trailhead.

From here it's all downhill. The Divide heads east down the mountain, while the CDT descends the peak's northern slopes, along a broad ridge. After about 0.5 mile, at N32°35'40", W108°25'45", elevation 7,630 feet, the CDT leaves the ridge to drop 0.4 mile into the head of Deadman Canyon. Throughout this, the CDT has followed a trail clearly marked with CDT signs.

About 0.3 mile down the canyon, a spur trail branches northwest to lead 0.3 mile to Mud Spring, N32°36'05", W108°26'06". Despite its unflattering name, Mud Spring is an excellent water source—and the only reliable one along the route, although water sometimes seeps into the canyon bottom about half way down.

SOUTHBOUND HIKERS: About 2 miles up the drainage from the parking area, an unmarked trail crosses the wash to head up slope to the south. The CDT, however, stays on the drainage's north side.

Once in the canyon, the CDT simply follows the valley downhill 2.4 miles to a small parking area (no facilities) at N32°36'56", W108°24'25", elevation 6,350 feet. From there it's another 0.2 mile over Forest Road 4249F to the dirt Tyrone Road. Although other trails sometimes branch from the canyon, the CDT is well-marked. The hiking is pleasant, and because the CDT follows a forested drainage beneath a north slope, it's conspicuously cooler than south of Jacks Peak.

SOUTHBOUND HIKERS: The CDT is not marked on the Tyrone Road; after 4 miles, look for a turnoff to the west and a small sign indicating Forest Road 4249F. Look for a CDT sign at the small parking area 0.2 mile from the Tyrone Road. You'll cross the dry wash, then almost immediately you'll leave the old road to pass through a gated fence. The CDT follows the wash upstream.

County maintained, Tyrone Road is wide and what traffic it receives often is fast, raising clouds of dust. It's 4.0 miles over this to NM 90, passing the mountainous waste piles of the Tyrone Mine en route.

SOUTHBOUND HIKERS: Tyrone Road is not marked as such; it's the first road heading north past the mine dump, with a sign indicating Burro Mountain Homesteads. Also, try to obtain water before embarking upon Tyrone Road, as the next water will likely be Mud Spring, 6.7 miles away.

Once you're at NM 90, it's about 16 miles into Silver City. The only good news is that the shoulders along the highway are wide. The segment ends at US 180, slightly north of the main part of town. As you approach from the south, you'll see signs to the historic downtown area; this route, along Bullard Street, is the most efficient and interesting end to the segment.

OTHER HIKES AND RIDES: JACKS PEAK

APPROXIMATE ONE-WAY DISTANCE: 4.5 miles
MODE OF TRAVEL: Hiking
DIFFICULTY: Moderate

Jacks Peak, at 7,986 feet the second highest summit of the Burro Mountains, makes for a relatively easy day hike, an interesting tour of the Lower Sonoran life zone, with expansive views of southwestern New Mexico. The trail to the summit coincides with the CDT, which is well-marked on the right side of NM 90, southwest of White Signal. The trail, also labeled here Trail 74, ascends steadily but not too steeply. Be sure to bring plenty of water, because the Burros are dry! The hiking gets easier and very pleasant when the trail reaches the ridge leading to Jacks Peak, a thicket of transmission towers but offering spectacular vistas. Burro Peak, 8,035 feet, is about 0.75 mile farther.

HISTORICAL NOTES

Mining in the Burro Mountains. Long before Europeans settled here, prehistoric Indians, members of the Mimbreno Culture dating from A.D. 800 to 1350, mined turquoise in these mountains. In 1875, John Coleman (later dubbed "Turquoise John") rediscovered the ancient diggings west of Saint Louis Canyon. Other turquoise mines were opened nearby; a 40-foot by 60-foot vein, known as the Elizabeth Pocket, in the Azure mine, produced $2 million in turquoise.

But the real mining boom came with copper, gold, and silver strikes in the 1870s. Most were toward the northern end of the range, where mining camps such as Telegraph, Paschal, Black Hawk, Oak Grove, Carbonate City, Fleming, and Penrose sprang up. Rattlesnake City and Gold Hill were gold camps at the range's south end, and Leopold was a copper camp in the Little Burro Mountains. Bullard Peak, 7,064 feet, at the range's north end, recalls Captain John Bullard, miner and prospector, who around 1870–1871 developed several claims around the peak now bearing his name. In 1871, while leading a campaign against the Apaches, Captain Bullard was shot and killed on another mountain, now also called Bullard Peak, west of Glenwood, just over the Arizona line. By mid-1882, the town of Paschal had approximately 1,000 residents and was one of the nation's leading copper camps. But after 1883, when copper prices fell and labor costs rose, the town began to die. Few of the camps survived into the twentieth century, although Leopold had 1,200 residents in 1907, and Tyrone still is an active town.

Cliff face and cave dwelling, Gila Cliff Dwellings National Monument. (See Segment 9)
Photo by William Stone.

SCALE 1/2 INCH = 1 MILE

1/4   1/4   1/2

- Continental Divide
- Continental Divide Trail (current segment)
- Continental Divide Trail (previous and next segments)
- Access route
- Intermittent river or stream
- Lake or pond
- Marsh or swamp
- Primary highway
- Secondary highway
- Light duty road
- Unimproved road
- Trail
- × Quarry or open mine pit

Segment 6
Silver City to Forest Road 506 (Little Walnut Road)

Bear Mountain and golden desert grassland, Silver City Range, Gila National Forest. Photo by William Stone.

12.4 miles (5.6 on trail)
Difficulty: Easy

You may encounter: motorized vehicles

Segment 6   **Total Elevation Gain:** 978 feet
From Mexico 126.25 miles
To Colorado 572.75 miles

CONTINENTAL DIVIDE
TRAIL ALLIANCE

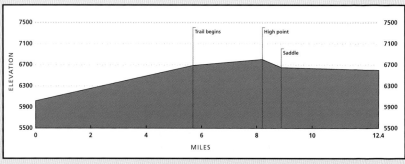

TRAIL OVERVIEW Expansive views from the Continental Divide distinguish this short segment. The route's main purpose is to return Continental Divide Trail hikers to the Divide after a much-needed layover in Silver City. Thus, more than half the segment is on road—and not very interesting or scenic road at that. But when you're striding along the Divide through grassy meadows, you are looking north as far as the Mogollon Mountains, south to Silver City, and south as far as Cookes Peak. Surrounding you are the hills and summits of the Silver City Range, while ahead to the east are the higher mountains of the Pinos Altos Range.

Dominating the landscape is Bear Mountain. At 8,036 feet, steep-sided all around, Bear Mountain is a commanding presence, especially from the trail's eastern sections. The Continental Divide goes over Bear Mountain, but the CDT doesn't. Similarly, the CDT declines to follow the Divide near the summit of Stewart Peak.

 This segment is dry; at its southern end, the only water pours either from a tap or a bottle in Silver City. At the northern end, you must hike 3.5 miles into the next segment to reach the tiny—and by no means assured—stream in Webb Gulch or down the road to Little Walnut Campground. The good news is that this segment's beginning and end connect to Silver City by well-traveled roads, making water caches less problematic to arrange.

This segment's trail portion does stay fairly constant to the Divide, and there's always a certain satisfaction to that.

Probably the most appealing day hike here is the trail section of the CDT itself. Spotting cars at both ends and then shuttling or arranging a key exchange allows for an outstanding half-day hike (longer if combined with a picnic in the meadows). Other hikes in the area are described below.

WATER NOTES

 This segment is bone dry—no water at all. There also is no water near the beginning of the next segment. Consider a water drop at the trailheads. Fortunately, this segment is short, easy, and scenic.

MOUNTAIN BIKE NOTES

 The CDT between Bear Mountain Road and Little Walnut Canyon Road is among the best mountain bike routes in the Silver City area, especially when combined with the trail system around Little Walnut Campground.

EQUESTRIAN NOTES

Similarly, only lack of water and corrals prevents these trails from being excellent equestrian routes.

SOUTHBOUND HIKERS

  Consider caching water at this segment's beginning. No water is available along the route until you arrive at Silver City.

MAPS

USGS QUADRANGLES: Silver City
OTHER MAPS: Gila National Forest

LAND-MANAGEMENT AGENCIES

Gila National Forest/Silver City Ranger District

BEGINNING ACCESS POINT

SILVER CITY: This segment begins toward the northern end of Silver City at the junction of NM 90 and US 180, as US 180 heads downhill south to the downtown area.

ENDING ACCESS POINT

FOREST ROAD 506 (LITTLE WALNUT ROAD): From Silver City, the Little Walnut Road heads north. The pavement stops after 5 miles, at the entrance to the Little Walnut Picnic Area. From there the road, now well-maintained dirt, continues another 1.9 miles to the CDT.

SUPPLIES, SERVICES, AND ACCOMMODATIONS

SILVER CITY. See Segment 4, page 81.

TRAIL DESCRIPTION From the US 180–NM 90 junction at the northern end of Silver City, the CDT follows US 180 west through the town about 0.7 mile to where the Bear Mountain Road heads north. It's paved until it reaches the Gila National Forest boundary at 3.25 miles. From there, it's 2.4 miles on well-maintained dirt to where the CDT leaves the road for trail, at N32°49'17", W108°20'33", elevation 6,690 feet. At the trailhead is a CDT information board and a small parking area, but no other facilities.

The trail, marked with CDT signs, crosses the dry drainage, then ascends the ridge to the north, where after 0.7 mile it joins the Divide. At 1.6 miles from the trailhead you'll reach a junction: Forest Road 858 heads east-southeast, Forest Road 4083B heads northwest, and the CDT, still marked with signs, heads east. Rerouting the CDT to follow its own course away from the roads was the first project of the local CDT volunteers. Here the route enters the ridge-top meadows that afford distant views: Silver City, Cookes Peak, the Mogollon Mountains far to the north, and the Pinos Altos Mountains to the east. Look to the east-southeast for a slender sliver of rock standing just beyond the north end of a long mesa; that is the Kneeling Nun, said to be the ossified figure of a nun jilted by her Mexican soldier lover. As you hike east, you gain increased appreciation of the size and significance of Bear Mountain, looming to the northwest. At N32°50'16", W108°19'15", you reach the segment's high point, 6,803 feet, 2.5 miles from the trailhead.

From this the CDT and the Continental Divide descend gentle slopes 0.75 mile north, then northeast toward a saddle (N32°51'07", W108°18'45") between Stewart Peak and Eighty Mountain. En route you'll see a metal sign on a hardened post denoting the CDT and proclaiming: "No Motorized Use." At the saddle, the Continental Divide continues north briefly, while the CDT runs northeast. After 0.75 mile, they intersect one more time at another small saddle (N32°51'08", W108°18'46"), elevation 6,570 feet. The CDT then continues its gradual descent northeast as it makes its way to the Little Walnut Road and the segment's end. Some hikers have confused the CDT with mountain-bike trails here. The main junction to watch for is at N32°51'35", W108°17'55", where a trail leading to Little Walnut Picnic Area heads downhill to the right. If in doubt, look for CDT signs, which continue until the segment ends at the small parking area on Little Walnut Road. From the parking area to Silver City is 6.9 miles.

OTHER HIKES AND RIDES: McCOMAS PEAK OR BEAR MOUNTAIN

APPROXIMATE ONE-WAY DISTANCE: 1.2 miles for each
MODE OF TRAVEL: Hiking
DIFFICULTY: Strenuous

From the height-of-land between 8,036-foot Bear Mountain on the north and 7,681-foot McComas Peak on the south, approximately 0.75 mile west of the CDT trailhead, an unmaintained "user" trail leads to these two summits, roughly following the Continental Divide. The routes, while short, are steep and not suited for mountain bikes.

SEE PAGE 103 FOR SEGMENT 6 MAP.

Segment 7
FR 506 (Little Walnut Road) to NM 15: Pinos Altos

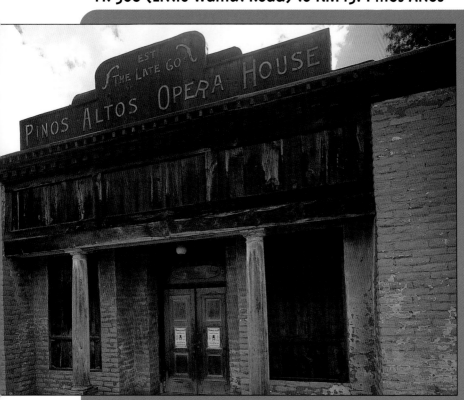

Pinos Altos Opera House in Pinos Altos near Gila National Forest. Photo by Tom Till.

8.2 miles
Difficulty: Easy to Moderate

You may encounter: hikers, mountain bikers, and equestrians

Segment 7   **Total Elevation Gain:** 1,569 feet
From Mexico 138.65 miles
To Colorado 560.35 miles

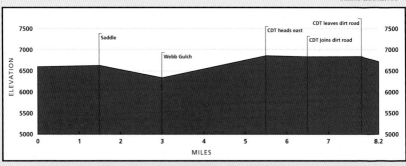

TRAIL OVERVIEW I've always maintained, when asked what my favorite places are among all I've visited in New Mexico, that my perceptions are colored by what happened at a place, so perhaps that explains why I had such a good time when I hiked this seemingly undistinguished stretch of the Continental Divide Trail. On this brilliant October day, I was guided on the first part of this segment by Bob Gosney, who has adopted this CDT segment and knows it better than anyone. By the time we parted company at Webb Gulch, I was thoroughly infected with his enthusiasm.

 Not that the trail doesn't have features to be enthusiastic about. The route is well-marked, and the trail is in good condition. Its mostly gentle contours wind through a forest of piñon and ponderosa pines, along with alligator and other junipers. It's primarily an upland trail, but it dips into several drainages, and although the CDT here has a reputation of being dry, I found water at several points. Not much, but cold and clear, unpolluted by cattle.

This is good wildlife habitat, and Gosney says deer and wild turkey are common, as are the tracks of coyote, black bear, and mountain lion.

The segment ends by going through a portion of the mineralized area that once made Pinos Altos a mining boomtown.

The only day hike here is the CDT itself. Parking a car at the segment's western end, then hiking east to another vehicle at the eastern end, followed by dinner or refreshment at the Buckhorn Saloon in Pinos Altos, would make an outstanding hiking day.

WATER NOTES

 The almost-permanent stream and nearby spring in Webb Gulch are the first water sources you've encountered since leaving Silver City. In a very dry year, both of these sources could be problematic. Inquire as to their status.

MOUNTAIN BIKE NOTES

This trail is a favorite of Silver City mountain bikers, lending itself well to the outing described above for hikers.

EQUESTRIAN NOTES

Though corrals are lacking at either the beginning or end of this segment, this route is deservedly very popular with local horseback riders.

SOUTHBOUND HIKERS

If fortune favors you with water in Bear Creek, then take advantage of it; although possible water sources exist along this segment, none is completely reliable. Similarly, if you encounter water in Webb Gulch, fill up; the rest of this segment—and all of the following segment—is dry. Your next certain source is Silver City.

MAPS

USGS QUADRANGLES: Silver City, Reading Mountain, Twin Sisters
OTHER MAPS: Gila National Forest

LAND-MANAGEMENT AGENCIES

Gila National Forest/Silver City Ranger District

BEGINNING ACCESS POINT

Smooth road to Trailhead

FOREST ROAD 506 (LITTLE WALNUT ROAD): This is a paved county road that heads north from Silver City, becoming dirt Forest Road 506 at the Gila National Forest boundary, about 5 miles from town. After another 1.9 miles, the graded Forest Road reaches the informal trailhead, with parking beside the road; N32°51'45", W108°17'22", elevation 6,600 feet. No facilities are here, but people clearly have parked, camped, picnicked, and partied here. It's a pleasant site, shaded by ponderosa pines.

ENDING ACCESS POINT

Smooth road to Trailhead

NM 15: This segment ends just east of paved NM 15, about a mile from Pinos Altos. No camping is available at the Arrastre Site, but informal campsites are available just 0.5 miles north, where the CDT crosses Bear Creek, immediately west of NM 15. The creek often (usually?) is dry, and no facilities are here, but the ponderosa pines contribute to a pleasant site nonetheless.

Note: The Bureau of Land Management is considering a BLM trailhead facility at Pinos Altos, but as of this writing nothing was imminent.

SUPPLIES, SERVICES, AND ACCOMMODATIONS

PINOS ALTOS has a population of only 300 people, so its services are limited. On the other hand, Silver City, with a complete array of services, is only 5 miles away on NM 15; see Segment 4, page 81.

Distance from Trail	1 mile	
Zip Code	88053	
Bank	See Silver City	
Bus	None	
Dining	Buckhorn Saloon and Opera House	(505) 538-9911
Emergency	911; non-emergency, Grant County Sheriff,	538-3797
	209 North Black Street, Silver City, 88061	or 538-2555
Gear	See Silver City	
Groceries	See Silver City	
Information	Silver City–Grant Chamber of Commerce,	538-3785
	1103 North Hudson Street, Silver City, 88061	(800) 548-9378
Laundry	Continental Divide RV Park and Campground, Silver City	388-3005
Lodging	Continental Divide RV Park and Campground;	
	Bear Creek Motel and Cabins, P.O. Box 53082,	(888) 388-4501
	Pinos Altos, NM 88053; www.bearcreekcabins.com	
Medical	See Silver City	
Post Office	See Silver City	
Showers	Continental Divide RV Park and Campground	

TRAIL DESCRIPTION CDT markers are prominent as the trail begins its journey east. The walking is easy, the gradients gentle as the CDT winds through piñon-juniper-oak forest. Gaps in the forest allow for vistas of the Pinos Altos Range.

After about 1.5 miles, the CDT intersects a gated fence at a small saddle, N32°52'34", W108°17'51", elevation 6,630 feet. About 1.5 miles north-northeast is Preachers Point, a formation said to resemble a man's head bowed in prayer (the resemblance, if any, is hardly compelling); equally implausible is that a mining-era preacher bellowed to miners in surrounding valleys from here. From the saddle, the CDT descends via some minor drainages 1.5 miles to Webb Gulch, N32°52'48", W108°16'49", elevation 6,340 feet, about 3 miles from the trailhead. Here a tiny stream trickles into some beautiful pools, watering as well a luxurious patch of spearmint. These pools are the best water source on this segment, and they are said to have water 8 to 10 months of the year.

If the pools are dry, however, you'll find a reliable spring about 0.6 mile farther down Webb Gulch. The spring is inconspicuous, but by watching for a junction with drainages from the west and southwest, then looking for a small rock outcrop next to where the bedrock streambed makes an abrupt drop, you should be able to find it. The spring's coordinates are N32°53'11", W108°17'05"; on the Reading Mountain quadrangle, the spring is located just east of the "e" in "Webb Gulch."

From Webb Gulch, the CDT ascends less than 0.5 mile to a ridge, elevation 6,480 feet, where it meets an abandoned two-track road. Marked by signs and a cairn, the CDT heads southeast on the two-track. The road doesn't stay long on the ridge but soon dips into a drainage running north-northwest. I found water here, but don't rely upon this source. After briefly paralleling the drainage, the two-track leaves it to begin climbing to another ridge. The ascent is steady but not brutally steep. Look on the hillsides here for the huge succulent basal leaves of the century plant, an agave whose flowering stalks often exceed 6 feet. Agaves were a staple of the Apaches' diet.

Soon after you cease climbing and begin walking a level course to the southeast, you'll notice beside the north side of the road two small cairns with a recently constructed trail between them. This is *not* the CDT, and should you follow this (as I did) you'll soon notice an absence of CDT markers. Rather, follow the CDT markers as the CDT continues south on the dirt road another 0.6 mile to a junction, well-marked by signs, where the CDT leaves the road at N32°52'56", W108°15'31", elevation 6,860 feet, to go east, climbing briefly over a ridge before descending. When walking along the dirt road, look to the south for a substantial building complex. This is Our Lady of Guadalupe Monastery, well-known locally.

After leaving the road, the CDT descends to cross the head of Long Gulch. I found a little water there, but one would not normally expect water here.

The CDT now follows a circuitous course through a complex of drainages and slopes until, after about a mile, it arrives at a dirt road, N32°53'01", W108°14'28", elevation 6,970 feet. CDT markers lead you east on this road less than 100 yards to where, at a junction with another dirt road, the CDT makes a 160-degree turn. The CDT follows this road as it climbs west, then north, then northeast. As you walk the road, look for signs of mining, as you're now within the mineralized area that was intensely prospected by miners from Pinos Altos beginning around 1860. Several smaller dirt roads intersect the CDT's road, but CDT markers and cairns make the route clear.

After about a mile of walking the road, the CDT leaves it to head east. This junction is well-marked; its coordinates are N32°52'53", W108°14'12". Visible beside the road less than 100 yards from this junction are the concrete remains of an old mill. If you walk past this mill, retrace your steps to the junction. You might find it tempting to continue walking the dirt road into Pinos Altos, but if Pinos Altos is your goal, you'll save time by staying on the CDT until it reaches NM 15, about a mile away.

The CDT now heads downhill to cross a small drainage, then climbs to intersect another dirt road after 0.5 mile from the old mine road. It crosses this road and descends a tributary of Bear Creek. It follows this tributary to Bear Creek (usually dry), on whose east side are pleasant campsites. Just uphill is NM 15, N32°53'09", W108°13'35", elevation 6,720 feet.

From this junction with the highway, the CDT goes about 0.5 miles through the forest—the route is not signed as of this writing—to the Arrastre Site, N32°52'59", W108°13'26", elevation 6,800 feet, and the end of this segment.

HISTORICAL NOTES

Pinos Altos conscientiously strives to preserve its character as an authentic frontier mining camp. But unlike so many of the West's mining camps that have become Beverly Hills in western drag, their core of self-consciously historic buildings cum boutiques surrounded by a rind of condos, Pinos Altos has remained a charming but unassuming village, dreaming of earlier days. Those early days, however, were anything but dreamy. In 1860, three prospectors, including Thomas "Three-fingered" Birch, found gold on Bear Creek. Soon, other prospectors and miners flocked to the area, and the fledgling mining camp was called Birchville, for Birch. But Apache raids in 1861 and 1864 drove away many settlers. Local lore says that when miners withdrawing from the wooden stockade here looked back, they saw the structure already in flames. The town eventually was resettled, taking the name used earlier by local Spanish speakers, *Pinos Altos,* "tall pines," for the towering ponderosas that grew here. Mining is no longer important in the area, but the scenic town still nestles among the pines that gave it its name—and certainly the Buckhorn Saloon remains pungent with Old West atmosphere.

Segments 6 & 7
1:100,000 MAP:
SILVER CITY

SCALE: 1/2 INCH = 1 MILE

••••	Continental Divide
—	Continental Divide Trail (current segment)
—	Continental Divide Trail (previous and next segments)
▨	Access route
	Intermittent river or stream
	Lake or pond
	Marsh or swamp
	Primary highway
	Secondary highway
	Light duty road
	Unimproved road
	Trail
✕	Quarry or open mine pit

Segment 7

Spring

Water (usually)

Important Junction

Campsites

Pinos Altos

Cross Mountain

Stewart Peak

Saddle

Silver City Trailhead

Segment 6

Silver City

Boston Hill

Whiskey Creek Airport

Turner Ridgeport Airport

Silver Acres

Segment 8
NM 15 to NM 35: Twin Sisters

*Collared lizard along the Continental
Divide. Photo by William Stone.*

21.3 miles
Difficulty: Strenuous
You may encounter: motorized vehicles

Segment 8

Total Elevation Gain: 5,113 feet
From Mexico 146.85 miles
To Colorado 552.15 miles

CONTINENTAL DIVIDE
TRAIL ALLIANCE

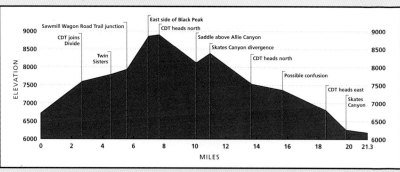

TRAIL OVERVIEW Challenging and interesting, this segment crosses rough, dry hills and through a region once scoured by Spanish-speaking prospectors. Their finds, if any, were meager; perhaps yours will be richer.

The Continental Divide Trail starts at the Arrastre Site by following an old mine road—poorly marked and with several junctions with other old mine roads. Tough navigation. Beyond this, however, the trail becomes clearer, with several reassuring CDT signs.

The route passes through relatively open piñon-juniper forest en route to ponderosa forest at higher elevations. Good wildlife habitat. In 1997, two CDT hikers noted, "A feature emerged along this section which remained constant throughout the trek—lots of bear scat and signs of an active carnivorous ecosystem." One has to wonder where the animals obtain their water; there sure aren't many sources for humans. Both north- and southbound hikers should begin this segment with full bottles.

The route outlined here is in a state of transition. A new route, described below, has been drawn on maps, and trail construction began in the summer of 2000. The previous route had descended to the Mimbres Valley via Allie Canyon; the new route goes down ridges west of Skates Canyon. The change obviates having to walk along narrow-shouldered NM 35 and will connect directly with the expanded Sapillo Campground, when that project is completed. Hikers wishing to attempt the new route should stop at the Silver City Ranger District offices in Silver City to check on current conditions and get maps showing the route.

Otherwise, CDT hikers should follow the old route down Allie Canyon. Actually, this route has the advantage of having water sources along it. The Allie Canyon route leads to the Gila National Forest's Wilderness Ranger District at Mimbres Station on NM 35. From there the options are walking along the highway to the Rocky Canyon Trailhead or walking a shorter distance along the highway to the North Star Mesa Road, which parallels the Divide and leads to the Trail 74 Trailhead.

The CDT itself offers perhaps the best day-hiking along this segment. The CDT route now being developed to the Sapillo Campground, also being developed, follows ridges west of Skates Canyon, but the bottom of the canyon makes for a very good day hike, with dramatic rock formations. Also, a 4WD road at the north end of Pinos Altos leads to a loop hike around the nearby unnamed 7,606-foot mountain.

WATER NOTES

Obtaining water on the new route on the ridges above Skates Canyon requires steep cross-country hikes down to springs in the canyons below. Nearby Pinos Altos is the water source closest to the beginning, unless there's water in Bear Creek. Barring unexpected water sources, plan for a dry camp and carry a two-day supply. Water is available at the Wilderness Ranger Station at the end of the segment. The former route is still a long stretch without water, but springs in Allie Canyon usually are reliable.

MOUNTAIN BIKE NOTES

 Again, the CDT itself offers good mountain biking. Also, mountain biking is very popular on the trails in the Fort Bayard area just to the south.

EQUESTRIAN NOTES

The terrain and trails here are well-suited for horse travel, assuming plans have been made for water.

SOUTHBOUND HIKERS

If you've come down Rocky Canyon to Sapillo Campground, you will possibly want to attempt the new route to Pinos Altos. If so, be sure to carry as much water as possible, as the new route, over the ridges west of Skates Canyon, has no water at all. If you choose instead to walk south on NM 35 to the Wilderness Ranger District at Mimbres Station and then take the Allie Canyon route, you'll encounter springs and possibly flowing water, but once you leave Allie Canyon you'll find no water for the rest of the segment.

MAPS

USGS QUADRANGLES: Twin Sisters, Allie Canyon
OTHER MAPS: Gila National Forest–Gila Wilderness

LAND-MANAGEMENT AGENCIES

Gila National Forest/Silver City Ranger District and Wilderness Ranger District at Mimbres Station

BEGINNING ACCESS POINT

  NM 15: The present trailhead is at the Arrastre Site, an interesting historic locality just east of paved NM 15, about a mile north of Pinos Altos. No camping is allowed at the Arrastre Site, but informal campsites are available just 0.5 mile north, where the CDT crosses Bear Creek, immediately west of NM 15. The Bureau of Land Management is considering establishing a CDT trailhead in Pinos Altos, which would be convenient for CDT users, but nothing is planned for the near future.

ENDING ACCESS POINT

  NM 35: This segment ends at Sapillo Campground, approximately 10 miles northwest of the Mimbres Ranger Station on NM 35. This Forest Service campground is scheduled for a major renovation in the near future that will include adding water and toilet facilities, as well as camping and picnic sites. The campground at present has camping sites but little else.

TRAIL DESCRIPTION

From the Arrastre Site, N32°52'59", W108°13'26", elevation 6,800 feet, the CDT follows an old mining road generally north then east to climb approximately 900 feet during the first 0.75 mile, a difficult beginning to a difficult segment. At around 7,600 feet the route, still heading east, levels off and even drops slightly to the intersection with another old mining road at the 1.5-mile point. The junction is marked, though by weathered signs difficult to spot.

From this junction, the CDT follows the jeep road northeast through piñon-juniper. Ahead are the Twin Sisters, two summits 0.4 mile apart, the southern 8,186 feet, the northern 8,347 feet. These are your destination, 1.5 miles farther and 1,000 feet higher. The CDT passes within several hundred yards of the saddle between the Sisters as it follows contour lines around to the west. Some CDT hikers reported having heard of old Spanish carvings on rocks in the saddle between the Twin Sisters, but 90-degree temperatures and an uphill bushwhack prompted them to settle instead for spectacular views of the Mogollon Mountains to the west.

Once past Twin Sisters, the CDT rejoins the Continental Divide as it follows the ridgetop northeast toward Black Peak. The CDT continues climbing ridges until, after almost 2 miles and more than 1,100 feet elevation gain, it arrives at 9,029 feet just southwest of the radio towers atop Black Peak's summit.

From Black Peak, the CDT heads north-northwest for 0.7 mile to an unnamed 8,939-foot summit, at N32°54'53", W108°09'56". Here the Divide and the CDT head down the hill's northeast slope to head generally east, staying atop the ridges as they descend toward the saddle between the Allie Canyon on the east and Meadow Creek on the west. The saddle is at N32°55'21", W108°08'06", elevation 8,118 feet, almost 3 miles from the unnamed summit. Crossing the saddle is a jeep road, one of many that lace this area.

SUPPLIES, SERVICES, AND ACCOMMODATIONS

PINOS ALTOS, described in Segment 7, page 100, is the community nearest this segment. Silver City, 5 miles from Pinos Altos, has a vastly greater choice of support resources; see Segment 4, page 81.

MIMBRES, south of the segment's end, has about the same choice of services as Pinos Altos, but the community is less centralized, the stores and services more difficult to locate and access.

LAKE ROBERTS, approximately 4 miles north of the segment's end, also has a general store and, in season, restaurants and lodging. See Segment 9, page 115.

TRAIL DESCRIPTION: THE ALLIE CANYON ROUTE The Allie Canyon route begins at an 8,118-foot saddle at N32°55'22", W108°08'06", 3 miles from Black Peak and 0.8 mile before the new Skates Canyon route. A jeep road crosses the saddle but does not go into the canyon, whereas the CDT jogs northeast 0.2 mile before beginning a steep descent down Allie Canyon's head. Once in the canyon, the CDT follows the drainage downhill for 6.3 miles, until it leaves the canyon to avoid private land. The streambed usually is dry, except in the spring and following heavy rains. The vegetation consists of piñon-juniper on the south-facing slopes, ponderosa pine on the north slopes. The canyon bottom itself consists of both types, along with some old-growth cottonwoods.

After 4.5 miles from the saddle, at the confluence of Allie and Hightower Canyons, are a couple of springs, at N32°55'14.5", W108°04'12", elevation 6,750 feet. At 6 miles from the saddle (1.5 miles east of the other springs) is Cabin Spring, N32°55'19", W108°02'59", elevation 6,575 feet.

At 0.3 mile farther down the canyon, at N32°55'26", W108°02'39", the CDT leaves Allie Canyon. It briefly enters a tributary entering from the north, passing by a spring just 0.15 mile from Allie Canyon, but at the spring the trail climbs out of the tributary, crosses a ridge, and then descends into an east-west canyon. The CDT follows this canyon downstream east for 1.5 miles until it reaches NM 35, immediately south of the Wilderness Ranger District offices at Mimbres Station.

TRAIL DESCRIPTION: THE SKATES CANYON ROUTE From the saddle, the Divide and the CDT follow a dirt road up ridges east-northeast for almost a mile to an unnamed 8,375-foot summit at N32°55'42", W108°07'26".

 Here the Continental Divide and the CDT diverge, the CDT heading west-northwest while the Divide heads east. Also here is the divergence from the previous CDT route that followed Allie Canyon. The present CDT descends over a long cascade of ridges running generally north almost all the way to the Mimbres Valley, a descent of more than 2,800 feet and nearly 11 miles. Until the very end, the CDT stays on the ridges west of Skates Canyon. Until now, you haven't passed a single natural water source, nor will you encounter any water until the end.

From the divergence point, the CDT descends a long, gradual west-northwest ridge for 1.75 miles; then the CDT slabs northwest down the ridge's north slope to intersect a jeep road after 0.75 mile, at N32°56'48", W108°09'01", elevation 7,560 feet.

 SOUTHBOUND HIKERS: This important junction might not be marked, so take care to look for it.

The CDT follows the dirt road west-northwest over generally level ground to a junction (after 0.4 mile) with a jeep road that heads northeast. Less than 100 yards west is another junction of dirt roads.

The CDT follows the dirt road that heads north over level ground until, after 0.4 mile, at N32°57'09", W108°09'27", the CDT heads north and the dirt road heads northwest.

The CDT continues north for less than 0.5 mile, however, before swinging northeast. Here it follows the relatively narrow ridge west of Skates Canyon. After 1.1 miles of gentle descent, the CDT arrives at an unnamed 7,409-foot summit, N32°58'00", W108°08'44".

Several ridges spread fingerlike from this summit, and it's important to choose the correct one. On your compass, set the heading at 37 degrees true (magnetic north is 11 degrees east). If you have a global positioning system (GPS) unit, use it to guide you downhill, then up briefly to a 7,281-foot height at N32°58'27", W108°08'15".

From here, it's straightforward, mostly downhill hike north for 1.2 miles to a long flat ridge at N32°59'19", W108°08'07". The temptation is to follow the flat ridge north-northwest, but in fact the CDT heads northeast, toward a 7,006 height, heading 30 degrees true, N32°59'46", W108°07'48". It reaches this after 0.6 mile.

After another 0.3 mile, the route swings east as it parallels Skates Canyon 200 feet below. Finally, just 200 yards above and west of Skates Canyon, the CDT declines to join the canyon but rather swings north at 0.3 mile before abruptly heading east after another 0.2 mile, then abruptly heading north-northwest, passing west of a ridge, to join NM 35 after 1.1 miles. Of course, you could also simply pick up the dirt road at the bottom of Skates Canyon and follow it north for about 0.8 mile to NM 35, then walk the highway west 0.75 mile to the same ending, the Sapillo Campground.

OTHER HIKES AND RIDES: SAWMILL WAGON ROAD

MODE OF TRAVEL: Biking or hiking
APPROXIMATE ONE-DAY DISTANCE: 8.8 miles
DIFFICULTY: Moderate to strenuous (because of distance)

Trail 243 connecting Fort Bayard with Twin Sisters along the old Sawmill Wagon Road has been designated a National Recreation Trail. From Silver City travel east on US 180 to the village of Santa Clara (formerly Central). Just north of the village is Fort Bayard and the trailhead. *Note:* Shorter trails also are found heading north from Fort Bayard.

HISTORICAL NOTES

The Arrastre Site. Luckless donkeys and mules hitched to a spoke, ceaselessly dragging boulders through a circular groove in bedrock—that was how miners and prospectors in primitive, remote areas extracted precious metals from the ore they mined. Spanish-speaking people developed this crude but effective mechanism and called it an *arrastre.* Operations such as the one at this segment's trailhead once were more common in the Southwest—more than 90 once operated in the Silver City area—always betokening that someone had found nearby ore rich enough to justify the enormous time and labor involved in crushing it, though most miners had little but time and labor. Arrastres were replaced around 1900 by more effective techniques, and now their remains, when found at all, seem like relics from a remote past.

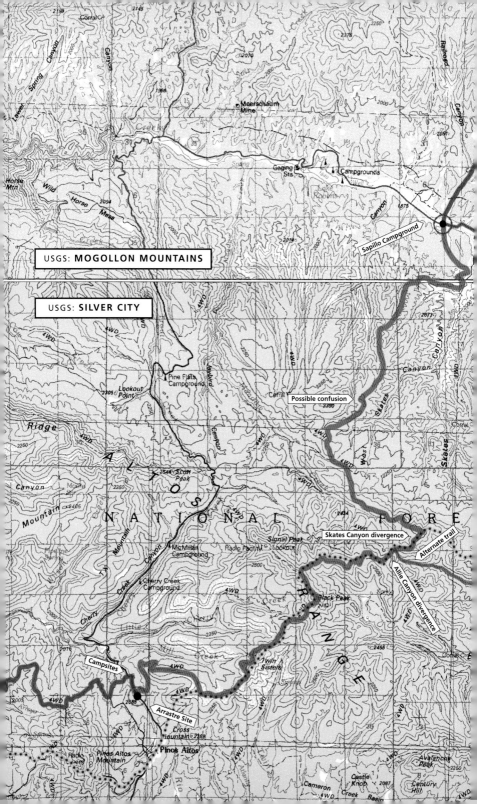

USGS: **MOGOLLON MOUNTAINS**

USGS: **SILVER CITY**

Sapillo Campground

Possible confusion

Skates Canyon divergence

Alternate trail

Allie Canyon divergence

Campsites

Arrastre Site

Pinos Altos

USGS: **TRUTH OR CONSEQUENCES**

USGS: **HATCH**

Alternate to Cooney Campground
and Segments 9 and 10

Cabin Spring

Trail leaves
Allie Canyon

Segment 8
1:100,000 MAPS:
SILVER CITY, MOGOLLON
MTNS, HATCH and TRUTH
OR CONSEQUENCES

1/4   1/4   1/2

SCALE: 1/2 INCH = 1 MILE

••••• Continental Divide

━━━ Continental Divide Trail
(current segment)

━━━ Continental Divide Trail
(previous and next segments)

━━━ Access route

Intermittent river or stream

Lake or pond

Marsh or swamp

Primary highway

Secondary highway

Light duty road

Unimproved road

Trail

✕ Quarry or open mine pit

Segment 9
NM 35 to Forest Road 150: Rocky Canyon

Cave dwelling structure,
Gila Cliff Dwellings National
Monument. Photo by
William Stone.

13.5 miles
Difficulty: Moderate to Strenuous
You may encounter: hikers and equestrians

Segment 9   **Total Elevation Gain:** 2,297 feet
From Mexico 168.15 miles
To Colorado 530.85 miles

CONTINENTAL DIVIDE
TRAIL ALLIANCE

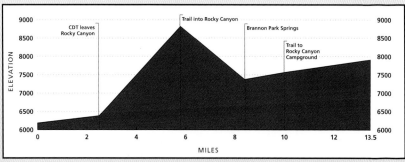

TRAIL OVERVIEW A verdant, narrow stream valley incised into arid uplands and flanked by volcanic cliffs—this for many people epitomizes the vast Gila Wilderness. And Rocky Canyon, along which much of the Continental Divide Trail runs in this segment, is just such a stream valley. The trail meanders back and forth in the mostly dry streambed, but isolated pools are interesting water sources.

Eventually, the CDT leaves the canyon and threads its away over the uplands, a very different environment. As elsewhere in the Gila Wilderness, wildlife is common: Among the animals you might see are deer, wild turkeys, bears, coyotes, javelinas, and tufted-eared squirrels. While hiking the uplands, you'll have occasional views into the canyon and thus can appreciate just what a deep and dramatic gorge it is.

Following the route in the canyon is easy, but when the CDT leaves the canyon, it's much harder to follow, as the rocky surface resists tread, and numerous cattle and game paths make for confusion. Water occurs, at least three places along the route: in the stream bed, at Brannon Spring, and at Rocky Canyon Campground. But even these sources are problematic in dry seasons. Water is available near the segment's beginning, and when the Sapillo Campground is completed, more and better water will be available. The eastern end is much drier. No water exists at the segment's end. It's 1.3 steep miles down to Rocky Canyon Campground, which has no developed water. As for the creek, well, it is called Rocky Canyon.

WATER NOTES

 Water is available at the beginning of this segment, either at the Sapillo Campground or in the lower reaches of Rocky Canyon. Other sources are available until you pass Brannon Park, whereupon water is generally lacking. Rocky Canyon Campground is supposed to have water, but it's a long, steep hike down and back—and I've seen the creek dry. No water is to be found at the segment's end. Nor is there any water along Segment 10, at least 13 miles, until its end at Reeds Peak. The Mimbres River alternative shortens this dry distance. Otherwise, plan on a water drop or carry a lot of water.

MOUNTAIN BIKE NOTES

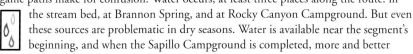 Mountain biking is prohibited in the Gila Wilderness, but portions of Forest Road 150 are well-suited for rides. Be aware, however, that the canyons through which this road passes are deep and steep, and the road sometimes is very rough and rocky.

EQUESTRIAN NOTES

Although ranchers and others clearly ride horses here, better places could be found for recreational riding. The horses certainly won't enjoy the narrow canyon, and the uplands are devilishly rocky. The ride into Brannon Park, however, on the CDT from the east is well-suited for horse travel.

SOUTHBOUND HIKERS

 Don't let the recently constructed tread at this segment's beginning lull you into inattention. South of the junction leading down to Rocky Canyon Campground, the trail becomes more obscure, the ubiquitous cattle and wildlife trails a further complication. This segment is scheduled for trail improvement by the Gila National Forest, perhaps by the time of your hike.

MAPS

USGS QUADRANGLES: North Star Mesa
OTHER MAPS: Gila National Forest–Gila Wilderness

LAND-MANAGEMENT AGENCIES

Gila National Forest/Wilderness Ranger District at Mimbres Station

BEGINNING ACCESS POINT

NM 35: This and the following segment underwent a rerouting just before this book was written. The previous route had followed Forest Road 150 from NM 35, 4.4 miles northwest of the Mimbres Ranger Station. This route followed the Continental Divide until just before the Aldo Leopold Wilderness. But although this route was direct and on the Divide, it required several miles of walking a rather unappealing dirt road. The new route goes through the Gila Wilderness and begins at Sapillo Campground, approximately 10 miles northwest of the Mimbres Ranger Station on NM 35. This Forest Service campground is scheduled for a major renovation in the near future that will include adding water and toilet facilities, as well as camping and picnic sites. The campground at present has camping sites but little else. The CDT, Trail 700, begins across the highway from the campground, where limited parking is available.

ENDING ACCESS POINT

FOREST ROAD 150: This segment ends on Forest Road 150, a well-maintained dirt road that separates the Gila and Aldo Leopold Wildernesses. There are no facilities at this junction, and while the Forest Service's Rocky Canyon Campground is 2.5 miles to the south, it is reached by a road far steeper and rougher than is suggested by the Forest Service map.

TRAIL DESCRIPTION

A CDT marker placed in the fall of 1999 on a weathered Gila National Forest sign is the main indicator that the recently rerouted CDT now coincides with Trail 700.

SOUTHBOUND HIKERS: This segment begins just across dirt Forest Road 150 from where the previous segment ended. It's a pleasant place here, beneath tall ponderosa pines—but no water is available.

This segment begins with the trail going through a metal pass-through in a fence and then crossing the marshy meadow of Sapillo Creek, usually dry, to enter the mouth of Rocky Canyon. At the mouth is an earthen dam. Past the dam, the CDT follows Rocky Canyon upstream and northeast. The CDT/Rocky Canyon Trail/Trail 700 meanders back and forth across the dry, gravelly streambed. Cairns attempt to distinguish this trail from the myriad of cow paths, but it doesn't really matter; you're

SUPPLIES, SERVICES, AND ACCOMMODATIONS

MIMBRES, a diffuse, small, but rapidly growing community along the Mimbres River, has many of the basic supplies needed by hikers, including a post office and limited groceries. Closer to the trailhead, you'll find basic supplies at the store at Lake Roberts, 4 miles west. The most complete array of services is in Silver City; see Segment 4, page 81.

Distance from Trail 11 miles

Zip Code:	88049	
Bank	None	
Bus	None	
Dining	None	
Emergency	911; non-emergency, Grant County Sheriff, 209 North Black Street, 88061	
Gear	None	
Groceries	La Tienda, 2574 Hwy. 35, San Lorenzo, 88041	(505) 536-3140
	Mimbres Store, 3090 Hwy. 35, Mimbres	536-9350
	Rio Mimbres Lodge, Feed and Supply, 3544 Highway 35 N., Mimbres	536-3777
Information	See La Tienda above	
Laundry	La Tienda, 2574 Hwy. 35, San Lorenzo, 88041	536-3140
Lodging	Casas Adobes RV Park, on NM 35, north of the NM 35–NM 152 junction	
Medical	Mimbres Clinic, at Casas Adobes north of the NM 35–NM 152 junction, Mon and Tue 9–5, Thur and Fri 9–5	536-3990
Post Office	Mimbres Post Office, next to the Mimbres Store on NM 35 (will hold general delivery 30 days)	536-3990
Showers	See Casas Adobes RV Park above	

LAKE ROBERTS is a small vacation community associated with scenic Lake Roberts. Lodging and limited supplies and groceries are available at the Lake Roberts General Store on NM 35, at the north end of the lake: HC 68 Box 95, Silver City, 88061, (800) 224-1080. Lodging and meals also are available at the Spirit Canyon Lodge and Cafe, on NM 35, at the lake's south end: HC 68 Box 60, Silver City, 88061-9341, (505) 536-9459; E-mail: info@spiritcanyon.com.

WILDERNESS ALERT: This segment is within the Gila Wilderness. Please observe these wilderness guidelines:

1. Camp out of sight, at least 200 feet from springs and drainages, on a dry, durable surface.

2. Use a stove instead of building a fire; use existing fire rings if you do build a fire.

3. Keep water sources pure by camping at least 200 feet from them.

4. Bury human wastes 6 inches deep and at least 200 feet from water sources; pack out toilet paper.

5. Dogs must be on a leash.

6. No mountain biking.

7. Pack out all trash; don't attempt to burn it.

not likely to confuse Rocky Canyon with any of its tributary drainages. Cliffs of buff-colored volcanic conglomerate flank the flat stream valley, and riparian plants such as willows and cottonwoods, walnuts and sycamores, make the stream a pleasant place. But remember: In the spring and during monsoon storms, the streambed can be full and swift.

After slightly more than 2.5 miles from the trailhead, at N33°02'46", W108°05'47", elevation is 6,380 feet. At this point, the canyon twists, constricts, and chokes with vegetation. Cairns here mark a trail out of the canyon, heading up a ridge to the north. The Gila National Forest map shows the CDT leaving the canyon here to parallel the canyon on the mesas above, though the North Star Mesa quadrangle, published in 1965, shows the Rocky Canyon Trail staying in the canyon. As of this writing, the most efficient route is by no means clear. Joseph Gendron and I, hiking south, arrived at the canyon here via a faint, poorly marked trail that had taken us over a mesa with the greatest density of foot-tripping rocks I had ever seen. Fortunately, planning is under way to improve this stretch.

The canyon is narrow above this junction, the steep cliffs over 400 feet high. Staying in the canyon makes a good side trip, though it requires a scramble around a pour-off up the side tributary. If you are able to stay in the canyon, continue up it for approximately 5.8 miles, to N33°04'05", W108°04'16", elevation 6,700 feet. Here a tributary enters Rocky Canyon from the north-northeast, and here, according to the North Star Mesa quadrangle, Trail 700 leaves Rocky Canyon. Water usually can be found here, but whether you encounter good water here or above, you should consider filling your bottles because the water not far ahead is polluted by cattle. The CDT follows the tributary upstream.

At 1.25 miles from Rocky Canyon, N33°05'00", W108°04'10", elevation 7,000 feet, you'll find the junction of two tiny drainages; in my visit, both had water.

The CDT here follows the drainage trending east-northeast, but only briefly before leaving it to climb onto the mesa. Cairns and blazes mark this sometimes faint stretch of the trail. After about 0.5 mile of walking gently uphill east-northeast on the mesa, you find yourself in a broad swale; this area is grazed heavily by cattle, some of which you're likely to meet. As you continue in this rather open area of easy walking, you'll notice water in low spots, especially as the trail swings north-northeast toward Brannon Park. The Gila National Forest map shows Brannon Spring here, but it doesn't appear on the North Star Mesa quadrangle. Most likely that's because the spring emerges over a broad area, accounting for the green grass here. When Joseph Gendron and I were here, we found a herd of javelinas rooting on the close-cropped grass. Surface water emerges in the area, but cattle have polluted it.

As the trail continues northeast, it enters Brannon Park, a delightful basin of grass and trees. Maps show Trail 95, the Brannon Park Trail, meeting Trail 700 from the north here. A sign is at the junction, but Trail 95 is faint. The CDT, Trail 700, continues northeast, climbing onto the uplands above the park. The terrain here is dry, the vegetation piñon, juniper, and oak. The trail climbs about 300 feet, trending generally northeast, until after about 1.6 miles it arrives at a saddle. Here at N33°06'24", W108°01'45", elevation 7,600 feet, look for a clear trail junction, though there's no sign. Trail 700 descends steeply east-southeast 1.7 miles to the Rocky Canyon Campground, but the CDT heads northeast over an easy-to-follow trail, constructed in August 1999. After about 1.5 miles from the junction, this trail takes you to a small saddle near a large rock outcrop, elevation 8,000 feet. From here, the trail descends approximately 0.75 mile to Forest Road 150, N33°07'23", W108°00'23", elevation 7,910 feet, and the end of this segment. No water or facilities exist at this point, but the Rocky Canyon Campground, with no developed water, is 2.5 long, steep, rocky miles south along Forest Road 150.

HISTORICAL NOTES

The Gila Wilderness. To borrow a Native American image, the Gila Wilderness is the grandmother of all wilderness areas. Until the Gila Wilderness was established by Congress in 1924, no area anywhere had been set aside solely to preserve its wilderness character. Scenery inspired the preservation of Yellowstone, watershed the protection of the White Mountains in New Hampshire, but the Gila was the first to be preserved just because it's wild.

Aldo Leopold, who spearheaded the preservation, came to the Gila country in 1909 as a young Forest Ranger (see Segment 10, page 126). He reveled in the wild vastness here, but unlike any before him, he could see that the wilderness was finite, that it was shrinking and in need of protection. At 558,065 acres, the Gila Wilderness is New Mexico's largest wilderness and almost twice as large as the second-place Pecos Wilderness; but when it was created in 1924 it was even larger, 755,000 acres, because it included the approximately 200,000 acres now part of the Aldo Leopold Wilderness. The two were separated in 1931–1932, when an administrative road was built from NM 35 to Beaverhead. But even with the administrative lines, the Gila Wilderness remains the wild core of one of the last and largest wilderness regions in the United States. Like the Aldo Leopold Wilderness, the Gila Wilderness also is near the Blue Range Wilderness to the northwest, itself adjacent to the much larger Blue Range Primitive Area in Arizona, the Peloncillo Mountains to the southwest, and nearby Bureau of Land Management and private lands that are often as wild as those in the Wilderness. For this reason, the Gila Wilderness is the nexus for the Sky Islands Alliance's dreams of a "super-wilderness" that will restore and protect species that need vast wildlands to survive.

Mimbres Culture. The Mimbres River takes its name from a Spanish word for "willows," a common riparian plant in New Mexico. But to most people, *mimbres* refers not to the river or to willows but to the prehistoric Mogollon culture that flourished here. By 300 B.C., these people were living in pit houses, in settlements as large as 50 units; around A.D. 1150 their culture underwent a dramatic shift, for reasons still unknown. Their pottery style changed, and they began living above ground, occasionally in masonry structures, the best surviving example preserved at Gila Cliff Dwellings National Monument. Suddenly the Mimbres people left, again for reasons unknown. By A.D. 1340, southwestern New Mexico was empty of the people who had lived here for more than a millennium. Where they went and who they became are subject to debate.

What attracts most modern people to the Mimbres culture is their extraordinary sense of design. Their finely crafted pottery is decorated with highly stylized paintings of animals, plants, people, and mythological figures; these paintings rank alongside the most beautiful and sophisticated prehistoric art anywhere in the world. So much so that intact decorated Mimbres pottery commands high prices among collectors, creating a black market for such items, resulting in extensive looting of Mimbres sites.

USGS: TRUTH OR CONSEQUENCES

USGS: HATCH

USGS: SILVER CITY

Alternate to Cooney Campground
and Segments 9 and 10

Cooney Campground

CONTINENTAL DIVIDE

Alternate to Cooney Campground
and Segments 9 and 10

Rocky Canyon alternate

CONTINENTAL DIVIDE

Trail poorly marked

Segment 10
Forest Road 150 to Reeds Peak

Thunderheads over the Blue Range, Blue Range Wilderness, Gila National Forest. Photo by Tom Till.

14.5 miles
Difficulty: Strenuous
You may encounter: hikers and equestrians

Segment 10 **Total Elevation Gain:** 4,041 feet
From Mexico 181.65 miles
To Colorado 517.35 miles

CONTINENTAL DIVIDE
TRAIL ALLIANCE

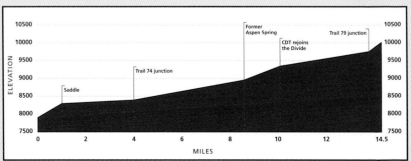

TRAIL OVERVIEW The Continental Divide Trail enters the Aldo Leopold Wilderness in this segment. Correy McDonald, New Mexico wilderness advocate, once described the Aldo Leopold Wilderness as "an archetype of a wilderness defending itself." Indeed it is.

The Aldo Leopold Wilderness and the surrounding Black Range—equally remote, forbidding, and wild—is arguably New Mexico's wildest wilderness. At 202,016 acres, the Aldo Leopold is third (barely) among New Mexico's Big Three of wildernesses. (The other two are the 557,873-acre Gila Wilderness and the 223,667-acre Pecos Wilderness.) But neither has the Aldo's unique combination of remoteness, limited access, punishingly rugged and steep terrain, lack of water, lack of public attractions such as hot springs or huge waterfalls—and paucity of visitors.

New Mexicans are barely aware the Black Range exists; even fewer have ever hiked there, despite the range's being among the state's largest mountain groups. In some parts of the West, the issue of the public's overusing wildlands—"loving the wilderness to death"—has raised concerns among environmentalists. If that issue speaks to you, then come to the Black Range. Trails are faced with abandonment because not enough people use them. Even major trails often are faint, more frequently used by wildlife than by hikers. Indeed, with Native Americans, explorers, soldiers, miners, prospectors, and homesteaders gone, the Black Range today probably has fewer foot or horse travelers today than it did 100 or 150 years ago.

The Black Range is dry. For example, along this segment, no natural surface water exists. The segments following face similar problems. And it is remote; no opportunities exist for resupply. Thus, prepare carefully before embarking upon this segment. Here more than elsewhere you should make contact with the local Forest Service districts, get the latest information about local conditions, and inform the Forest Service of your plans.

At least 200 miles of trails exist in the Aldo Leopold Wilderness, which includes this segment; clearly a large number of day hikes are possible. Almost all, however, share remoteness and rugged terrain. Also, because almost all are seldom traveled, tread is likely to be faint—or less—so solid route-finding skills are essential. Perhaps the best day hike here—and the easiest—is Trail 77 along the Mimbres River (see page 125).

WATER NOTES

No water is available along the official route, from Forest Road 150 to Reeds Peak via Signboard Saddle, until the end—either at Squeaky Spring or the cistern at Reeds Peak. But hikers who elect to follow the Mimbres River alternative will find water plentiful in the river.

MOUNTAIN BIKE NOTES

Though mountain bikes are prohibited in the Aldo Leopold Wilderness, the nearby Forest Road 150 affords interesting—and challenging—mountain biking. One good ride would be along Forest Road 150, at the segment's beginning; the Rocky Canyon Campground and the Upper and Lower Black Canyon Campgrounds are about 7 miles apart. *Note:* Stay on the roads here; the trails are fragile and rarely suited for mountain biking.

EQUESTRIAN NOTES

Corrals are at the alternative access point (described below), the head of Trail 74. Unfortunately, no water is available until Reeds Peak, more than 12 miles away. For equestrians, the Trail 74 route is preferable to the Trail 76–CDT route to Signboard Saddle, because the other route traverses steep, rocky slopes where forest fires have removed vegetation and the footing is treacherous.

SOUTHBOUND HIKERS

Following the Divide, the CDT, and Trail 74 downhill over forested ridges is a pleasant hike, but an alternative at least as pleasant— and with water— is to hike Trail 79, the Crest Trail, south from Reeds Peak about 0.25 mile to where Trail 77, the Mimbres River Trail, enters from the southwest. After an initial steep descent, this well-marked trail follows the Mimbres River 12 miles to the Gila National Forest's Cooney Campground. From here, Forest Road 150A leads uphill 2 miles to Forest Road 150, which leads after 5.75 miles to the Rocky Canyon Campground and then connects with the CDT 2.5 miles farther north.

If you follow the CDT down from Reeds Peak, be sure to top off your water containers, as water is lacking along this route and also at its end.

MAPS

USGS QUADRANGLES: North Star Mesa, Bonner Canyon, Reeds Peak
OTHER MAPS: Gila National Forest; Gila National Forest–Aldo Leopold Wilderness

LAND-MANAGEMENT AGENCIES

Gila National Forest/Wilderness Ranger District at Mimbres Station and Black Range Ranger District

BEGINNING ACCESS POINT

FOREST ROAD 150: This and the previous segment were rerouted just before this was written. The previous route had followed Forest Road 150 from NM 35, 4.4 miles northwest of the Wilderness Ranger Station at Mimbres Station. This previous route followed the Continental Divide until just before the Aldo Leopold Wilderness. But although this route was direct and on the Divide, it required several miles of walking a rather unappealing dirt road. The new route is on trail and begins on Forest Road 150, about 15 miles from NM 35, 2.5 miles from the Rocky Canyon Campground. No facilities or water are at the trailhead, but the Rocky Canyon Campground is 2.5 miles to the south along Forest Road 150.

ALTERNATE ACCESS

FOREST ROAD 150–TRAIL 74: The previous CDT route still provides access to this segment. At 4.4 miles northwest of the Wilderness Ranger Station at Mimbres Station on NM 35, Forest Road 150 branches northeast, following the Continental Divide. About 8 miles from NM 35, a rougher Forest Road branches right, or northeast, and after less than a mile stops at the trailhead. A sign here says Signboard Saddle is 3.25 miles, Reeds Peak is 12.25 miles, both via Trail 74. The hike to Signboard Saddle and the present CDT is a very pleasant and relatively easy hike.

ENDING ACCESS POINT

REEDS PEAK: Reeds Peak is accessible to backpackers from the south via the McKnight Road. This road heads east from NM 35 about 1.2 mile north of the Wilderness Ranger District at Mimbres Station. The McKnight Road gets rougher as it climbs and is vulnerable to bad weather, but normally you can drive it in high-clearance vehicles. Drive to its end just south of McKnight Mountain, then hike north along the Black Range Crest Trail, No. 79, for 11 miles; water is available at McKnight Cabin. Should this be too algae-ridden, water likely would be available at Mimbres Lake 3 miles north or at North Seco Spring, 3.5 miles north.

SUPPLIES, SERVICES, AND ACCOMMODATIONS

MIMBRES is the community nearest this segment. Its CDT support resources are described in Segment 9, page 115. Although maps show Mimbres as a distinct village, in reality the community is spread out for several miles along NM 35. For supplies and groceries not available in Mimbres, see Silver City, Segment 4, page 81.

LAKE ROBERTS is a small vacation community associated with scenic Lake Roberts. Lodging and limited supplies and groceries are available at the Lake Roberts General Store on NM 35, at the north end of the lake: HC 68 Box 95, Silver City, 88061, (800) 224-1080. Lodging and meals also are available at the Spirit Canyon Lodge and Cafe, on NM 35, at the lake's south end: HC 68 Box 60, Silver City, 88061-9341; (505) 536-9459; E-mail: info@spiritcanyon.com.

TRAIL DESCRIPTION

A pleasant grove of oaks begins this segment. At the trailhead, a sign informs you that Signboard Saddle is 4 miles distant and Reeds Peak 13 miles. At this point, you should make sure that your stomach and water bottles are full, for the next water is at Reeds Peak. If necessary, obtain water at the Rocky Canyon Campground, 2.5 miles south on Forest Road 150.

The CDT and Trail 76 begin this journey by heading uphill from Forest Road 150. The trail climbs rather steeply from 7,910 feet elevation to a ridge at 8,195 feet in about half a mile. From here the trail continues east another half mile to reach a saddle at N33°07'25", W107°59'12", elevation 8,300 feet. A sign at the saddle says Signboard Saddle is 3 miles, Reeds Peak is 12, and Forest Road 150 is 2 miles via a spur trail here, 1 mile via the main Trail 76. From the saddle, Trail 76 climbs again to pass just north of a knob at N33°07'25", W107°58'58", elevation 8,696 feet. From here, the trail descends as it continues east, swinging around another knob before heading south.

Although the trails here are indicated on maps and well-marked with signs— but no CDT markers—the trails are very faint and often difficult to follow. Blazes and cairns help, but a good map, compass, and GPS unit help even more. Much of the difficulty is caused by sparse vegetation and topsoil, the result of forest fires, which leaves the trail rocky and subject to erosion. As the trail heads south, it crosses a steep west-facing slope that is a good example of this.

The trail slabs along this slope, then climbs to a saddle at 8,750 feet. From here Trail 76 crosses east slopes as it descends gradually to end at the junction with Trail 74, just north-northeast and slightly downhill from Signboard Saddle, N33°06'13", W107°57'41", elevation 8,400 feet. The swale here is very pleasant, shaded by ponderosa pines, and the grass in the swale is green, as if water were near the surface. At this junction is a sign that says State Road 61 (Forest Road 150) via Rocky Point (the trail you just hiked) is 4 miles; Forest Road 150 (NM 61) is 3.75 miles via Trail 74. Trail 75 begins here, heading north down the valley toward Black Canyon, 5.25 miles.

Trail 74, which had been trending north, now heads east-northeast toward Reeds Peak, 8.25 miles away. It follows the Continental Divide along a ridgeline, through pleasant ponderosa forest interspersed with oak and, at higher elevations and north slopes, mixed conifers. After about 4.6 miles, Trail 74 and the CDT pass by what appears on the map as Aspen Spring. Unfortunately, attempts to "improve" the spring instead destroyed it completely; nothing is there now. The Forest Service is planning to reroute the CDT near here to bring it closer to Aspen Canyon, but for now . . .

From the former Aspen Spring, the CDT descends briefly before ascending through a saddle on the south side of Aspen Mountain. Rather than heading over 9,606-foot Aspen Mountain, as does the Continental Divide, the CDT follows contour lines along the mountain's south and east slopes to rejoin the CDT after 1.5 miles from Aspen Spring at N33°07'37", W107°53'58", elevation 9,360 feet. It descends via some switchbacks before climbing again onto a ridge and the Divide.

At 3 miles from the spring, still on the ridge, the CDT climbs more steeply, using switchbacks, until at 5.2 miles from the spring it reaches the junction with Trail 79 at N33°08'34", W107°51'29". From here, at elevation 9,760 feet, it's a steep and steady climb of 0.25 mile to the top of 10,015-foot Reeds Peak. From the Trail 79 junction, it's 0.4 mile north to Squeaky Spring, a reliable water source, though many hikers will get water from the cistern atop Reeds Peak.

ALTERNATIVE TRAIL: THE MIMBRES RIVER The CDT route, following a ridge to Reeds Peak, has no reliable water along its course. An appealing alternative is to follow the Mimbres River to its headwaters near Reeds Peak.

From the previous segment's end, you'll follow Forest Road 150 south for 7.25 miles to where Forest Road 150A descends 2 miles to Cooney Campground, on the Mimbres River. *Note:* Low-clearance vehicles face a river crossing at the campground. After the crossing, follow a dirt road upriver to a wide gravel area, with gates and private residences. The sign for the Mimbres River Trail, Trail 77, is at the parking area's south end.

The route follows a road above the river, skirting the private property below. Several false trails descend prematurely to the river, but when the private property ends, the main trail is easy to follow. The hiking is pleasant: broad, grassy clearings; several easy river crossings; tall ponderosas, large Gambel oaks, and narrow-leaf cottonwoods. The Mimbres River, the Aldo Leopold Wilderness's largest stream, supports a protected population of the endangered Gila trout. Campsites are numerous here, the gradients gentle.

After 6.25 miles, you reach the junction of the Mimbres River's North and Middle Forks. *Note:* The Middle Fork, as shown on the Gila National Forest–Aldo Leopold Wilderness map, is labeled the South Fork on the Hay Mesa quadrangle. The coordinates are N33°05'38", W107°53'29", elevation 7,675 feet. The route to Reeds Peak, 5.75 miles, runs via the North Fork and Trail 77. The canyon becomes steeper and narrower now as it makes its way north, then northeast up to the south side of Reeds Peak. There Trail 77 ends at the Crest Trail, Trail 79. From here, the Crest Trail heads steeply north, up the south slope of Reeds Peak before a more gradual descent northwest and a reunion with the CDT, almost a mile from Trail 77.

WILDERNESS ALERT

This segment is entirely within the Aldo Leopold Wilderness. Please observe these wilderness guidelines:

1. Camp out of sight, at least 200 feet from springs and drainages, on a dry, durable surface.

2. Use a stove instead of building a fire; use existing fire rings if you do build a fire.

3. Keep water sources pure by camping at least 200 feet from them.

4. Bury human wastes 6 inches deep and at least 200 feet from water sources; pack out toilet paper.

5. Dogs must be on a leash.

6. No mountain biking.

7. Pack out all trash; don't attempt to burn it.

HISTORICAL NOTES

Aldo Leopold is regarded as the father of wildlife ecology, but his influence was much more far-reaching than just that discipline. It was Leopold who articulated for much of the world the concept of a land ethic, and it was Leopold who spearheaded the drive to create the world's first formally protected wilderness area—the Gila Wilderness of New Mexico.

Leopold, born and raised in Iowa and educated in New Jersey, came to the Southwest in 1909 as a 22-year-old Forest Ranger. He was an avid hunter and a seasoned outdoorsman, and he soon came to know well the wildlands of southwestern New Mexico. Leopold rose rapidly in the Forest Service and became acquainted with others in the agency who were beginning to espouse the innovative concept that wilderness should be preserved simply because it is wild. Leopold, then working in Albuquerque, was especially concerned about the threatened wildlands of southwestern New Mexico. In 1924, his vision was realized when the Gila Wilderness was created as the nation's first area set aside solely to preserve its wild character. (The area presently within the Aldo Leopold Wilderness originally was part of a much larger Gila Wilderness; the two were separated in 1931–1932 with the creation of the North Star Road, Forest Road 150.)

Leopold left the Forest Service and moved to Wisconsin, where he devoted himself to university teaching and writing. His *Game Management* (1933) remains a classic of wildlife management, and in books such as *A Sand County Almanac* he articulated a philosophy of a land ethic that profoundly influenced conservationists worldwide. In it he wrote: "There are some who can live without wild things and some who cannot. These essays are the delights and dilemmas of one who cannot."

Coyote Peak and a CDT sign on the southern edge of the Plains of San Agustin.
Photo by William Stone.

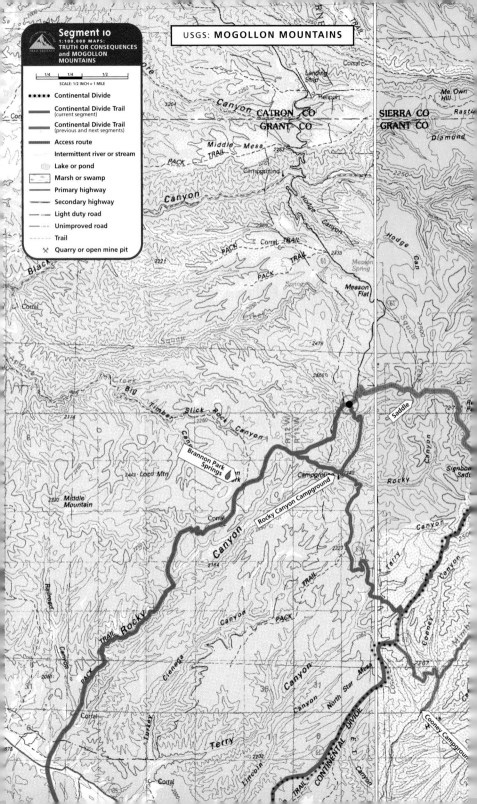

Segment 10
1:100,000 MAPS:
TRUTH OR CONSEQUENCES
and MOGOLLON
MOUNTAINS

SCALE: 1/2 INCH = 1 MILE

••••• Continental Divide

───── Continental Divide Trail
(current segment)

───── Continental Divide Trail
(previous and next segments)

▓▓▓▓▓ Access route

───── Intermittent river or stream

⬭ Lake or pond

Marsh or swamp

───── Primary highway

───── Secondary highway

───── Light duty road

───── Unimproved road

───── Trail

✕ Quarry or open mine pit

Squeaky Spring

Reeds Peak Lookout

Alternate route

Trail leaves Mimbres River

USGS: **TRUTH OR CONSEQUENCES**

Segment 11
Reeds Peak to Diamond Peak

Rio Grande Valley ridges, Aldo Leopold Wilderness. Photo by Tom Till.

9.5 miles
Difficulty: Strenuous
You may encounter: hikers and equestrians

Segment 11   **Total Elevation Gain:** 2,639 feet
From Mexico 196.15 miles
To Colorado 502.85 miles

CONTINENTAL DIVIDE
TRAIL ALLIANCE

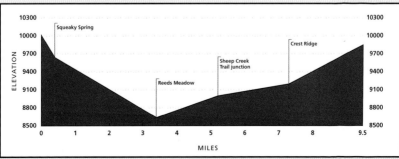

TRAIL OVERVIEW   This segment can be called the New Mexico Continental Divide Trail's crux, to borrow a climbing term for a route's most difficult pitch. It is remote. No towns are nearby for resupply, nor do any major roads approach this segment. Even the secondary and dirt roads are few, long, seldom-traveled, and often rough, making food and water caches difficult. One experienced party simply ran out of food here. The Gila National Forest–Black Range Ranger District staff, based both in Truth or Consequences and at the Beaverhead Work Center, are very supportive and helpful, but their resources are limited. Nor are they exactly metropolitan themselves. Worse, the remoteness, difficult terrain, aridity, and sometimes obscure route don't end at paved NM 59. Indeed, from the highway those conditions continue—with fewer trails—for several long segments, as far as NM 12.

In planning your hike for this segment, allow more time than the distance would suggest. The hiking is rough, with lots of relief and lots of steep and rocky sections. But what really impedes travel here is the Black Range's having undergone numerous forest fires in recent times; these fires have left downed and soon-to-be-downed trees everywhere, along with dense stands of aspen and other trees and shrubs that appear after fires. These burned areas require hikers with heavy packs to climb over, under, and around countless snags, plowing through dense brush, tripping, and losing the trail. The dead snags are especially dangerous in high winds because they can fall at any moment. The Forest Service Black Range and Wilderness Districts have cleared the route and hope to do so yearly, and, as time passes, the cut logs will help define the trail.

 The burned, dead trees and successional vegetation mean the landscape is constantly changing; this makes following the trail difficult sometimes and enlarges the importance of cairns and blazes. It's always a good policy, when tread is faint or lacking, not to lose sight of one cairn or blaze before having sighted the next. The Black Range is among the worst possible places to get lost.

Forest managers welcome the burns as promoting natural succession and species diversity, and hikers should just accept them. The fires are essential for natural processes, and, because of the numerous burns of different ages, the Black Range is among the best places in the Southwest to observe fire ecology. As the successional aspens mature, in 50 years or less, the crest in the fall will turn golden.

Along with its challenges, the Black Range also offers rewards. In this segment, you'll be in the heart of what perhaps is New Mexico's wildest wilderness where wildlife is plentiful. You'll be on the Continental Divide, not just in a vague, almost abstract sense as so often in New Mexico, but in an intimate, physical sense. The staff of the Gila National Forest–Black Range Ranger District know this area as well as anyone. They say, "When you're walking on the CDT here, you *know* you're walking on the Continental Divide because it's all downhill on both sides."

Note: Because the crest is a lightning magnet, plan to hike early in the day and be prepared to retreat from the crest to seek shelter during storms. Equestrians should be especially careful with horses.

Come prepared for difficult, challenging hiking, but prepared as well for some of the wildest, most beautiful country in New Mexico.

Note: The vast and complex Aldo Leopold Wilderness can exact a high price from travelers who don't know the region. A great way to become familiar with this area is to accompany a Forest Service trail crew as a volunteer. The work can be rough, but volunteer opportunities abound, with crews departing every two weeks in the summer; opportunities exist at other seasons as well. Contact the Black Range Ranger District for information (see Appendix A, page 306).

This is spectacular though challenging hiking country, but the distance of this segment from a road means that any hiker here almost by definition is a backpacker.

WATER NOTES

Sufficient water exists at Reeds Meadow near the beginning of this segment and at Diamond Peak Spring near its end, so hikers should be able to carry enough water to see them through this stretch.

MOUNTAIN BIKE NOTES

This segment is entirely within the Aldo Leopold Wilderness and thus is off-limits for mountain biking.

EQUESTRIAN NOTES

Rough terrain, paucity of water, and, most important, the numerous downed trees and snags argue for this segment's being suited for hardy, mountain-trained horses only. Equestrians should inquire about current conditions and maintenance at the Black Range (505-894-6677) or Wilderness (505-536-2250) Ranger Districts.

SOUTHBOUND HIKERS

By this time you've encountered the downed timber, dead snags, and other forest fire aftermath that make the Black Range Crest a challenge. This segment is more of the same. Fill your water bottles at Diamond Peak Spring; your next water is at Reeds Meadow 6 miles away. Be sure to descend from the Crest if lightning threatens.

MAPS
USGS QUADRANGLES: Reeds Peak
OTHER MAPS: Gila National Forest–Aldo Leopold Wilderness, Gila National Forest

LAND-MANAGEMENT AGENCIES
Gila National Forest/Black Range Ranger District

BEGINNING ACCESS POINT

REEDS PEAK: See Ending Access Point in Segment 10, page 123. Backpackers can access Reeds Peak only via hiking and horses over trails.

DIAMOND PEAK: The only access to this segment is via foot or horse via the CDT or other trails, such as Trail 68 along South Diamond Creek, cleared by the Forest Service–Wilderness Ranger District in 1998.

SUPPLIES, SERVICES, AND ACCOMMODATIONS

MIMBRES is the community nearest this segment. Its CDT support resources are described in Segment 9, page 115.

LAKE ROBERTS, approximately 4 miles north of the segment's end, also has a general store and, in season, restaurants and lodging. See Segment 9, page 115.

TRAIL DESCRIPTION Technically, Reeds Peak is not on the CDT, as Trail 74, coinciding with the CDT, joins Trail 79, the Black Range Crest Trail, about 0.3 mile west of the summit. It's all but inconceivable, however, that CDT hikers, having come this far, 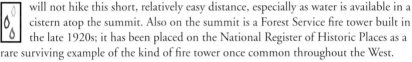 will not hike this short, relatively easy distance, especially as water is available in a cistern atop the summit. Also on the summit is a Forest Service fire tower built in the late 1920s; it has been placed on the National Register of Historic Places as a rare surviving example of the kind of fire tower once common throughout the West.

 From the summit, a trail with no trail number heads north about 0.25 mile to a junction. The left fork, difficult to find, descends northeast about 250 feet to join Trail 74 at Squeaky Spring, N33°08'49", W107°51'23", elevation 9,640 feet. This is a fairly reliable spring, rebuilt by New Mexico Volunteers for the Outdoors (NMVFO) in 1997.

If you don't descend to Squeaky Spring, you would take the right fork north-northeast as it descends more gently to join Trail 74. This trail section connecting the peak with Trail 74 was rebuilt in 1997 by NMVFO. The top of Reeds Peak is rocky, good tent sites are few. Better is the meadow between the CDT–Reeds Peak Trail junction north of the peak and Squeaky Spring. There are softer, more sheltered sites in the trees on the north and southwest sides of this meadow.

 Where the CDT runs through this meadow, the trail is sometimes obscure. Bear to the meadow's east side and pick up the trail where it enters the trees. Squeaky Spring is about 60 feet off of Trail 74 and about 100 feet back in the trees on the meadow's south side.

At about where you rejoin Trail 74–CDT, Trail 73, the Falls Canyon Trail, enters from the northwest. Trail 74 and the CDT, marked and signed, continue north along the crest and the Continental Divide, descending and then climbing along the Black Range crest, with dramatic views to the east into deep, rugged canyons. This is a rough, difficult section; hikers should have no problems, but it's punishing for horses. Just before a 9,450-foot summit, the trail (a 1998 NMVFO project) descends via switchbacks to a small saddle on the crest; from here it dips down to slab below the crest to the east.

From this east-facing vantage, you'll have great views of the very rugged eastern Black Range. About 0.25 mile or less on the east slope, the trail reportedly passes a small spring. The trail continues below the crest to the east for about 1.25 miles.

Keeping to the trail here, especially to the north, can be difficult because the forest was burned, and the trail is often obscured by the dense growth of young aspens. If it's any consolation, the aspens colonizing such burned areas will, in time, turn the Black Range Crest into one of the Southwest's premier fall foliage hikes with waves of shimmering gold.

After running north and staying near the 9,250-foot contour, Trail 74 briefly heads east to descend to a small saddle. It descends north briefly at the head of a small drainage, but soon swings west to parallel the 8,800-foot contour to make a long 1.5-mile switchback down to Reeds Meadow. En route it passes a spring, then at the meadow it crosses the Black Canyon drainage near its head, meeting the Black Canyon Trail, Trail 72, as it arrives from the west; water usually is available here, though another spring is just a short distance away. Water also can be found by descending into Black Canyon.

Reeds Meadow, N33°10'49", W107°51'05", elevation 8,640 feet, deservedly is a favorite place among CDT hikers as well as Forest Rangers. It combines meadow with mixed conifers and aspens. It has water, and is sheltered because it is off the crest. (Reeds Meadow takes its name from a man named Reed who built a cabin here and grew potatoes for about 30 years around 1900.) Water is available here, in small pools as well as in Black Canyon, and the meadow is frequented by such wildlife as deer, elk, and wild turkeys.

From Reeds Meadow, the 6 miles to Diamond Peak are difficult but rewarding. This area has been burned within the last 15 years; dead trees are perennially falling, obstructing the trail with deadfalls and threatening hikers, especially during high winds. The CDT stays close to the crest, thus following the Continental Divide. The views from the crest are spectacular, especially around Diamond Peak. But because the CDT does cling to the crest, there's a lot of up-and-down walking. Also, there's little to no water until Diamond Peak; springs are shown on the map, but they're not reliable. The next reliable water is at Diamond Peak Spring, so fill your bottles and your stomach at Reeds Meadow.

From Reeds Meadow the CDT heads due north, climbing gradually until, after about a mile, the trail swings northwest to follow briefly along the south side of a small drainage before coming out into a large meadow. Here, as in other such meadows, the trail is often obscured, especially as the blazed trees marking the route may have been destroyed by fire. Two hikers who came through in 1997 during Uniting Along the Divide reported: "Then the trail becomes hopelessly lost in a semi-marshy glade-saddle, which I call 'Sleepy Hollow' because it's a pretty spooky place with dense vegetation growing out of an old burn, and the surrounding country-side is simply a jumble of similar ridges and canyons." If you lose the trail, head northwest across the meadow to the junction with Trail 481, the Sheep Creek Trail, at N33°11'52", W107°51'39", around 9,000 feet. *Note:* The two hikers did find the trail again, but noted that old burns and dense vegetation continued to make route-finding difficult until they got onto the ridge running toward Diamond Peak. Since their reconnaissance, several work parties have been in the area, so the trail likely has become more distinct, but be prepared nonetheless.

From here the CDT passes between two small hills as it continues northwest on the Continental Divide, climbing from 9,000 feet to 9,200 feet in about 0.5 mile before heading north along the east slopes of a mountain. It continues north to a saddle, N33°12'32", W107°51'57", at around 9,200 feet, where it mounts the crest ridge running northeast. The CDT climbs along the axis of this ridge, then descends to another saddle at about 0.8 mile from the previous saddle. Here Trail 69, the Burnt Canyon Trail, enters from the west to meet Trail 74 at N33°13'00", W107°51'29", 9,067 feet.

From the Trail 69 junction, the CDT and Trail 74 promptly begin climbing along the ridge again, staying on the crest and the Continental Divide until they reach Diamond Peak after about 1.5 miles and almost 800 feet of elevation gain. Along this section, the burned areas are fewer and the trail is much easier to follow. The ridges offer spectacular views, but they also expose hikers to lightning strikes and storms. Diamond Peak is at N33°13'45", W107°50'38", 9,850 feet. The summit is an appealing place to camp—fairly flat, green, with water nearby, though a lightning storm quickly voids its appeal. Diamond Peak Spring, N33°13'55", W107°50'40", on the CDT just north of Diamond Peak, is small, sometimes just a trickle, but it trickles year-round. Diamond Peak once was topped by a Forest Service fire lookout tower, but now only its foundations remain.

According to a ranger who knows the place well, the knoll just north of the summit is a great place to rest—"and to gaze off to the east across that spectacular, eternal landscape of south-central New Mexico."

SEE PAGE 143 FOR SEGMENT 11 MAP.

WILDERNESS ALERT:
This segment is within the Aldo Leopold Wilderness. Please observe these wilderness guidelines: **1.** Camp out of sight, at least 200 feet from springs and drainages, on a dry, durable surface. **2.** Use a stove instead of building a fire; use existing fire rings if you do build a fire. **3.** Keep water sources pure by camping at least 200 feet from them. **4.** Bury human wastes 6 inches deep and at least 200 feet from water sources; pack out toilet paper. **5.** Dogs must be on a leash. **6.** No mountain biking. **7.** Pack out all trash; don't attempt to burn it.

Segment 12
Diamond Peak to Lookout Mountain

Double rainbow over the Continental Divide, Gila National Forest. Photo by Tom Till.

15.8 miles
Difficulty: Strenuous

You may encounter: motorized vehicles (a remote possibility)

Segment 12 **Total Elevation Gain:** 2,946 feet
From Mexico 205.65 miles
To Colorado 493.35 miles

CONTINENTAL DIVIDE
TRAIL ALLIANCE

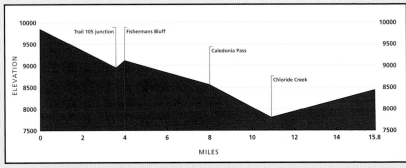

TRAIL OVERVIEW Like the last segment, more or less—more gentle terrain, less water. Actually, the crest along which the Divide and the Continental Divide Trail run remains narrow for about 6 miles north of Diamond Peak. Eventually, though, as the trail begins its long, gradual descent, relief becomes less stark, and ponderosa pines subtly replace mixed conifers, except on north slopes.

The CDT leaves the Aldo Leopold Wilderness in this segment, and indeed the Black Range here is penetrated by a network of Forest Roads and two-tracks. Rangers traveling to the Lookout Mountain fire tower generally do so via vehicle, not with horses or on foot. But don't expect to find this segment any less wild than the previous segments, and don't expect that when you finally arrive at paved NM 59 that you've reached civilization. The Gila National Forest's Beaverhead Work Center is 18 miles away to the west; the nearest settlement to the east is the faded mining town of Winston, 24 miles away.

As with the Black Range generally, this is good wildlife habitat. Elk, deer, and wild turkey, as well as tufted-eared squirrels, are the animals you're most likely to see. Also here but less common are black bear, lions, coyotes, foxes, bobcats, and javelinas.

Hikers willing to hike Forest Roads will find very pleasant hiking here. The roads run primarily through ponderosa and mixed conifer forest, but the main appeal probably is the abundance of wildlife. Good day hikes include climbing to Lookout Mountain from Monument Park and hiking parts of the CDT from Forest Road 226, Forest Road 226A, or Forest Road 500. Only high-clearance vehicles should attempt these roads.

WATER NOTES

 Begin this segment with full water bottles from Diamond Peak Spring or from Diamond Creek, off the CDT. And replenish your bottles from Caledonia Creek or Chloride Creek as you near the segment's end. If you can arrange a water drop, Lookout Mountain would be a good place for it.

MOUNTAIN BIKE NOTES

 Aside from remoteness and lack of water for extended trips, this segment offers excellent mountain biking over the network of Forest Roads.

EQUESTRIAN NOTES

Were it not for paucity of water, this would rank with the state's best horse country. The Forest Rangers responsible for this CDT segment use horses when working on the trail.

SOUTHBOUND HIKERS

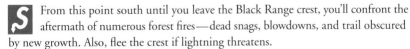 From this point south until you leave the Black Range crest, you'll confront the aftermath of numerous forest fires—dead snags, blowdowns, and trail obscured by new growth. Also, flee the crest if lightning threatens.

MAPS

USGS QUADRANGLES: Reeds Peak, Lookout Mountain, Sawmill Peak
OTHER MAPS: Gila National Forest, Gila National Forest–Aldo Leopold Wilderness

LAND-MANAGEMENT AGENCIES

Gila National Forest/Black Range Ranger District

BEGINNING ACCESS POINT

DIAMOND PEAK: Reached only by hikers and horseback riders over trails. See Ending Access Point in Segment 11, page 133.

ENDING ACCESS POINT

LOOKOUT MOUNTAIN: See Beginning Access Point in Segment 13, page 146.

SUPPLIES, SERVICES, AND ACCOMMODATIONS

None exist anywhere remotely near this segment. The nearest human habitation is the Gila National Forest's Beaverhead Work Station, 19 miles west of the CDT on NM 59.

TRAIL DESCRIPTION

Beginning at Diamond Peak, N33°13'45", W107°50'38", 9,850 feet, your first task should be to fill your water containers (including yourself) as full as possible at Diamond Peak Spring, N33°13'55", W107°50'40"on the CDT just north of Diamond Peak. Small but reliable, sometimes just a trickle, this spring flows year round. But if it should be dry, then drop down the Fishermans Cutoff into Diamond Creek, 3 miles north of the peak. You can return to the CDT via Trail 40, the Diamond Creek Trail, or Trail 42, the Caledonia Trail.

Just north of Diamond Peak Spring, Trail 67 enters from the northwest. Though very obscure above the head of Doubtful Canyon, if followed down the canyon it will take you to Diamond Creek—and water. From near the spring, the Continental Divide, the CDT, and Trail 74 head generally north-northeast. The trail descends on the north side of Diamond Peak to follow a long ridge. From here the CDT continues along the ridge, up and down over the hills along the narrow crest, crossing from saddle to saddle. This continues throughout most of this segment. Because the crest and the Continental Divide coincide with the boundaries of grazing allotments, the CDT often follows along barbed wire fence. The Gila National Forest–Black Range Ranger District and the volunteers with whom they work have improved much of the Black Range CDT, and they plan to work on this stretch, taking the trail around the ridge knobs rather than over them, but there are other priorities now.

The crest here is narrow, and sometimes exposed. Get off it quickly if lightning threatens.

The hiking here is rough! Dead snags are scattered everywhere; they're especially dangerous in high winds. The forest is almost a textbook exhibit of fire ecology. The different ages of the burns are revealed in the species and maturity of the plants that have colonized the charred forest. The vegetational diversity makes for especially rich wildlife habitat. I always associate the Black Range with wild turkeys, and if you haven't seen any by now, here would be a good place to resume looking. You're still in the Aldo Leopold Wilderness here.

From here the CDT continues running generally north, following the Continental Divide, descending gradually and leapfrogging from saddle to saddle. At N33°15'53", W107°49'35", Trail 105, from the North Fork of Palomas Creek, enters from the northeast, while Trail 48, the Fishermans Canyon Trail, enters from the northwest. Should you desperately need water, you could follow Trail 48 steeply downhill through Fishermans Canyon about 1 mile to Diamond Creek. North of this trail junction is another burned area, with numerous charred stumps.

After about 3 miles from the wilderness boundary, the CDT arrives at Fishermans Bluff, a 9,200-foot butte, N33°16'12", W107°49'30", whose cliff-guarded sides the CDT chooses to bypass. On the bluff's south side the trail enters a meadow. (The meadow once was a "helispot," where helicopters landed in a doomed attempt to contain the Divide Fire to the west side of the Divide.) The trail then swings west and north around the bluff, to enter another meadow, where charred stumps mark a cemetery of trees killed by fire. Here the trail is sometimes difficult to follow as it heads north.

After less than 0.5 mile, the trail again descends via a broad switchback, then resumes ridge-hopping, heading north.

At about 2 miles north of the butte, the CDT reaches the Aldo Leopold Wilderness's northern boundary, at N33°17'20", W107°49'02", 8,950 feet, atop a small rise.

The Continental Divide, the CDT, Trail 74, and the wilderness boundary coincide as they head north, descending until after 0.75 mile the wilderness boundary runs west, while the others continue ridge-running north. Just about 0.3 mile north of where the wilderness boundary heads west is a large saddle that has earned renown among Forest Service employees for its raspberry patch in the fall. Alas, the site has no water.

From this saddle, Trail 74 curves around the northeast side of one small hill, then around the southeast side of another to reach another saddle at N33°18'19", W107°49'44", elevation 8,560 feet. New tread and a switchback have been constructed here to take a gentler course down to the saddle; the old trail went more steeply downhill. This saddle is known as Caledonia Pass among Forest Service personnel. Here at the saddle, Trail 74 ends at its junction with Trail 42 entering from the southwest. From here, the CDT follows Trail 42, which on the west connects to trails first in Turkey Run and then along Diamond Creek. Also here Trail 46—very faint—enters from the west, having come up the valley of Blackhawk Gulch. The 1993 Blackhawk Fire left the area filled with charred stumps and blowdowns, but by Caledonia Creek the hiking gets easier.

At Caledonia Pass, the CDT leaves the Continental Divide, which heads northwest by climbing the ridge to yet another knob. From Caledonia Pass north to

NM 59, the CDT tread is too new to be reflected on any National Forest or USGS map; the map in this book was drawn from handwritten notes by the trail builders.

The CDT, now following Trail 42, heads due north, contouring along the ridge's eastern slopes, then briefly turns west to switchback down to the headwaters of Caledonia Creek, a small, intermittent stream not labeled on the USGS quadrangle. Until here, the terrain has been littered with charred stumps and blowdowns from the 1993 Blackhawk Fire, but the CDT now runs through predominantly green vegetation, mixed conifer on north slopes, ponderosa pine elsewhere. Near where the CDT joints the drainage, at about 8,120 feet, the tailings of a long-abandoned mine are visible. Numerous abandoned mines that once produced silver, tin, and kaolinite scatter the area.

Trail 42 and the CDT follow Caledonia Creek north for about 1.75 miles to the creek's junction with Chloride Creek, elevation 7,800 feet. Here, Trail 42 heads abruptly west along Chloride Creek until, after less than 0.5 mile, it meets Forest Road 226 in a flat at N33°20'04", W107°49'53". Forest Road 226 enters down a small drainage from west-northwest.

Caledonia Creek and Chloride Creek are your last likely water sources (neither is perennial in dry times) heading north, and even here the flow—such as it is—often disappears into the sand but resurfaces over rocks; so you definitely should fill up here.

The CDT follows Forest Road 226 as it heads up the drainage, then wiggles onto the Divide.

The reunion is brief, however, because after about 0.3 mile, at N33°20'23", W107°50'35", elevation 8,170 feet, the CDT heads northwest across a flat, then swings northeast, paralleling the 8,200-foot contour and entering Seventy-four Draw less than a mile from Forest Road 226. The CDT then follows the draw north about a mile until it meets Forest Road 226A at 8,430 feet. Forest Road 226A and then Forest Road 226

WILDERNESS ALERT

Portions of this segment are within the Aldo Leopold Wilderness. Please observe these wilderness guidelines:

1. Camp out of sight, at least 200 feet from springs and drainages, on a dry, durable surface.
2. Use a stove instead of building a fire; use existing fire rings if you do build a fire.
3. Keep water sources pure by camping at least 200 feet from them.
4. Bury human wastes 6 inches deep and at least 200 feet from water sources; pack out toilet paper.
5. Dogs must be on a leash.
6. No mountain biking.
7. Pack out all trash; don't attempt to burn it.

head approximately 11.6 miles to NM 59, which Forest Road 226 joins about 1.8 miles west of the Continental Divide. If people were to meet you, this good dirt road would provide access. Walking it to NM 59 would take about 5.5 hours; you'd be better to stay on the trail.

From the junction with the CDT, Forest Road 226A heads southeast, then climbs Lookout Mountain's steep slopes via switchbacks to reach the top after 2.3 miles. Besides the fire tower, a heliport also is at the summit—but not water.

OTHER HIKES AND RIDES: LOOKOUT MOUNTAIN

> **APPROXIMATE ONE-WAY DISTANCE** (Chloride to Monument Park, at mountain's base): 11.2 miles
> **MODE OF TRAVEL:** Biking
> **DIFFICULTY:** Moderate

Forest Road 226 and 226A: From the east, Forest Road 226 follows Chloride Creek west from the former mining camp of Chloride. To reach the roadhead, take NM 52 west from Interstate 25 north of Truth or Consequences to the former mining town of Winston. Go down the main street and turn west on a county road at the end to reach Chloride after about 1 mile; the county road ends at Forest Road 226.

OTHER HIKES AND RIDES: LOOKOUT MOUNTAIN

> **APPROXIMATE ONE-WAY DISTANCE:** 1.5 miles
> **MODE OF TRAVEL:** Hiking
> **DIFFICULTY:** Strenuous

From Forest Road 226, Trail 43 leads to the top of Lookout Mountain and spectacular views.

OTHER HIKES AND RIDES: DIAMOND CREEK

> **APPROXIMATE ONE-WAY DISTANCE:** 2 miles or more
> **MODE OF TRAVEL:** Hiking
> **DIFFICULTY:** Easy to moderate

Diamond Creek, Trail 40: Take Forest Road 226 to Forest Road 500, then drive to the trailhead near the road's end. Trail 42 heads east, reaching Caledonia Pass in 2 miles, or south, to reach Diamond Creek in 1 mile. Diamond Creek is a perennial stream in a beautiful canyon. If you follow it upstream, you join the CDT via Fishermans Canyon or Trail 67 via Doubtful Canyon. Following Diamond Creek downstream leads after 14 miles to Forest Road 150.

HISTORICAL NOTES

Volunteers on the CDT. Perhaps no segment in the entire CDT more epitomizes the cooperative spirit among people involved in the trail than this segment. Recruited under the aggressive leadership of the Gila National Forest–Black Range Ranger District, squads of volunteers penetrate the Black Range each year to improve the CDT. As a result, new tread now or soon will exist all the way from north of Diamond Peak to NM 59. Among the groups who swung pulaskis and pried out boulders were AmeriCorps, National Civilian Community Corps, Trinity University, Montana State University, University of Texas–Austin, University of Texas–Dallas, Southern Methodist University, University of Pittsburgh, Warburg College, Vanderbilt, Armand Hammer United World College, Goddard College, Central Texas Trail Tamers, Hot Springs High School in Truth or Consequences, Alabama A&M University, and New Mexico Volunteers for the Outdoors. The Continental Divide Trail Alliance also has been involved in trail building here.

The CDT may last a thousand years (why not?), but in all its history it can only be born once—and that is happening now.

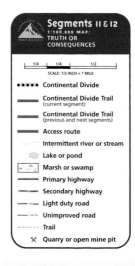

Segments 11 & 12
1:100,000 MAP:
TRUTH OR
CONSEQUENCES

| 1/4 | 1/4 | 1/2 |
SCALE: 1/2 INCH = 1 MILE

●●●●● Continental Divide

▬▬▬ Continental Divide Trail (current segment)

▬▬▬ Continental Divide Trail (previous and next segments)

▬▬▬ Access route

Intermittent river or stream

Lake or pond

Marsh or swamp

Primary highway

Secondary highway

Light duty road

Unimproved road

Trail

✕ Quarry or open mine pit

Segment 13
Lookout Mountain to NM 59

Abandoned log cabin in a ponderosa pine forest northwest of Lookout Mountain, Gila National Forest. Photo by William Stone.

12.25 miles
Difficulty: Moderate
You may encounter: motorized vehicles

Segment 13   **Total Elevation Gain:** 1,222 feet
From Mexico 221.45 miles
To Colorado 477.55 miles

CONTINENTAL DIVIDE
TRAIL ALLIANCE

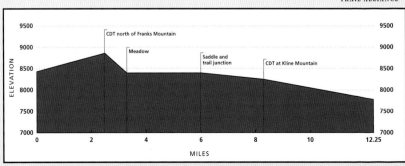

TRAIL OVERVIEW Finally, after long miles of struggling with nightmarish blow-downs and snags, of marching up and over countless knobs, you get a break. Sure, the Continental Divide Trail for the most part still follows a ridge, and there's still some climbing, but the burned areas are behind you, the gradients are gentle—and mostly downhill. If you need to make up some time, this is the place to do it.

This is classic ponderosa forest: tall straight trunks of deep-orange bark. Sniff the bark, and you're likely to smell a faint vanilla scent. Sometimes, especially after rainstorms, you can detect the scent while walking through the forest. Beneath the rather open canopy, forest grass flourishes.

This is outstanding wildlife habitat, especially for elk. Wild turkeys are also found here, though they're more elusive. Walk softly; the Black Range may have other surprises for you.

 From Forest Road 226A north to NM 59, the CDT stays near the Continental Divide, though often to one side to avoid fences. Except around Franks Mountain, tread generally is lacking, though the route is marked with signs and blazes. Because blazes on piñon-juniper often are obscure, you should not leave one blaze without having sighted the next.

 Appealing campsites are plentiful, but regrettably they're dry. No reliable year-round water source exists along this stretch; there are a few stock tanks, and should you encounter any with water you should take advantage of them.

Hikers willing to hike Forest Roads will find very pleasant hiking here. The roads run primarily through ponderosa and mixed conifer forest, but the main appeal probably is the abundance of wildlife.

WATER NOTES

 Not as dry as Segment 14 and much shorter, this segment nonetheless poses a water challenge. There's no water at Lookout Mountain, so Caledonia and Chloride Creeks, neither of which is reliable in dry weather, are your nearest sources. Lookout Mountain would be a good place for a water drop. Otherwise, plan to carry plenty of water and hope to get lucky with intermittent sources. Also, no water exists at the end of this segment, another logical place for a water drop.

MOUNTAIN BIKE NOTES

 Aside from remoteness and lack of water for extended trips, this segment offers excellent mountain biking over the network of Forest Roads.

EQUESTRIAN NOTES

Were it not for paucity of water, this would rank with the state's best horse country. The Forest Rangers responsible for this CDT segment use horses when working on the trail.

SOUTHBOUND HIKERS

S You are about to embark upon the New Mexico CDT's most challenging segment. The four segments ahead total more than 50 miles, with no good prospects for resupply. Indeed, even after 50 miles you're still 27 miles from Mimbres, the nearest settlement—and a meager one at that! So before setting out, you should make sure you have adequate food and other supplies.

You'll need all the energy you can muster. The terrain ahead is among the state's most difficult. The CDT heads along the rugged crest of the Black Range, and through the Aldo Leopold Wilderness, the state's wildest. The forest here has been burned repeatedly; snags and blowdowns are everywhere, obscuring the trail and making maneuvering difficult. You are unlikely to encounter other hikers with whom you can commiserate.

Take extra care, therefore, in preparing for the segments ahead, and if ever there was a stretch where it's important to inform the Forest Service of your plans, this is it.

MAPS
USGS QUADRANGLES: Lookout Mountain, Sawmill Peak
OTHER MAPS: Gila National Forest–Aldo Leopold Wilderness

LAND-MANAGEMENT AGENCIES
Gila National Forest/Black Range Ranger District

BEGINNING ACCESS POINT

LOOKOUT MOUNTAIN: 1.8 miles west of the Continental Divide on NM 59, Forest Road 226 heads south through Burnt Cabin Flat and follows a winding course through pleasant grasslands and ponderosa pine forest until after 5.2 miles Forest Road 226A branches southeast. Follow Forest Road 226A as it continues a gradual climb to reach the CDT after 6.55 miles from Forest Road 226. The road continues to zigzag up the steep slopes of Lookout Mountain to reach the summit after 2.3 miles.

ENDING ACCESS POINT

NM 59: The only practical access to the CDT and this segment's end is from the east, via NM 59. West of the CDT the pavement ends at Beaverhead. From here, dirt Forest Road 150 heads south toward the Continental Divide at NM 35, but the road can be rough, especially in bad weather. The same is true for Forest Road 150 north of Beaverhead; this dirt road, generally in good condition, eventually (!) can be taken either to NM 12 or to US 60, but these routes are long. NM 59 becomes Forest Road 59 at Beaverhead; it continues west until finally arriving at Alma on US 180 after an even longer and more mountainous course.

SUPPLIES, SERVICES, AND ACCOMMODATIONS
Sorry, but no town could even remotely be considered near this segment; Truth or Consequences is 60 miles to the east of the Continental Divide. The Beaverhead Work Center of the Gila National Forest is 19 miles away, and although its staff are very welcoming to CDT hikers, and willing to assist with food and water drops, they are not equipped for resupply.

Autumn along the Continental Divide, Lookout Mountain, Gila National Forest. Photo by Tom Till.

TRAIL DESCRIPTION From Forest Road 226A, the CDT heads east about 1 mile to join the Continental Divide, but only briefly, declining to accompany the Continental Divide over 8,880-foot Franks Mountain. Instead, the CDT heads along the mountain's west slopes over recently constructed tread (AmeriCorps volunteers in fall 1998), then up a drainage to rejoin the Continental Divide about 2.25 miles from Forest Road 226A.

Back on the Divide, the CDT follows it northwest over modest ridges until after 3.3 miles the CDT enters a broad, level meadow, a great campsite—if it had water. About 1.2 miles north of the meadow, in yet another saddle on the ridgeline, the CDT runs into a junction with an unnamed trail joining Bear Creek on the east; a branch of Stiver Canyon is on the west. Near this junction, the Sawmill Peak quadrangle shows an unnamed spring at N33°23'54", W107°50'39", near the eastern trail, about 0.25 mile down from the saddle. This spring's reliability is unknown.

From this saddle-trail junction, at approximately 8,100 feet, the CDT stays with the Continental Divide, though often side-hilling around ridgetops, as it meanders generally north, with little elevation change until after 2.3 miles; at the south side of 8,475-foot Kline Mountain, the trail swings west to contour the mountain's southern slopes, at about 8,250 feet.

From here, the Continental Divide and the CDT run northwest down the mountain's slopes, then swing north, descending gradually until after about 2.75 miles from Kline Mountain the Divide and the CDT reach NM 59 at N33°26'53", W107°52'06", around 7,780 feet elevation. From here, the Gila National Forest's Beaverhead Work Center is 19 miles west.

OTHER HIKES AND RIDES: LOOKOUT MOUNTAIN

APPROXIMATE ONE-WAY DISTANCE: 13.6 miles
MODE OF TRAVEL: Biking
DIFFICULTY: Moderate

Forest Road 226 and 226A: About 1.75 miles west of the CDT on NM 59, Forest Road 226 heads south at the west end of scenic Burnt Cabin Flat. It follows gentle gradients before descending briefly into Scales Canyon. It soon climbs back up until after 5.8 miles from NM 59, Forest Road 226A branches southeast. This leads after 6.4 miles to the CDT, on the west side of Lookout Mountain. From there, Forest Road 226A climbs rather steeply to the top, reaching it after 2.3 miles.

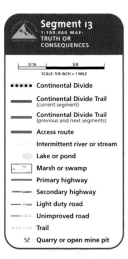

Segment 13
1:100,000 MAP:
TRUTH OR
CONSEQUENCES

5/16   5/8
SCALE: 5/8 INCH = 1 MILE

••••• Continental Divide

——— Continental Divide Trail
(current segment)

——— Continental Divide Trail
(previous and next segments)

——— Access route

——— Intermittent river or stream

◯ Lake or pond

Marsh or swamp

——— Primary highway

——— Secondary highway

— — Light duty road

— — Unimproved road

------ Trail

⚒ Quarry or open mine pit

Segment 14
NM 59 to NM 163: Wahoo Peak

Winter ponderosa pines west of the Continental Divide, Black Range, Gila National Forest. Photo by William Stone.

25.8 miles
Difficulty: Moderate

You may encounter: livestock and vehicles

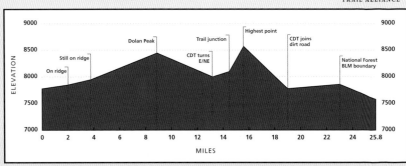

Segment 14 **Total Elevation Gain:** 2,127 feet
From Mexico 233.75 miles
To Colorado 465.3 miles

CONTINENTAL DIVIDE
TRAIL ALLIANCE

Elevation profile labels:
- On ridge
- Still on ridge
- Dolan Peak
- Trail junction
- CDT turns E/NE
- Highest point
- CDT joins dirt road
- National Forest BLM boundary

ELEVATION (9000, 8500, 8000, 7500, 7000)

MILES (0, 2, 4, 6, 8, 10, 12, 14, 16, 18, 20, 22, 24, 25.8)

TRAIL OVERVIEW "Pretty mellow country" is how a Gila National Forest Ranger describes the stretch from NM 59 to NM 163. Generally easy gradients, mostly cross-country but along a rolling ridge, in an open ponderosa forest with grass underneath. A good place to make time, should you need to. If you get tired of seemingly endless ups and downs as the Continental Divide Trail follows a ridgeline, blame it on the Continental Divide, because throughout its length here, the CDT never is more than 0.5 mile from the Divide. This is excellent habitat for wild animals, which are hunted in season but otherwise left to themselves in this remote wilderness.

But for all its potential mellowness, this segment *is* a challenge—long up-and-down miles over rocky ground with *no* reliable water. None. You'll encounter a few stock tanks, but they're least reliable during dry seasons—when you need them most! Moreover, most such tanks are earthen dams, which allow cattle to wade and urinate and defecate in the water. Such water—massively treated—is better than none in an emergency, but that doesn't make it less disgusting.

 What's worse, packing enough water and force-marching through this segment in less than two days only brings you to the next segment, also dry; no water awaits you at NM 163. The nearest water along the CDT here is at North Garcia Tank, approximately 6 miles away, but it's on private land. If you were to arrange for a water or food cache, NM 163 would be the place for it.

Also, while volunteer work parties organized by the Continental Divide Trail Association and the Gila National Forest have marked the route signs and cairns, no tread exists, except around Dolan Peak and the descent into the south side of North Wahoo Canyon. Consult your compass, Global Positioning System unit, and map often.

Approach this segment prepared and positively. Then, perhaps, it will reveal itself as "pretty mellow country."

Lack of trails, paucity of water, and pleasant but undistinguished scenery make this an unlikely focus for day hikes.

WATER NOTES

 There is no water at the beginning of this segment, just a questionable stock tank at the end, and nothing much in between. Plan on a dry camp, with water drops at the beginning and end. Also, inquire locally as to water status.

MOUNTAIN BIKE NOTES

 Remoteness, private land, and the CDT going cross country make this unsuitable for most mountain biking.

EQUESTRIAN NOTES

Only lack of water and corrals prevents this from being excellent horse country.

SOUTHBOUND HIKERS

The caveats above for northbound hikers apply as well to southbound hikers, including the one that no water exists at the segment's end.

MAPS

USGS QUADRANGLES: Sawmill Peak, Wahoo Peak, Paddys Hole
OTHER MAPS: Gila National Forest

LAND-MANAGEMENT AGENCIES

Gila National Forest/Black Range Ranger District

BEGINNING ACCESS POINT

NM 59: The only practical access to this segment's beginning is from the east, via NM 59. West of the CDT, the pavement ends at the Forest Service's Beaverhead Work Station.

ENDING ACCESS POINT

NM 163: To reach this segment's end, take US 60 west from Magdalena for 19 miles to where all-weather dirt NM 52 branches south. Drive on this 22 miles to where all-weather dirt NM 163 (labeled NM 78 on the Paddys Hole quadrangle) branches southwest. After about 22.5 miles, you reach a junction with a private road branching left (southeast), while NM 163 continues generally southwest. Pointing down this private road are Adobe Ranch signs; the National Forest is not accessible via this route. Near this junction look for cairns indicating the CDT.

SUPPLIES, SERVICES, AND ACCOMMODATIONS

No support facilities exist anywhere near either the beginning or end of this segment; not even tiny villages are near here. But because the CDT often follows Forest Roads, used by local people, the sense of isolation isn't quite as great as you might expect.

TRAIL DESCRIPTION

Classic ponderosa pine forest begins the CDT here, at N33°52'06", W107°51'55", around 7,780 feet elevation. From here the Continental Divide and the CDT head northeast along a ridgeline. The gradients are gentle, and the forest pleasant. From the ridge you might glimpse stock tanks in the valleys below, but unless you see water and need it badly, climbing down for it is not worth the effort.

Once on the ridge, the north-trending Continental Divide is relatively level for at least 3.5 miles, when it jogs briefly east and then north to climb about 200 feet as the ridge gets higher. Then the ridge again levels off briefly before leapfrogging ridgetops again. It continues this for 3 miles, trending generally northeast, with little net elevation gain, until southwest of 8,445-foot Dolan Peak. This important summit is not identified on the Wahoo Peak quadrangle, except by elevation, nor on the Gila National Forest map; its coordinates are N33°31'42", W107°48'00". Reaching Dolan Peak's summit requires a climb of about 245 feet in slightly more than a mile. The CDT swings east-southeast to join a ridge, which it then follows northward to the top. Tread had been constructed, following contours around Dolan Peak's west side.

From Dolan Peak, the CDT descends somewhat to a saddle, then up and over a hill before the gradients become gentler. The country east of the ridge is a chaos of steep hills and ridges, a maze of deep canyons. The country west of the Continental Divide also is complex but not as steep. At about 4.5 miles north of Dolan Peak, at the head of Silver Creek Canyon, at about 8,000 feet, at N33°34'37", W107°48'45", the Continental Divide and CDT swing east-northeast to follow a ridge to an unnamed 8,365-foot summit. From here, the CDT and the Divide descend a northern ridge for less than 0.5 mile before swinging east again, through a low saddle. Just downhill southeast of this saddle, Trail 59 from the northwest and Trail 60 from the northeast meet at a stock tank with the unwelcoming name of Dry Time Tank. From the saddle, the Divide and the CDT climb more steeply to an unnamed 8,535-foot summit. From here, the Divide and the CDT head north 0.5 mile along a ridge to an unnamed 8,570-foot summit, at N33°35'49", W107°47'38", this segment's highest point.

The CDT descends from this summit as steeply as it went up, then becomes more gradual as it meanders northwest to reach the National Forest–Bureau of Land Management boundary, N33°38'55", W107°48'42", marked by signs and a fenceline, after 2.75 miles from the summit. Here, as the CDT emerges from the Gila National Forest, it also emerges from the forest to enter the open grasslands that will characterize most of the next segment.

From the boundary fence the CDT, marked by cairns and posts, heads downhill over rolling grassland toward a private graded dirt road and nearby the junction with NM 163, where the CDT is marked by a stake.

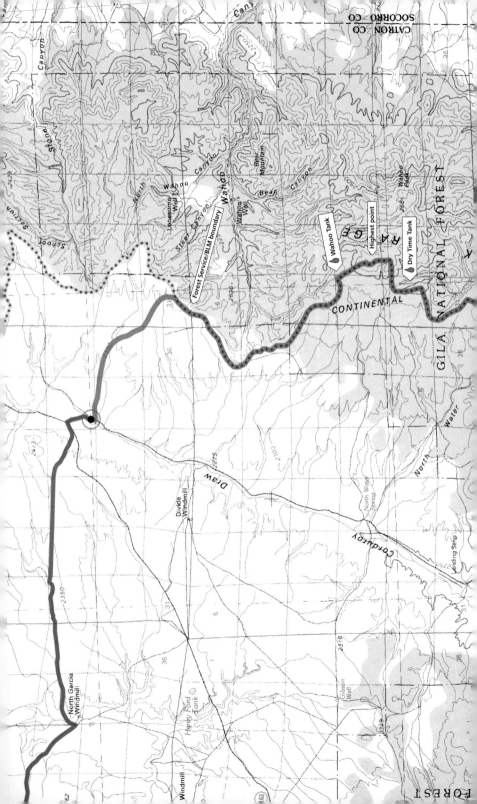

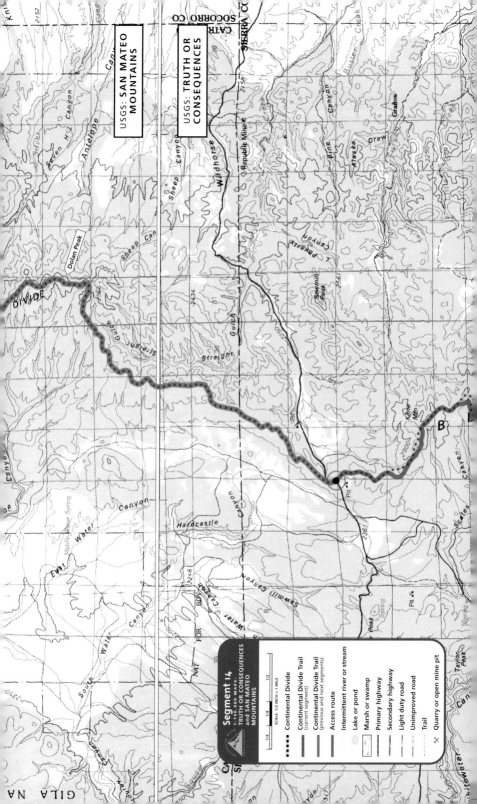

Segment 15
NM 163 to Coyote Peak Stock Tank: Pelona Mountain

Tularosa Mountains from above West Canyon, western flank of Pelona Mountain, Continental Divide Wilderness Study Area. Photo by William Stone.

**32.5 miles
Difficulty: Strenuous**
You may encounter:
hikers and equestrians

Segment 15 **Total Elevation Gain:** 3,399 feet
From Mexico 259.5 miles
To Colorado 439.5 miles

CONTINENTAL DIVIDE
TRAIL ALLIANCE

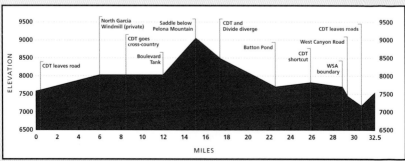

TRAIL OVERVIEW By almost any standards, Pelona Mountain is a modest summit, lacking a distinctive profile, cliffs, dramatic rock formations, or other striking features, barely distinguishable from nearby mountains of comparable height, rising a mere 1,600 feet above the surrounding high plain. Even its name defies respect: *pelona* is Spanish and means "bald," yet the slopes and even the top of Pelona Mountain are forested, indeed the only forest for miles around; what are bald are the surrounding plains!

But by the time you reach Pelona's summit, you'll experience a sense of achievement comparable to summiting a major Fourteener in Colorado; you'll also be rewarded with a view that, though very different, is equally awe-inspiring.

This Continental Divide Trail segment is difficult, challenging, and beautiful. The best advice I can give to someone attempting it was inspired by a lesson Joseph Gendron said he learned during his trek over the also-daunting Little Hatchet segment: "Don't fight it."

Actually, only a single major obstacle makes this segment such a challenge: lack of water. Pelona Mountain and the surrounding plains are part of the vast Datil-Mogollon Volcanic Plateau physiographic region. The widespread and cataclysmic volcanism that occurred here 40 to 25 million years ago produced a varied and interesting landscape, but it also produced one whose soils and rocks don't retain water on the surface. Not that there's much to retain to begin with; average precipitation here is only 15 inches, and much of it is captured by the nearby western mountains before it can fall in the great basins here. Aridity more than anything else accounts for the vast grasslands, devoid of trees.

Ranchers have attempted to overcome this obstacle by creating impoundments to capture runoff, but these are infrequent and, almost by definition, dry during dry weather. More reliable are windmills tapping subsurface water, but in the entire 32.5 miles of this segment, only one windmill exists—on private land, 9 miles into the route from the southeast. When I hiked this route with Joseph Gendron and Jim Scanlon, we did find water in stock tanks at the route's western end, but this also coincided with an unseasonable spate of monsoon rains. Not wishing to rely upon these fickle sources, we carried enough water for the entire two-day trip: approximately 2.5 gallons per person, 20 pounds. We finished the trip with water to spare, but only because the weather blessed us the second day with relatively cool temperatures and overcast skies. Completely overcast skies in this part of New Mexico are about as common as typhoons!

The walking is tough here. From a distance the grasslands appear golf-course smooth, but beneath the grass are volcanic cobbles. The CDT route coincides in a few places with two-track dirt roads. I viewed these roads with mixed emotions; although I appreciated their relatively level surfaces after stumbling over lava, I nonetheless resented their intrusion into the area's seemingly pristine vastness. I found comfort in remembering that the land surrounding Pelona Mountain is within the Bureau of Land Management Continental Divide Wilderness Study Area, mandated to be managed to preserve the area's substantial wilderness characteristics. At 68,761 acres, the Continental Divide WSA is among New Mexico's largest WSAs; if the New Mexico Wilderness Alliance's recommendation of 105,704 acres is adopted, the wilderness here will be half as large as the 202,016-acre Aldo Leopold Wilderness just to the southeast, one of New Mexico's three wilderness giants. Within the WSA, the area immediately around Pelona Mountain has been designated a Special Management Area.

Route-finding is not too difficult in this CDT segment; the route is marked with cairns and posts, and, except in the far western section, the land is conspicuously open; you can see your destination and route from miles away. At the end of the first day of our reconnaissance, from the saddle just beneath Pelona Mountain, Jim Scanlon looked east and said, "This is the first time I've hiked 12 hours and been able to look back and see the trailhead where I started." But sure enough, there it was, far, far in the distance.

Difficult and challenging as this segment is, it is also beautiful and special. People who drive on US 60 always are awed by the distances of the Plains of San Agustin, but those motorists see only a fraction of the vast, all-but-uninhabited spaces in this part of New Mexico. From high atop Pelona Mountain, with a view encompassing 360 degrees and extending for miles and miles, you could look out at night and perhaps not see not a single light: Here is uninhabited vastness such as Paleo-Indians experienced when they hunted the Pleistocene megafauna (Bat Cave nearby is among New Mexico's oldest and most significant archaeological sites); here is uninhabited vastness such as the mountain men beheld when they ventured into the Gila Country in the early 1800s. Sure, cattle now graze here, and two-tracks lead to stock tanks and elk-hunting camps, but they're ephemeral, easily erased from one's consciousness by time and distance. As I hiked down a ridge from Pelona Mountain in early morning and close gray clouds swirled above and below me, I looked down into the nearby valley and realized that this remarkable, perdurable land, this weather, had made transparent all the thousands of years separating me from those Native Americans of so long ago.

This segment likely will never attract many day-hikers. It's remote, with poor access, lacking water, with no defined tread (though some two-tracks are here), over treacherous volcanic cobbles—and its main feature, Pelona Mountain, is in the middle of it all. Having said that, I also must say this region has a powerful allure for people with a rarified taste for solitude, space, and silence. And defined trails, after all, would detract from this wilderness experience. West Canyon at the segment's western end makes a pleasant southwestern New Mexico canyon walk along Forest Roads.

WATER NOTES

 This segment has muddy, unreliable stock tanks at both ends and problematic water in between. Fortunately, if water karma favors you and all the tanks have potable water, the spacing allows a well-hydrated trip. But be sure to always have enough water with you in case the next source is dry. This is a good place to hedge your bets.

MOUNTAIN BIKE NOTES

 While the long, little-traveled dirt roads here would seem to invite mountain biking, remoteness, lack of support facilities, and possible conflicts with private landowners mean this area is less suited for mountain biking than more accessible areas. Also, mountain bikes will be excluded, when this area is designated wilderness.

EQUESTRIAN NOTES

The grass-filled basins here would seem well-suited for equestrian travel; the country just looks like a scene from a Western movie epic. But paucity of water sources and abundance of volcanic rocks underfoot, as well as possible conflicts with private landowners, make it advisable to consult local ranchers or the BLM before planning a trip here.

SOUTHBOUND HIKERS

 Be sure to top off your water bottles at Coyote Tank. The next reliable water source is Green Tank, at least 6.5 miles away, while Batton Pond is 10 miles distant.

MAPS

USGS QUADRANGLES: Paddys Hole, Mojonera Canyon, Pelona Mountain, Rail Canyon, Salvation Peak
OTHER MAPS: BLM 1:100K Tularosa Mountains, San Mateo Mountains

LAND-MANAGEMENT AGENCIES

BLM/Socorro Field Office

BEGINNING ACCESS POINT

  NM 163: See Ending Access Point in Segment 14, page 152.

ENDING ACCESS POINT

  COYOTE PEAK STOCK TANK: This segment's western end is reached by taking NM 12 southwest from Datil. About 11 miles west of New Horse Springs (Old Horse Springs is 3 miles farther east—and neither place has any supplies or services), Forest Road 28 heads south. Take this as it winds along the southwestern edge of the Plains of San Agustin. You're driving along the shore of a long-vanished Pleistocene lake, so the driving is pretty flat. After about 27 miles, the road begins to wind among some hills. After 3.5 miles from the Forest Road leading east into West Canyon, at about 30 miles from NM 12, the CDT crosses the road; about a mile farther southeast the Continental Divide crosses the road. The CDT is marked by a stake, but not conspicuously, so look for the Coyote Peak stock tank, just off the road to the west. Access to the stock tank allows for parking. The Global Positioning System coordinates here are N33°39'04", W107°16'25".

SUPPLIES, SERVICES, AND ACCOMMODATIONS

There are no supplies, services, or accommodations anywhere near this segment. The nearest supplies of any kind are in the general stores in Magdalena or Datil.

WILDERNESS ALERT

Much of the CDT here is within the BLM Continental Divide Wilderness Study Area and deserves the same respect as wildernesses already designated. Please observe these wilderness guidelines:

1. Camp out of sight, at least 200 feet from springs and drainages, on a dry, durable surface.

2. Use a stove instead of building a fire; use existing fire rings if you do build a fire.

3. Keep water sources pure by camping at least 200 feet from them.

4. Bury human wastes 6 inches deep and at least 200 feet from water sources; pack out toilet paper.

5. Dogs must be on a leash.

6. No mountain biking.

7. Pack out all trash; don't attempt to burn it.

TRAIL DESCRIPTION This segment begins at NM 163, at the junction with the private road leading to Adobe Ranch. Before you begin this segment, carefully assess your water needs. Take on as much water as you can. This route can be physically demanding, and no natural water source exists along it. Windmills can be turned off, and stock tanks go dry in dry seasons. When Joseph Gendron, Jim Scanlon, and I reconnoitered this route, we each carried at least 2 gallons of fluid (including electrolyte replacement). As we grunted and hoisted our too-heavy packs setting out, we said, "Think of how great it will feel as the packs get way lighter by the trip's end!" But never did the packs lose an ounce; at least that's what our shoulders told us. So much for gravity!

Walk north up the graded road about 0.5 mile to its junction with a larger graded dirt road, NM 163, N33°41'09", W107°50'55", elevation 7,612 feet. Here you'll see signs for the Adobe Ranch, a large private landowner in this area. At the junction, the CDT, marked by stakes and cairns, enters a shallow dry wash, filled with low scrub, that initially runs west but after 0.4 mile swings slightly west-northwest. After another 0.25 mile, it climbs out of the wash on its west side to a fence corner. From here, you'll follow the fence west, staying on its south side. A worn cattle path adjacent to the fence doesn't really make the walking easier over the numerous volcanic cobbles.

About half a mile along the fence, look south; about 0.25 mile away is a strange can-shaped structure with a flared top. This is a catchment tank to gather rainwater and make it available for pronghorn (a fence keeps cattle out). A small amount of water is found in the feeder tank, but you'll probably prefer to push on to the stock tank ahead.

And speaking of pronghorn, this segment is especially rich habitat for them; your chances of seeing them here are excellent. Pronghorn aren't uncommon in New Mexico, but they seem especially beautiful in this setting of rich, vast grassland. Pronghorn aren't the only animals who live on the grasslands here; elk and deer venture down from the forested slopes of Pelona Mountain. As you walk, the stones underfoot will force you to keep your eyes on the ground, so you're likely to see horned toads. Notice how closely their color matches that of the surrounding soil, a good example of protective adaptation. Snakes live here, too. Joseph, Jim, and I encountered a baby rattlesnake. After intense discussion, we concluded it was a blacktail. Joseph said blacktails are conspicuously unaggressive; this one certainly was—but then it was just a baby.

The CDT continues following along the fence as it runs west, descending into a broad valley and joining a dirt road that also runs west before turning south to reach North Garcia Windmill. The CDT continues west and does not include the windmill, operated privately by the Adobe Ranch, whose permission should be obtained before getting water. Should you choose, you also could leave the fence to ascend the broad ridge just to the south and follow it west to reach the windmill. The ridge offers great views, but whether the walking there is easier is debatable.

North Garcia Windmill, N30°40'58", W107°56'57", is a larger-than-usual windmill that pumps water into a large metal tank. Several dirt roads and numerous cow paths converge here—and for good reason: This is the only reliable water for miles, but it is on private land.

The windmill and water tank are the first real landmarks you've encountered in the approximately 11 miles from the National Forest (or 7 miles from the graded road), not to mention the first water. Should you camp here, you'd be wise to do so some distance from the windmill, as the water naturally attracts cattle and their attendant deposits. And it is private land.

From North Garcia Windmill, a dirt road runs northwest, ascending gradually and entering the 68,761-acre Continental Divide Wilderness Study Area. The walking is easy, the views expansive. You can make out Pelona Mountain in the distance. The road continues northwest about 1.4 miles before heading west in a shallow valley. You'll find CDT posts here, but after 1.2 miles, at a manmade impoundment, you'll need to leave the road and begin heading cross-country when the road again begins swinging northwest, away from Pelona Mountain. After walking cross-country 1.5 miles southwest, you'll encounter yet another road, which roughly coincides with the Continental Divide. In July 1999, the BLM had completed a prescribed burn north of this road. This you can follow 3.5 miles to a stock impoundment called Boulevard Tank. The walking here is easy and pleasant, with expansive views in all directions. Ahead, Pelona Mountain gets closer and closer.

At or just before Boulevard Tank, you'll hike about 0.5 mile into the next drainage to the south, which you'll follow all the way to the saddle just south of Pelona Mountain. You'll be off the Continental Divide, but not by much.

For the first time since you left the National Forest, you'll be in what could be described as forest. Diffuse forest, to be sure, but piñons, junipers, and, looming above, ponderosa pines. The Pelona Mountain quadrangle doesn't show a road leading into the canyon, but there is a two-track that becomes progressively more narrow and more scenic as you ascend it. The hiking is gradual until the final couple of hundred yards at the canyon's head, where a series of switchbacks leads to the saddle, N33°40'18", W108°06'11". Pleasant campsites exist in the canyon east of the saddle, sheltered by trees and shrubs. Regrettably, there's no water.

Once at the Pelona Mountain saddle, you'll pass through a gate—be sure to close it—then follow posts and cairns west on the CDT, now a trail rather than a two-track. But before you do that, try to summon the energy to make the steep but short climb to Pelona's top. There's not really a single trail, and you'll know you're at the top only when you can't go up anymore, but you'll behold a landscape vast and seemingly pristine, entire mountain ranges empty of humans, canyons with no names, plains inhabited only by elk, deer, and pronghorn. Were you to resurrect the mountain man James Ohio Pattie and bring him here, he likely would not know that nearly 200 years had passed since he was here in 1825.

 Use your compass to keep on a westward bearing as you descend from Pelona Mountain. (I didn't do this and would have followed a southwesterly ridge had not Joseph Gendron corrected me.) We camped on the CDT at a saddle (dry) between two canyons, about 0.75 mile west of the Pelona Saddle, just east of the elevation marked 8,945 on the Pelona Mountain quadrangle. The CDT, marked by cairns, runs past this height, then follows the Continental Divide along a ridge, descending gradually westward. There's no tread, but you're back in open grassland, and the route is still marked with posts, visible atop rounded summits in the distance. When I hiked here, the remnants of the previous night's rain swirled about the area and threatened more precipitation. No place to be in a thunderstorm, but the weather imparted a sense of mystery to this empty, barren land, and I was reminded of walking on Exmoor in southwestern England. Ahead, to the west, you can see mountains, valleys, and trees, and indeed you'll soon be hiking in forest again.

In Section 25, at a prominence marked 8,485 feet on the Rail Canyon quadrangle, 8,484 feet on the BLM Tularosa Mountains map, at N33°40'41", W108°08'27", the CDT and the Continental Divide diverge. The Continental Divide runs west-southwest, on the south side of a drainage, while the CDT heads west-northwest on the drainage's north side.

You'll follow the ridge about 1.3 miles toward another prominence marked 8,310 feet on the USGS 7.5-minute Rail Canyon Quadrangle, unmarked on the BLM map, N33°41'01", W108°09'45". Upon reaching this prominence, you'll begin descending west into the unnamed east-west canyon. The canyon progressively narrows and steepens as you descend about 0.75 mile to north-south Rail Canyon; on the canyon's south slopes is a rough trail, marked with CDT posts.

 At this junction, you'll find Batton Pond, N33°41'15", W108°11'07", elevation 7,700 feet. This manmade impoundment is larger than most and is a real pond and not just a muddy depression, as so many manmade stock impoundments are. The BLM reports that this tank usually contains water. The next water is at Green Tank, N33°42'12", W108°12'48", also reported to usually contain water.

 SOUTHBOUND HIKERS: You should top off your water supplies at Batton Pond, as the next reliable water is many miles away.

From Batton Pond, don't attempt to follow the Rail Canyon drainage beneath Batton Pond, but rather climb the slope just west of the pond less than 75 yards to find a dirt road. You'll follow this as it winds and climbs through pine, juniper, and oak forest. After 2 miles, you'll arrive at a north-south ridge separating Rail Canyon from another tributary of Cottonwood Canyon; the Rail Canyon quadrangle marks the elevation here at 7820 feet, in Section 17, N33°41'53", W108°12'27". The official CDT route continues on the road as it loops around a couple of summits to the north, but others have noticed that if you're willing to endure a steep, rocky descent, you'll save about a mile if at this point you head due west downhill, following a route vehicles have taken. If you were hiking the CDT north to south, following the road wouldn't necessarily save you a climb, as you still ascend to the ridge, though the climb likely is less steep.

Upon reaching the bottom, you head to the canyon's west side to follow the jeep road south. You climb to a ridge (kind of a bummer to regain the elevation you just shed) about 0.5 mile to a saddle and a fence. A sign here notes the boundary of the Continental Divide WSA. From the saddle, the jeep road descends steeply about 0.5 mile to join West Canyon at N33°41'36", W108°13'20".

If you've found the walking difficult since Pelona Mountain (or even before), finally you get a break. The road descending West Canyon is smooth and gentle, and the terrain along the broad canyon bottom is scenic and interesting. Follow the road about 1.4 miles as it swings west. Just after the canyon's mouth, at N33°41'40", W108°14'35", a CDT stake marks the CDT leaving the road to head southwest. Here the CDT, still marked by cairns and posts, heads south, climbing into the hills; here it climbs and descends repeatedly for about 4.5 miles before joining Forest Road 28 at N33°39'04", W108°16'25", 1 mile northwest along the road from the Continental Divide at N33°38'35", W108°15'46", elevation 7,540 feet.

Note: Because the mountains are administered by the BLM and the foothills are state land, the CDT heads into the hills, over some rough country, rather than following the gentle slopes on the mountains' western foothills. This is a valid reason for the land manager, but I can't imagine a CDT hiker, especially a northbound one, going over a difficult stretch just to observe an administrative nicety. I know I didn't. Still, the route presented here is the "official" route. The route on the map is approximate.

The next segment begins just across the road at Coyote Tank. It stays briefly on BLM land before entering the Gila National Forest.

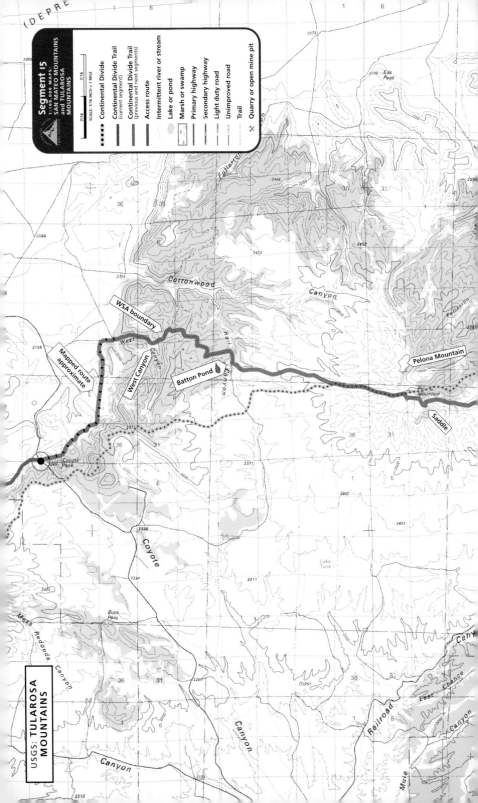

WSA boundary

Mapped route
approximate

West Canyon

Batton Pond

Cottonwood

Canyon

Eds
Peak

Fullerton

Pelona Mountain

Pelona
Mountain

Saddle

Coyote
Peak

Coyote

Buck
Pass

Mesa
Redonda
Canyon

Lake
Tank

Railroad

Last Chance

Canyon

Mule

USGS: TULAROSA
MOUNTAINS

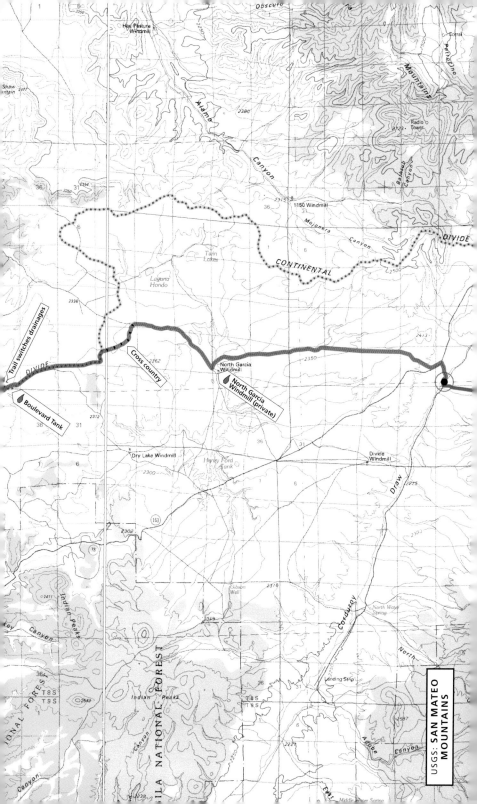

USGS: SAN MATEO MOUNTAINS

Segment 16
Coyote Peak Stock Tank to NM 12: Tularosa Mtns.

*Derelict ranch house at Horse Springs on
the edge of the Plains of San Agustin.
Photo by William Stone.*

52.25 miles
Difficulty: Strenuous

You may encounter: motorized vehicles

Segment 16   **Total Elevation Gain:** 7,802 feet
From Mexico 292 miles
To Colorado 407 miles

CONTINENTAL DIVIDE
TRAIL ALLIANCE

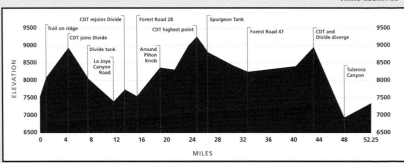

TRAIL OVERVIEW The Tularosa Mountains are among several modest ranges in this part of New Mexico, all having in common rolling topography along with volcanic cliffs, little natural surface water (it's the volcanic soil), abundant wildlife, extensive Forest Roads, remoteness, and except for hunters, very few recreational visitors.

The terrain is pleasant: open ponderosa pine forests on rolling hills and mountains, waves of grass. Good country in which to see animals, especially elk (deer seem to be declining here), with the possibility of wild turkeys, black bears, coyotes, squirrels, foxes, and bobcats.

If you meet any animals in this segment, ask them where they go for water. Water is this segment's unavoidable problem. Water is available here, but the source often is an earthen dam (labeled a "tank" on most maps) whose water is muddied (or worse) by cows. Furthermore, such tanks, dependent upon runoff, are least reliable when they're needed most—in dry spells. Other and more desirable sources also exist along the route, but the availability of water dictates hiking plans here. The really bad news is that when you arrive at the segment's end on NM 12 to begin the next segment, you find that it, too, is dry.

The Continental Divide Trail is blazed, signed, or marked with cairns throughout this segment. Much of the route is cross-country, though in some areas new tread has been constructed, primarily around steep mountains. Elsewhere, the CDT follows existing trails (many made by cattle), two-tracks, or other roads.

For much of this segment, the CDT stays true to the physical Continental Divide. Following the Continental Divide over the ridges of the Tularosa Mountains yields a satisfaction not always accessible on the CDT.

Remoteness, rough terrain, and lack of trails mean that this segment will have little appeal for day-hikers, though those who undertake exploring here will feel rewarded.

WATER NOTES

This segment is similar to Segment 15—but much longer. And it has nothing but stock ponds at both ends and a sprinkling of stock watering places and springs in between. Fortunately, the most reliable sources are fairly well-spaced, and just a short distance off the route are even more water sources. Still, this segment is characterized by long, dry stretches. Carry enough to cover contingencies, and consider a water drop at the end.

MOUNTAIN BIKE NOTES

The CDT itself isn't suitable for mountain biking, but the Forest Roads the CDT follows or intersects are excellent riding. The Tularosa Mountains abut the Plains of San Agustin, and Forest and County Roads go around the southwestern shoreline of this former Pleistocene lake. But while the riding is easy here, the area is indeed remote and lacking support services. More strenuous and more remote still is the road network around John Kerr Peak, but the ponderosa pine forests are delightful.

EQUESTRIAN NOTES

Gila National Forest Rangers used horses when scouting and designating this trail, so it clearly is suitable for horse travel, though some sections more than others. Facilities for horses are lacking, however, and the scarcity of reliable water is a serious obstacle.

SOUTHBOUND HIKERS

 Unfortunately, no reliable water source exists near where this segment begins on NM 12. Heading south, the nearest water source is Damian Spring, almost 8 miles away. There are several tanks and wells not far from the CDT before then, but none are reliable.

MAPS

USGS QUADRANGLES: Salvation Peak, O Bar O Canyon West, Pitchfork Canyon, Collins Park, John Kerr Peak, Tularosa Canyon

OTHER MAPS: Gila National Forest

LAND-MANAGEMENT AGENCIES

Gila National Forest/Reserve Ranger District

BEGINNING ACCESS POINT

 COYOTE PEAK STOCK TANK: See Ending Access Point in Segment 15, page 159.

Smooth road to Trailhead 30 miles

ENDING ACCESS POINT

 NM 12: This segment ends at NM 12, across the road from the next segment's beginning, where Forest Road 218 heads north from NM 12, approximately 39.8 miles from Datil, 27.8 miles from Reserve, and 15.7 miles east of the Apache Creek Store and Gas Station.

Smooth road to Trailhead

TRAIL DESCRIPTION As if by divine grace, this conspicuously dry segment begins at a water source (not a great one, but in this country . . .); you'll find Coyote Peak Tank where the previous segment ends, just 1 mile northwest of the Divide, at N33°38'35", W108°15'46", elevation 7,540 feet. The water behind this dam is likely to be fouled by cattle, but at least some water is usually here. Fill up, because the next reliable source is 7.5 miles away.

For about 2 miles, the CDT traverses Bureau of Land Management land. The route, marked by cairns, goes through grassland as it heads southwest into a small drainage for 0.5 mile, where it begins climbing more steeply up a grassy ridge, topping out after less than 0.5 mile at 8,075 feet. The CDT now follows a more gradual course along the ridgetop, sidehilling around some prominences, heading over others, a pattern that continues throughout the segment.

After 2 miles, you reach the BLM–Gila National Forest boundary near the head of a small drainage; along the east slopes the route climbs back toward the ridge-

SUPPLIES, SERVICES, AND ACCOMMODATIONS

RESERVE, population 400, is the nearest community that can offer the most supplies and services, although the Apache Creek Store, 14 miles west, is a closer but more limited alternative. Because of this, and because many CDT thru-hikers choose to depart from the "official" route and go through Reserve to experience the Gila Cliff Dwellings and the Gila Wilderness, Reserve's accommodations are listed here.

Distance from Trail 27.8 miles

Zip Code	87830	
Bank	Catron County Bank, Mon–Thur 9–2, Fri 9–2, 4–6	(505) 533-6226
Bus	None	
Dining	Several options	
Emergency	911; non-emergency, Catron County Sheriff	533-6222
Gear	Mostly hunting and fishing supplies at several stores	
Groceries	Jake's Groceries on Main Street	533-6565
Information	Reserve Area Chamber of Commerce,	533-6116
	P.O. Box 415, Reserve; website: reservecc@gilanet.com	
Laundry	Inquire locally	
Lodging	Rode Inn Motel, P.O. Box 167, Main Street	533-6661
	Elk Country Café and Village Motel,	533-6615
	P.O. Box 408, South Main Street	or 533-6600
Medical	Catron County Medical Center, on a hill in the village,	533-6456
	hours Mon–Fri 8–5	all other times call 911
Post Office	Mon–Fri 8:30–12:30, 12:30–5, Sat 9:30–11:30;	533-6333
	will hold packages as long as necessary for CDT hikers	
Showers	Inquire locally	

APACHE CREEK: Where the Tularosa River and Apache Creek join, NM 32 heads north from NM 12. The Apache Creek Store is here, with basic groceries and hardware. The hours are 8–6, though they're open later during hunting season. Apache Creek Store, HCR 62, Box 6700, Apache Creek, NM 87830; (505) 533-6800.

Distance from Trail 15.7 miles

Zip Code 87830

line, having declined to go over an 8,245-foot top. The terrain continues grassy until after a mile from the National Forest boundary; here the route, following cattle trails, enters the open ponderosa pine forest that's a feature of this segment. Now that trees are available, the route is marked by signs and blazes as well as by cairns. As you head south up a small valley, you come to North Tank, N33°37'00", W108°18'45". During my visit, this was dry, but it usually contains water; as an earthen dam, though, it's likely polluted.

The CDT follows the valley uphill south until it tops out at a sharply defined saddle at N33°36'15", W108°18'51", 8,930 feet, where it joins the Continental Divide. From the saddle, O Bar O Mountain, at 9,417 feet the area's highest point, is about 0.75 mile south. Less than 0.5 mile south of the saddle, but 330 feet below, you'll find Mesa Redonda Tank, a reliable water source, but difficult to reach—

and on private land. Another reliable source and more easily accessible is Divide Tank on the CDT 3.1 miles west of the saddle.

From the saddle, the CDT follows the Divide as it climbs steeply west, then less steeply northwest, to an unnamed 9,320-foot summit. In 1994, the Gila National Forest–Reserve Ranger District put in tread over this difficult section. They also blazed a short (about 0.25 mile) spur trail due north to a 9,390-foot height for which a scenic vista site has been proposed.

Having climbed the mountain, the Continental Divide follows a ridge downhill westward through ponderosa pines and mixed conifers, over tread constructed in 1998, until after almost 3 miles from the spur trail, at around 8,200 feet, the CDT leaves the Divide to jog north less than 0.25 mile along the slopes to Divide Tank, N33°36'20", W108°21'10"; this is an earthen dam and a reliable water source, located in the valley of La Jolla Canyon.

From Divide Tank, the CDT follows a two-track down La Jolla Canyon for about a mile to approach the Divide. It doesn't join it, however, because the CDT, at N33°35'48", W108°22'03", turns northwest to follow the north side of a drainage uphill to mount a northwest-trending ridge. There's no tread here, but the CDT is marked with signs and blazes. The CDT continues northwest, over the ridge, until the route descends a small drainage to enter the grassy flats, N33°37'15", W108°24'06", elevation 7,380 feet, of West La Jolla Canyon, 4.3 miles from Divide Tank. In these flats, the CDT crosses a two-track. If followed southwest, this road would lead after 1.2 mile to Forest Road 30 (labeled NM 78 on the Pitchfork Canyon quadrangle). The well-maintained Forest Road 30 is this region's primary vehicular link, used by ranchers, woodcutters, Forest Service personnel, hunters, and others. If you follow

---

A NOTE ABOUT CATRON COUNTY

With 4,414,720 acres and 2,900 people, Catron is New Mexico's largest county—and among its least populated. Within its boundaries are the Gila Wilderness and the vast Plains of San Agustin, as well as many less well-known forests, mountains, and plains. New Mexico's last grizzly lived here, as did the last free-roaming Apaches. If you ever wanted to experience the Old West, you'll find its environment and spirit surviving here.

You'll also find surviving here the independence and distrust of government that characterized the Old West. The county has received considerable publicity for its conservatism and opposition to the federal government (more than half the county's land is federally owned), including many programs most CDT hikers would support; these include wilderness preservation, wolf reintroduction, and regulation of grazing. You'll not see many Sierra Club bumper stickers on the pickups here, but don't let any of this prejudice you in your dealings with the local people. In addition to their other Old West values, they have retained western friendliness, generosity, and, above all, obligatory hospitality. Even people who don't necessarily support the CDT nonetheless are usually open and helpful.

Forest Road 30 northwest 4.25 miles you will reach Forest Road 94, another well-maintained road that goes to Apache Creek on NM 12.

From the two-track in La Jolla Canyon, the CDT heads cross-country, following signs and blazes gently uphill to a flat-topped mesa. After about 1.5 miles from the two-track, it crosses another dirt road as it continues northwest to climb a 7,733-foot hill at N33°38'14", W108°25'31", to rejoin the Continental Divide.

From here, the CDT follows the Divide northwest along the ridgeline until, after 2.1 miles along the Divide, the CDT jogs north to sidehill around a 7,850-foot rise, rejoining the Divide at Forest Road 28.

The Collins Park quadrangle shows Ghost Lake just east of this junction, but barring heavy precipitation, this intermittent lake is indeed a phantom. If you follow Forest Road 28, 2 miles southwest, you'll reach Forest Road 94 and the broad open grassland of Collins Park. Several tanks and wells are here, but most are unreliable. Following Forest Road 28 to the east takes you to the Plains of San Agustin, then north to NM 12.

The CDT crosses Forest Road 28, then continues west-northwest over a small hill, leaving the Continental Divide briefly to follow relatively recent tread around the north side of a 8,033-foot hill. Then the CDT rejoins the Divide to climb to the top of an 8,137-foot knoll with long views in all directions. No tread has been created here, but the route, which stays with the Divide on a ridge, is marked with blazes and signs, then with cairns. About 1.25 mile west-northwest of the knoll, the CDT leaves the grassland to reenter ponderosa pine forest as the Divide climbs a long, fairly gentle ridge to arrive at the northeast side of 8,665-foot Piñon Knob. The Continental Divide heads over the knob, but the CDT takes a shortcut to the northeast.

SOUTHBOUND HIKERS: As the CDT swings southeast from Piñon Knob, it follows a ridge downhill until, in less than a mile, it reaches a small grassy hill, at N33°40'26", W108°28'46", elevation 8,350 feet. At this point, one's natural tendency is to continue following the ridge as it now heads east, on the north side of a drainage, but in fact the Continental Divide and the CDT head more south, then southwest along the top of another ridge, south of the drainage.

Heading north from Piñon Knob, the Divide and the CDT descend to a saddle, then climb to the top of an 8,712-foot forested summit. From this, the route runs generally northeast atop a long ridge. It's pretty country—open ponderosa pine forest, good habitat for elk and wild turkey. About 600 feet below, on the north side of Cox Canyon, is Davis Spring, N33°42'02", W108°29'02", a metal tub that's a fairly reliable water source; the next reliable water source on the CDT is Spurgeon Tank, 6 miles away.

From the 8,712-foot summit, the CDT runs north-northeast, along the ridge, heading over some hills, around others, gradually gaining elevation until after 5 miles the CDT arrives at the southwest side of a 9,403-foot summit. The Divide climbs straight up the steep, rocky side of this, but the CDT heads north at N33°44'15", W108°26'34", elevation 9,250 feet, to contour via recent tread along the hill's western slopes. Even without going over the top, the CDT here reaches its highest point during this segment.

The CDT quickly rejoins the Divide as together they descend a northwest-running ridge, then bend north briefly to join a two-track. The Collins Park quadrangle shows a spring just east of this junction. It's not reliable, but you might be lucky. If not, follow the CDT and the two-track 0.75 mile northwest to Spurgeon Tank, a dependable earthen dam at N33°44'54", W108°27'32". If you don't like or don't need the water at Spurgeon Tank, Five Springs, N33°44'33", W108°29'30", is 2 miles farther, not on the CDT, but near. Five Springs has a metal tank and is a reliable source of good water.

From Spurgeon Tank, the CDT follows the Divide and the two-track west to its junction with good dirt Forest Road 94, which you could follow less than a mile west to Five Springs. The map shows Aspen Tank northeast of the junction, but this source is not reliable.

SOUTHBOUND HIKERS: When you reach the Forest Road 94 junction, you should evaluate your water supplies. Five Springs, less than a mile west on Forest Road 94, is a reliable source of good water, and about 1.5 miles east on the CDT is Spurgeon Tank, another reliable source. (*Note:* This Spurgeon Tank is not to be confused with another Spurgeon Tank on the John Kerr Peak quadrangle.) But south of Five Springs and Spurgeon Tank are many long miles with no dependable water.

Heading north from Forest Road 94, the CDT follows the two-track north along the ridgeline. After about 1.5 mile, from atop an 8,975-foot mountain, tread has been constructed north for about 3.5 miles to the junction at a saddle with Forest Roads 47 and 289, both good dirt. Forest Road 289 leads north to Apache Creek, while Forest Road 47 heads east to intersect Forest Road 28 at the west side of the Plains of San Agustin.

From the saddle at 8,238 feet, the Continental Divide goes up over 8,868-foot John Kerr Peak, but the CDT follows Forest Road 289 around its east side. After 0.6 mile, at 8,460 feet, a good dirt road branches west to spiral up the peak to the fire lookout on its top. The CDT, however, follows Forest Road 289 north for less than a mile to where, at the head of Squirrel Springs Canyon, at N33°48'43", W108°28'27", CDT travelers face a choice.

One route, marked by signs and blazes, follows the Continental Divide east-northeast as it leapfrogs along a ridgeline connecting five 9,000-foot summits, rejoining the other route after about 4.5 miles. No tread exists along this route, which is unsuited for horses.

The other route, almost 6 miles, follows a dirt road shown neither on the John Kerr Peak quadrangle nor on the Gila National Forest map. It runs north then northeast to contour around the north side of an 8,970-foot mountain. At N33°49'00", W108°27'09", about 2.5 miles from its beginning, the road takes you to a CDT information bulletin board and a short spur road that heads south uphill to connect with the CDT. The road route, on a two-track, continues contouring hillsides to join the Continental Divide. Their junction is at N33°50'11", W108°25'31", elevation

Sunrise from the top of Mangas Mountain, Cibola National Forest. Photo by Tom Till.

8,600 feet. Pit Tank, N33°49'16", W108°26'48", is along this route, but it's not a reliable water source.

SOUTHBOUND HIKERS: At this point, you face the same choice as northbound hikers: a relatively easy walk along a two-track for almost 6 miles or a hilly cross-country hike along the Divide for 4 miles.

From where the road joins the Divide, the CDT follows the Divide generally northwest along a route marked by blazes and signs. Less than 0.25 mile west of the Divide is an unnamed earthen dam that usually has water behind it, at N33°51'06", W108°26'27". After 3 miles, on the ridge of Wagontongue Mountain, the Divide plunges due north down the mountain's steep slopes, but the CDT follows tread northwest to follow a more gradual course down the mountain. The CDT continues downhill north on tread to reach a metal tank, shown neither on the Tularosa Canyon quadrangle nor on the Gila National Forest map. The tank's coordinates are N33°52'39", W108°27'32", elevation 7,510 feet. If the metal tub is empty, walk up the drainage less than 0.25 mile to Damian Spring, which feeds the tub and is a reliable source. *Note:* This likely will be your last good water source before NM 12, almost 8 miles away—and there's no water there! So replenish your supplies here.

SOUTHBOUND HIKERS: Damian Spring will be your last good water source before a long, difficult stretch to Spurgeon Tank or Five Springs. Stock up here.

At the Damian Spring tank, the CDT follows Forest Road 4036Y downhill through a deep canyon. After 2.5 miles, the road climbs northeast out of the canyon to drop into another, which it follows downhill north for 1.5 miles to join east-west Forest Road 4036, 4.5 miles from Damian Spring. This dirt road parallels NM 12 just to the west as it runs through the broad grassy bottom of Tularosa Canyon. The CDT follows Forest Road 4036 east along the drainage gradually uphill for 2.5 miles, to where it swings northeast to reach the highway after 1 mile. The Tularosa Canyon map shows Aragon Well by the CDT, but it's both unappealing and unreliable. At the highway is an information bulletin board and the end of this segment.

OTHER HIKES AND RIDES   No other well-established hiking or biking trails are accessible from this segment. However, the route from Silver City to Reserve is a great route and does not have most of the navigating and water problems of the eastern routes. But because this route is so far from the CDT, where a comparably scenic route has been designated, it is not included in this book.

HISTORICAL NOTES

Gila National Forest and Vicinity. Of the more than 4.4 million acres in Catron County, 2.8 million acres, or 63 percent, are federally owned; the Gila National Forest manages not only the vast Gila Wilderness but also Apache National Forest lands within New Mexico. Another 533,000 acres, or 12 percent, are owned by the state. This region was settled by non-Indians in the late 1870s, and Reserve then was known as Upper San Francisco Plaza, or simply Upper Frisco Plaza, one of three closely related settlements along the San Francisco River. The locality also was known locally as Milligans Plaza, or simply Milligan, for a prominent merchant and saloon keeper. The establishment of the sprawling Gila River Forest Reserve here in 1899 had an enormous impact on the region; when the community applied for a post office in 1901, they named it Reserve to commemorate the Forest Reserve and the Forest Service ranger headquarters here. John Kerr Peak, a landmark on this route, was named after a Forest Service employee.

Damian Spring

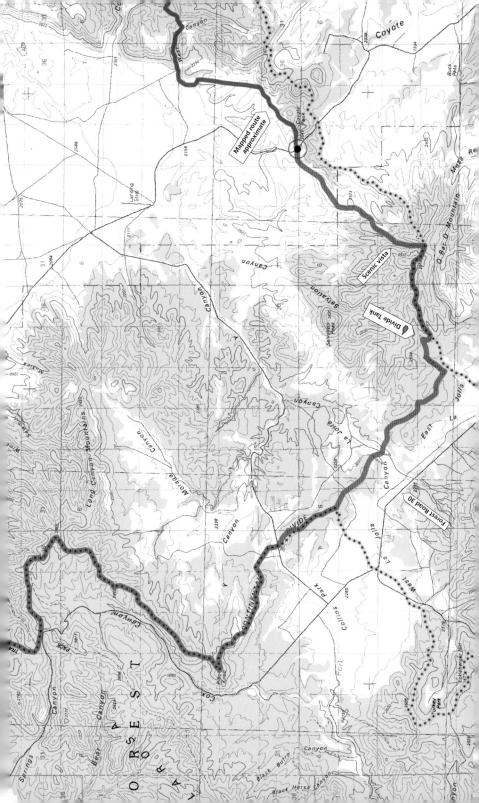

Segment 17
NM 12 to Valle Tio Vences Campground

Threadleaf groundsel on the Plains of San Agustin. Photo by Tom Till.

11.2 miles
Difficulty: Easy
You may encounter: motorized vehicles

TRAIL OVERVIEW Pleasant is the word that comes to mind for this short segment. Not spectacular, not challenging, not tedious, just . . . pleasant. It passes first through piñon-juniper forest (you've already seen lots of this—and you'll see *lots* more ahead), then through ponderosa pine forest carpeted with grass. There are a few small meadows, and even some water, though not much. A good place to watch for wildlife.

This is excellent elk habitat—open ponderosa pine forest with a grassy understory—and the campsites you'll encounter along the road were made by hunters. As you walk, you might ponder the remarkable recovery elk and other wild animals have made in New Mexico after undergoing a holocaust of hunting in the 19th century. The greatest slaughter was done by market hunters, and so relentless were they that by 1900 elk were completely gone from the state. In all New Mexico, not a single elk survived.

They did not return until 1915, when 40 animals were imported from Wyoming. Gradually they were reintroduced into their former habitats throughout the state, but it was a slow process. In 1934, 100 permits were issued to hunt elk; only 3 were taken.

But elk are a prolific, resilient species, and through responsible game management elk populations have recovered to the point that in Catron County, site of this CDT segment, some residents complain about elk being a nuisance, a sentiment not likely to be shared by CDT hikers!

The Gila National Forest–Quemado Ranger District has marked the route with Continental Divide Trail markers and redwood posts, and plan to put up more.

Opportunities for day hikes along the route are limited by lack of trails.

WATER NOTES

Finally, this is a segment where water isn't a significant issue. There's no good, reliable water at the beginning of this segment, so a water drop would help. But the segment is short and relatively easy, with a few well-spaced sources in between and a great source at the Valle Tio Vences Campground.

MOUNTAIN BIKE NOTES

The CDT route here is well suited for mountain biking, despite a few steep, rocky sections. Longer trips are possible when combined with the routes described in the next segment.

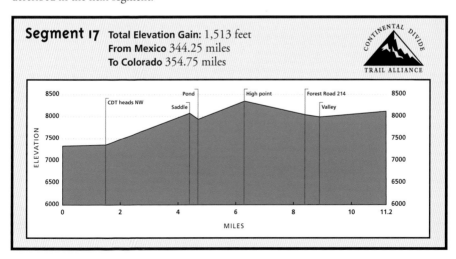

Segment 17 **Total Elevation Gain:** 1,513 feet
From Mexico 344.25 miles
To Colorado 354.75 miles

CONTINENTAL DIVIDE
TRAIL ALLIANCE

EQUESTRIAN NOTES

This CDT segment is well-suited for horse travel. Indeed, Back Country Horsemen of New Mexico–Northwest Chapter, in cooperation with Quemado Ranger District of the Gila National Forest, has constructed horse corrals and water tanks at Valle Tio Vences Campground.

SOUTHBOUND HIKERS

 The route through this segment is relatively uncomplicated, but it would be a good idea to stock up on water at the Valle Tio Vences Campground. There's water farther along the route, but it's subject to livestock contamination. The route gets progressively drier as you approach NM 12, and there's no water at the end of this segment or the beginning of the next. The next reliable water on the CDT south of NM 12 is at Damian Spring, 8 miles from the highway.

MAPS

USGS QUADRANGLES: Tularosa Canyon, Bell Peak, Mangas Mountain
OTHER MAPS: Gila National Forest (the best small-scale depiction of this route),
    BLM 1:100K Tularosa Mountains, Quemado

LAND-MANAGEMENT AGENCIES

Gila National Forest/Quemado Ranger District (this is within the Apache National Forest, but because that is mostly in Arizona, the Gila National Forest administers the New Mexico section)

BEGINNING ACCESS POINT

 NM 12: See Ending Access Point in Segment 16, page 168.

ALTERNATE ACCESS

 FROM US 60, COUNTY ROAD A95: Valle Tio Vences Campground also can be reached from US 60 via County Road A95, which branches south 12.6 miles west of Pie Town. This well-graded gravel road reaches the campground after 22.4 miles, going through the old community of Mangas and up San Antone Canyon, an interesting and scenic drive.

ENDING ACCESS POINT

 VALLE TIO VENCES CAMPGROUND: From NM 12, Forest Road 214, a well-graded and pleasant road, branches north, 34 miles west of Datil, to reach Valle Tio Vences Campground after 9.3 miles.

SUPPLIES, SERVICES, AND ACCOMMODATIONS

RESERVE is the support community nearest this segment and seat of Catron County. Many CDT hikers bypass the eastern route and go through Reserve, primarily because it's direct and goes through perhaps the most scenic section of the Gila Wilderness, past the Gila Cliff Dwellings National Monument, then along the Middle Fork of the Gila River (no water problems there) to Snow Lake, then via Forest Roads 142 and 141 and NM 435 to Reserve, which is described in more detail in Segment 16, page 169.

APACHE CREEK: For hikers on this segment, the nearest supply source is the Apache Creek Store, 15.7 miles to the west, at the junction of NM 12 and NM 32, at the confluence of the Rio Tularosa and Apache Creek. The store has basic groceries and hardware. Their hours are 8–6, though they're open later during hunting season. Apache Creek Store, HCR 62, Box 6700, Apache Creek, NM 87830; (505) 533-6800.

TRAIL DESCRIPTION Easy uphill walking begins this segment as Forest Road 218, marked with a sign, heads north from NM 12, 0.33 mile east of where the Continental Divide crosses the highway, also marked by a sign. Just across the highway from Forest Road 218 is a CDT information board and the end of the previous segment, but you'll find no water near here. As Forest Road 218 runs northeast through piñon-juniper-oak forest, it parallels the Divide until after about 1.4 miles from NM 12 the road forks. The right fork is Forest Road 218 and has a CDT marker. At 2 miles, you'll find an earthen dam, which may have some water behind it.

At 2.2 miles Forest Road 218 and the CDT begin climbing out of the valley, and at 3 miles ponderosa pines appear among the piñons and junipers. Stay left at the fork at 3.1 miles. After a small valley, Forest Road 218 begins climbing to a height-of-land at 4.3 miles from NM 12. As you descend from here, you'll notice campsites used by hunters, and in the small, grassy valley below, at 4.6 miles, you'll see an earthen dam down the valley that is a reasonably reliable water source, though the water likely has been polluted by cattle. At 5.25 miles, just as you begin to leave the valley, at N33°59'17", W108°22'44", you reach a milestone—the halfway point of the CDT in New Mexico.

From this valley the road begins climbing again. It passes by another pleasant grassy valley, then continues climbing, the road becoming steeper and more rocky, until at 6.3 miles it tops out. It drops into yet another grassy valley before climbing again to top out at 7.2 miles. Throughout this roller-coaster ride, you'll hike through ponderosa pine forest with a delightful grassy carpet interspersed with volcanic boulders. You're likely to see Aberts squirrels—large and gray, with tufted ears—as well as elk and deer.

Forest Road 218 continues its easy descent until at 8.4 miles it joins Forest Road 214. The CDT follows this north. After just 0.2 mile, the road enters a broad meadow, Valle Tio Vences ("Uncle Vences's Valley"). The road crosses the meadow and at 0.8 mile reaches a spring-fed stock pond, a reliable water source.

Another 0.8 mile farther you'll reach Valle Tio Vences Campground, with picnic tables, toilets, corrals, and water at horse troughs. The horse tanks are fed by Valle Tio Vences Spring, about 0.25 mile northeast of the campground. Although I located tanks and concrete enclosures, I found no surface water because the flow now fills the horse troughs; however, where the pipeline crosses the road there's a T in the line where spring water can overflow.

This completes Segment 15. The next segment begins across the road, where Forest Road 11 and the CDT, marked by signs, begin their ascent of Mangas Mountain.

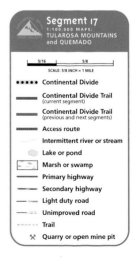

Segment 17

1:100,000 MAPS:
TULAROSA MOUNTAINS
and QUEMADO

| 5/16 | 5/8 |
SCALE: 5/8 INCH = 1 MILE

●●●●● Continental Divide

━━━━━ Continental Divide Trail
(current segment)

━━━━━ Continental Divide Trail
(previous and next segments)

━━━━━ Access route

──── Intermittent river or stream

🔵 Lake or pond

Marsh or swamp

──── Primary highway

━━━━━ Secondary highway

── ── Light duty road

── ⋅⋅ Unimproved road

------- Trail

⚒ Quarry or open mine pit

Segment 18
Valle Tio Vences Campground to Pie Town: Mangas Mtn.

*Leafy aster and Sawtooth
Mountains, Cibola National
Forest. Photo by Tom Till.*

28.8 miles
Difficulty: Moderate to Strenuous
You may encounter: motorized vehicles

TRAIL OVERVIEW Alegres Mountain, New Mexico's highest point on the
Continental Divide, dominates this segment, acting as an axis for this vast, sparsely
populated region of long vistas and subtle delights. No public access currently exists
to Alegres Mountain (Allegros Mountain on some maps), but perhaps an easement can be
obtained in the future. Lacking that, Continental Divide Trail hikers longing for views

must adjust their perspective down 553 feet and settle for those from atop 9,691-foot Mangas Mountain. Not too much of a sacrifice, as Mangas Mountain is far easier to reach than Alegres Mountain.

This is ranching country, and here as elsewhere in southwestern New Mexico, hikers must accept water sources intended for cows. The ranches here are fewer and larger than in earlier times; throughout the region you'll see the ruins of log cabins where doughty homesteaders tried to wrest a subsistence from this parsimonious land. The ranchers here now are also pretty hardy and have evolved a lifestyle and culture based on a curious mixture of self-reliance and mutual dependence. How many of us can even imagine living, say, 20 miles over dirt road from the nearest town (Pie Town)—and then that town having just 55 people? But then, how many ranchers can imagine walking from New Mexico to Canada? I want to believe that ranchers and CDT hikers have more in common than either group suspects, especially in their particular mixture of self-reliance and mutual dependency.

No hiking trails exist along this route, though the one-mile road walk to the lookout tower atop Mangas Mountain is an interesting side trip.

WATER NOTES

There is good water at the beginning and the end of this segment, and scattered but fairly reliable stock tanks in the southern half, but then next to nothing between the A56–A58 junction and Pie Town. Doubtless there are stock tanks and windmills scattered along the route, but they're off the road, on private land, and unreliable. Inquire in Pie Town about possible sources as well as water drops.

MOUNTAIN BIKE NOTES

Despite being long and steep, this segment offers scenic and interesting mountain biking along the lightly traveled dirt roads.

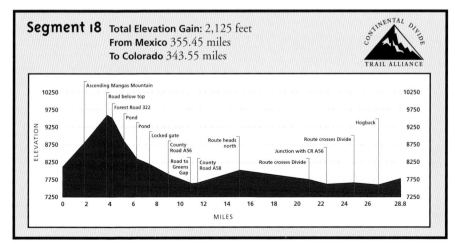

Segment 18   Total Elevation Gain: 2,125 feet
From Mexico 355.45 miles
To Colorado 343.55 miles

CONTINENTAL DIVIDE
TRAIL ALLIANCE

EQUESTRIAN NOTES

This segment is excellent for equestrian travel. Corrals and water tanks are available at Valle Tio Vences Campground. The 10-mile round trip to the top of Mangas Mountain is an outstanding ride.

SOUTHBOUND HIKERS

Be sure to fill your water bottles—and perhaps arrange for a water cache—before heading south from Pie Town. You'll be walking well-graded but lightly-traveled dirt roads for almost all of this segment.

MAPS

USGS QUADRANGLES: Mangas Mountain, Wallace Mesa, Alegres Mountain, Cox Peak, Pie Town

OTHER MAPS: Gila National Forest; BLM 1:100K Quemado

LAND-MANAGEMENT AGENCIES

Gila National Forest/Quemado Ranger District (this is within the Apache National Forest, but because that is mostly in Arizona, this New Mexico section is administered by the Gila National Forest)

BEGINNING ACCESS POINT

  VALLE TIO VENCES CAMPGROUND: See Ending Access Point in Segment 17, page 180.

ALTERNATE ACCESS

 US 60: The campground also can be reached from US 60 via County Road A95, which branches south 12.6 miles west of Pie Town. This well-graded gravel road reaches the campground after 22.4 miles, going through the old community of Mangas and up San Antone Canyon, an interesting and scenic drive.

ENDING ACCESS POINT

 PIE TOWN: Pie Town is reached via US 60.

TRAIL DESCRIPTION A gradual but steady ascent begins this segment, as Forest Road 11, marked with signs and a CDT marker, climbs east to the top of 9,691-foot Mangas Mountain. Be sure to stock up on water at the Valle Tio Vences Campground because there's no other water until you begin your descent on the mountain's east side. The walking is pleasant among the ponderosa pines and grassy understory. This is excellent habitat for elk and deer, and your chances of seeing them, as well as wild turkey and black bear, are good. Also, as you ascend, you'll either hike on or near the Continental Divide.

SUPPLIES, SERVICES, AND ACCOMMODATIONS

PIE TOWN. Most people's first impression of Pie Town is that it's all they expected—and less. The village, born with an influx of homesteaders fleeing the Dust Bowl and nurtured by construction of US 60, has seen better days. Most buildings have been abandoned, most shops and services closed. There's the Pie-o-neer Restaurant and store, where a few basic supplies are available. There's a post office, for supply drops, and a free public campground, with minimal facilities. And that's about it. Yet curiously, the CDT hikers who stop at Pie Town rarely seem disappointed. On the contrary, they speak warmly of the villagers' friendliness, their helpful hospitality.

Distance from Trail	Pie Town is on the CDT
Zip Code	87827
Bus	None
Bank	None
Dining	Pie-o-neer Restaurant, open for breakfast and lunch (legendary pies); P.O. Box 656, Pie Town (505) 772-2900 (pielady@gilanet.com)
Emergency	911; non-emergency, Catron County Sheriff 533-6222
Gear	None
Groceries	Pie-o-neer
Information	Pie-o-neer
Laundry	None
Lodging	A free (donations appreciated) campground with toilets and picnic tables is located one block south of US 60, approximately opposite the Pie-o-neer Restaurant
Medical	None
Post Office	Open Mon–Fri 8–12, 12:30–4:30 772-2637 will hold general delivery packages for CDT hikers as long as necessary
Showers	None

QUEMADO, OMEGA, and **DATIL.** Eighteen miles west on US 60 is the village of Omega, which makes Pie Town seem positively urban; don't even think of finding supplies and facilities there. Four miles farther west on US 60 is Quemado, larger than both Pie Town and Omega, with more shops and services but still modest. Twenty-one miles east of Pie Town is Datil, smaller than Pie Town but with a well-stocked, usually open store combined with an outstanding cowboy restaurant. One mile west of Datil off US 60 is the Bureau of Land Management's Datil Well National Recreation Site, an exceptionally well-maintained campground (fee charged) and an excellent source of water.

The ascent gets progressively steeper as you climb until at 3.8 miles from the campground it levels off at a cattle guard. Another 0.6 mile brings you to the junction with Forest Road 322, marked with a CDT sign. Before descending, consider walking less than a mile to the Forest Service lookout on top of Mangas Mountain. The site has a picnic table and views that make the side trip worth it.

Forest Road 322 is considerably rougher than Forest Road 11. It descends steeply, continuing to follow the Continental Divide through a forest of Douglas fir, aspen, southwest white pine, and other trees of the northern coniferous forest lifezone. At about 2.0 miles from the junction, when you've left the ridge and are in a small valley, you reach the first of two small ponds behind earthen dams, N34°04'14", W108°16'21", for the first pond. Like most such manmade ponds, their reliability in dry times is doubtful, though the elevation of these makes them better than most. At 3.1 miles from the junction is the second pond. I found two mule deer drinking here.

By now, at about 8,600 feet, ponderosa pines, oaks, and alligator junipers begin to replace the higher-elevation trees. At 3.8 miles, Forest Road 322 makes a brief jog. Look for CDT markers and a cairn on the right as you're descending. The road heading up the low ridge will not seem to be the right route because it's much rougher than the road you've been following, but have faith. Follow this east for 0.3 mile to a gate, not locked. About 75 yards south of the gate you'll find a stock tank with water. *Note:* If you're going straight through to Pie Town on the shortest route, this could be your last water source for about 20 miles.

Go through the gate, closing it behind you, then follow the rough road another 0.1 mile to where Forest Road 322 encounters a locked gate, which Forest Road 322 jogged to avoid.

SOUTHBOUND HIKERS: As you're ascending Forest Road 322, you'll encounter a locked gate. Forest Road 322 at this point follows the fence line to the right to an unlocked gate. Go through this and follow the rough two-track 0.3 mile to where it joins a better road.

Forest Road 322, now much smoother and gentler, continues heading northwest downhill through pleasant ponderosa forest. At 0.9 mile from the gate, you'll find a pond of dubious reliability. After 1.6 miles you'll reach the junction with County Road A56, N34°03'09", W108°17'53". Until now you've been on or near the Continental Divide.

The Gila National Forest map shows the CDT turning right at this junction, to parallel Nester Draw as it runs east-southeast; note that the Quemado Ranger District argues against this route because the road crosses stretches of private land and hikers might encounter locked gates. And sure enough, when I ventured down this road, I soon found myself in a rancher's front yard and went no farther.

Instead, turn left, or northwest, at this junction. This route isn't much longer than the other, the road is better, there's water (though not much), it's scenic — and it crosses the Continental Divide.

Antennas of the Very Large Array radiotelescope facility on the Plains of San Agustin. Photo by William Stone.

County Road A56 heads downhill for about a mile through ponderosa pine forest in a broad, shady valley before reaching meadows, which allow good views of the forested Mangas Mountains to the west. After 2.0 miles from the Forest Road 322 junction, you reach a bigger junction, where a sign points toward Chavez Canyon to the south (down which you just hiked), Mangas to the north, and Greens Gap to the east, via County Road A56. *Note:* These road numbers don't appear on the roads themselves.

County Road A58 on the west joins the direct, scenic, and dry route to Pie Town. The shortest, most direct route to Pie Town is to continue north from this junction. After 0.6 mile, you'll reach a junction where County Road A56 enters from the south; County Road A58 enters from the west, and then continues north. (County Road A58 on the west joins County Road A95 at Mangas after 2.7 miles.) *Note again:* These road numbers don't appear on the roads themselves. You continue north also on County Road A58. This well-maintained dirt road quickly heads northeast, toward Pie Town. Between 2 and 4 miles you'll see ahead massive and impressive Alegres Mountain. Just to the north you'll see twin conical formations; the road passes between them.

At 4.2 miles you'll see an old log cabin on the right. At 5.5 miles are some recently or currently inhabited buildings and a windmill.

At 7 miles, the county road reaches a height-of-land and begins a long, gradual descent. To this point, you've found no natural water, and very likely no human-captured water, nor will you until Pie Town. You'll wonder how such sparse water can support such a handsome forest. Dry country, but attractive country. Going north, at 7 miles you'll walk downhill to a panorama of the Sawtooth Mountains behind Pie Town. Going south at this point, you'll have some of the closest and best views of Alegres Mountain on the CDT without traveling over Alegres Mountain itself, the apex of the Continental Divide in New Mexico. It's an impressive mountain from any angle, and its presence enriches this segment.

The vegetation here, as throughout the area, is piñon-juniper, interspersed with ponderosa and oak. By 9 miles, the descent has ended and the road now traverses the rolling country. At 11.2 miles, look for some ranch buildings on the right, followed by more panoramic views of the Sawtooths. At 11.5 miles, you again meet County Road A56, which enters from the south. You'll follow this north the remaining 6.1 miles to Pie Town.

At 12.2 miles the road swings northeast. At 15.8 miles, you confront a striking hogback formation. You'll pass through this hogback and at 17.6 miles you reach Pie Town. One solution to the water problem is to enlist the help of a local resident in dropping one or more water caches; this is easier for southbound hikers starting in Pie Town. You can also probably carry enough water to get you through this stretch. For northbound hikers the last fairly reliable water is the stock tank on Forest Road 322 about 20 miles from Pie Town. Southbound hikers face the same situation but in reverse.

PIE TOWN VIA GREENS GAP

From the Forest Road–County Road A56 junction, the most direct route to Pie Town runs north then northeast over County Road A58, but many CDT hikers enter and leave Pie Town from the south via County Road A56.

County Road A56, should you choose this route, leaves the meadow of piñon-juniper and rabbitbrush, climbing gently uphill east to enter a small valley. Looming conspicuously ahead is 10,244-foot Alegres Mountain, an important landmark. Its Spanish name means "happy, bright." The Continental Divide heads over the summit of Alegres Mountain, making it the highest point on the Divide in New Mexico. At 1.8 miles from the junction, you reach Pipe Spring beside the road on your right. The spring feeds a small pond; nearby stand the decaying wooden structures of a tiny settlement. The road becomes somewhat steeper as it continues climbing the drainage.

At 3.5 miles from the junction, you climb out of the drainage to the Continental Divide, N34°08'03", W108°12'58", on the ridge between Alegres Mountain and Little Alegres Mountain to the south. Don't expect a marker or anything else, but it's certainly an appropriate place to raise your water bottle in a toast. Don't drink too much, however, because water is scarce ahead.

As you descend from the Divide, you begin skirting a broad, attractive valley to the north, affording spectacular views of Alegres Mountain. At 1.9 miles from the

Divide, you cross the valley at a shady oak grove with abandoned wooden structures. The Forest Service map says Oak Spring is here. County Road A56 continues southeast. At 5.9 miles southeast of the Divide, County A56 swings abruptly north, at its junction with B40, to run 17.3 miles to Pie Town.

A56 now is wider and more heavily traveled than the previous dirt roads, but traffic is still light. (Fewer than 3,000 people live in the county—except during hunting season.) The road runs due north to Pie Town and lacks some of the variety of the Forest Road, but the views of Alegres Mountain are awesome. The road runs primarily through open piñon-juniper country, over rolling hills. After 1.8 miles, at N34°05'44", W108°08'32", you reach the junction known as Greens Gap, an interesting name because there's no gap here and no one by any name, much less Green. Continue north. At 2.6 miles, N34°06'21", W108°08'24", is a windmill that was pumping water during my visit.

 The next possible water (underline "possible") is 5.2 miles from Greens Gap junction at a water tank. The road continues north, gradually climbing as it heads over rolling hills. You'll pass other water tanks; some might have water, many won't.

 At 7.3 miles, at N34°09'59", W108°07'22", from Greens Gap junction is a metal tank to the west; it contained water during my visit. As there's no guarantee of water ahead, you should stock up at any productive water source. Some small earthen dams might have water, but then they might not.

The rolling hills continue, as does the dry piñon-juniper land beside the road. Much of this land is private, and most is posted. At 2 miles from Pie Town, you'll notice some interesting volcanic dikes to the east. At 1.5 miles from Pie Town, you'll see a small lake to the southeast, but unless you're desperate you should push on to the village.

After 17.3 miles from Greens Gap, you arrive in Pie Town, elevation 7,900 feet, population 55. Head east to reach the Pie-o-neer Restaurant, the post office, and the free campground. Pie Town may not seem like much at first, but the people are friendly and welcoming, and the pies at the Pie-o-neer Restaurant are legends in their own time!

HISTORICAL NOTES

Mangas Coloradas. The name Mangas, found on many features in this segment, recalls Mangas Coloradas, the leader of the Mimbres Apaches, whose territory included southwestern New Mexico. Born in 1797, Mangas Coloradas earned respect for his intelligence and stature. In 1837, he united several Apache bands to combat white scalp hunters paid by Mexico. He pledged peace when the United States acquired the region in 1846, but, following a flogging by gold miners, he led his people in warfare until he was killed by Union soldiers in 1863.

Segment 18

1:100,000 MAP:
QUEMADO

SCALE 1/2 INCH = 1 MILE

1/4   1/4   1/2

.... Continental Divide

———— Continental Divide Trail
(current segment)

———— Continental Divide Trail
(previous and next segments)

———— Access route

～～ Intermittent river or stream

⬭ Lake or pond

🟦 Marsh or swamp

════ Primary highway

──── Secondary highway

──── Light duty road

──── Unimproved road

········ Trail

✕ Quarry or open mine pit

Pie Town

Powerline

Hogback

Bright
Lake

Long
Lake

Alternate

Wyche Draw

Chavez Draw

Ignacio Creek

San

Views of Sawtooth and Alegres Mountains

Thaeger Draw

Pancake Draw

Muncie Draw

Draw

Hubble Draw

del Macho

Creek

Well

Creek

2267

2262

2296

2250

2227

2223

2209

2223

2253

2213

2189

2250

2219

2251

2350

2465

2361

2367

2468

2368

2485

2253

2950

2950

Segment 19A
Pie Town to NM 117

Sawtooth Mountains at sunrise,
Cibola National Forest near Pie Town.
Photo by William Stone.

31.6 miles
Difficulty: Moderate
(would be easy except for length and paucity of water)

You may encounter: motorized vehicles

Segment 19A   **Total Elevation Gain:** 321 feet
From Mexico 384.25 miles
To Colorado 314.75 miles

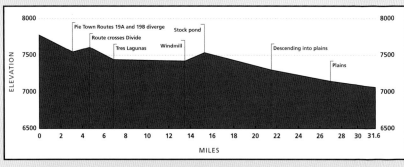

TRAIL OVERVIEW Long, dry, and monotonous. Indeed, this segment's redeeming feature is that it's the most direct connection to the next segment, which, although also long and dry, is not monotonous. On this segment, you're walking a dirt county road through rolling uplands sparsely forested with piñon-juniper. Traffic is usually light on this road, but the dust from the occasional vehicle can be annoying. A few residences exist along the road, mostly ranches.

 Except for privately owned stock tanks and windmills, there is no natural surface water. You'll either want to carry or cache water, or rely upon these cattle facilities. If you use stock tanks, try to obtain the owner's permission, and by all means don't damage fences or harass livestock. Most land along this segment is private, although a few parcels of state and Bureau of Land Management land exist toward the north.

Note: The route described here is not the "official" route, which is described under Segment 19B. That route, however, although not quite as monotonous, is even longer (by 16.7 miles) and drier than this route, and few thru-hikers follow it.

In the north this segment parallels the 62,800-acre Cebolla Wilderness, whose main hikes are described below. Trails generally are lacking, however.

WATER NOTES

 No natural water exists along this road, but ranchers maintain wells and stock tanks. These, however, are on private land, so ask permission, or consider water drops and dry camps. At the end are two good windmills.

MOUNTAIN BIKE NOTES

 Riding along the dirt county road described here could be dangerous because high-speed vehicles coming over hills would not be prepared for mountain bikes. The dirt roads that provide access to the Cebolla Wilderness offer excellent and scenic recreational riding.

EQUESTRIAN NOTES

Although natural surface water is lacking, stock tanks exist along the route and adjacent dirt roads; see Mountain Bike Notes above.

SOUTHBOUND HIKERS

 Except for monotony, southbound hikers report few problems with this segment. The route could hardly be easier to follow. Reliable water is available from two windmills near the segment's beginning, but the next water is 7.8 miles away. It would be prudent to keep your bottles topped off throughout this segment.

MAPS

USGS QUADRANGLES: Pie Town, Red Flats, Tres Lagunas, Third Canyon, Bonine Canyon, Sand Canyon (*Note:* At least some of these maps have not been updated recently.)

OTHER MAPS: BLM 1:100K Quemado, Fence Lake, Acoma Pueblo. These maps are useful in showing the configuration of land ownership around El Malpais National Monument. Although the routes in this segment are straightforward—you simply walk your choice of well-marked roads—and the USGS quadrangles might not seem necessary, you might want to get them anyway because they sometimes show the stock tanks and windmills so critical to this section. Should you cache water or make other arrangements, the quadrangles probably will not be necessary.

LAND-MANAGEMENT AGENCIES
BLM/Socorro Field Office

BEGINNING ACCESS POINT
  PIE TOWN: This segment begins at the west end of Pie Town, where NM 603 heads north from US 60.

ENDING ACCESS POINT
 NM 117: Access to this segment's terminus is via NM 117, 31.8 miles south of Interstate 40. This drive, along the eastern side of El Malpais National Monument, is among the most interesting and scenic in New Mexico.

SUPPLIES, SERVICES, AND ACCOMMODATIONS
PIE TOWN, described in Segment 18, page 187, is the only source of supplies and services.

TRAIL DESCRIPTION
About water on this segment: In the 31-plus miles of this segment, there is no natural surface water. All water you use here must either be carried, cached, or obtained from windmill-fed tanks or stock ponds. During my visit I checked these sources, and I've listed those that not only contained water then but also seemed likely to do so in the future. But windmills and stock tanks are built and maintained for cattle, not hikers, and a windmill working now could be disconnected in the future. Also, most of these windmills and stock tanks are on private property; please obtain the landowner's permission before using them. If you must obtain water at these installations, at least take care not to damage fences or harass livestock. Should you make camp along this segment, the same cautions apply.

At the west end of Pie Town, wide, well-graded gravel NM 603 branches north from US 60. It runs through rolling piñon-juniper uplands for 3.1 miles until the road forks, NM 603 continuing left and northwest, County Road A83 heading right and northeast (this later becomes County Road C41). Proceed on A83 as it continues through rolling piñon-juniper uplands; this will be your route for the next 28.5 miles. As you head north, look south occasionally for good views of the Sawtooth Mountains.

The BLM 1:100K maps show a locality called Tres Lagunas ("Three Lakes") about 6.5 miles from the fork, but the Tres Lagunas quadrangle shows this before the fork, not after. In any case, not much is there, including the lakes.

About 4.7 miles from US 60, road A41 crosses the Continental Divide at a small saddle at coordinates N34°21'40", W108°07'13", elevation 7,600 feet. Don't expect a marker.

At 11.1 miles from US 60, you'll pass a couple of mud holes, but you'll find a better water source at 13.2 miles, where a metal tank beside the road on the east had flowing water when I tried it.

At 13.5 miles, you'll pass by an abandoned stone building and some decaying wooden structures. Nearby is a windmill, but it, too, is abandoned.

At 15.3 miles, you'll notice on your right a large earthen dam; behind this dam is a large stock pond that has a better chance of having water than most stock ponds. Regrettably, that is your last water source for about 8 miles.

At 21.5 miles, you begin descending out of the piñon-juniper uplands onto the plains south of El Malpais National Monument. Ahead, to the northeast, you'll glimpse the sandstone cliffs and bluffs of the Cebolla Wilderness.

At 23.1 miles you'll see a windmill, a metal tank, and stock pond to your east. At 24.3 miles, look for another windmill about 0.3 mile west; all of these contained abundant and good water for me.

By 25 miles from US 60, the piñons and junipers have all but vanished, but ironically, water is more available here than farther south—thanks to ranchers and their windmills.

At 27.8 miles, you'll see a sign pointing east toward Armijo Canyon. A small but easily passable dirt road leads 1.3 miles to a fence, marking the boundary of the Cebolla Wilderness. About 0.5 mile northeast of the fence is the Dittert Site, the remains of an Ancestral Puebloan village occupied around A.D. 1200.

Continuing north on A41, at 30.9 miles from US 60 and Pie Town, you encounter to the east a windmill that, when I visited, was working and pumping water. But another 0.7 mile farther north, near the junction with NM 117, you'll find Point Windmill, also working and with water.

OTHER HIKES AND RIDES: DITTERT SITE

APPROXIMATE ONE-WAY DISTANCE: 0.5 mile
MODE OF TRAVEL: Hiking
DIFFICULTY: Easy

Approximately 800 years ago, Ancestral Puebloans began constructing a small settlement whose remains—rubble mounds, a few low masonry walls—today are known as the Dittert Site, for the archaeologist who investigated them. This short but interesting side trip begins at the Armijo Canyon trailhead (see page 198). No sign or even clear trail shows the way to the Dittert Site, but if you head northeast across a broad arroyo, you'll have no trouble finding it. A pamphlet available at the El Malpais National Monument Visitor Center north on Highway 117 gives more information.

OTHER HIKES AND RIDES: ARMIJO CANYON

ONE-WAY DISTANCE: 2 miles
MODE OF TRAVEL: Hiking
DIFFICULTY: Easy

Located in the Cebolla Wilderness, Armijo Canyon combines thirteenth-century Puebloan ruins with a ruined Hispanic homestead. To reach the trailhead, drive about 33 miles on Highway 117 south from Interstate 40 to the unpaved Pie Town Road, a well-maintained County Road. Drive on this 3.3 miles to a still smaller dirt road heading east and ending after 1.3 miles at the wilderness boundary. The Dittert Site will be about half a mile to the northeast. The mouth of Armijo Canyon is not obvious, but if you head southeast from the Dittert Site you'll enter it. Follow an abandoned ranch road until you reach the ruins. Here, opposite the buildings, follow a very rough old road up the mesa to Armijo Spring. Inside the recent protective structure is the niche where the Hispanic ranchers once placed a *santo* to bless and protect the place.

HISTORICAL NOTES

Why is it called Pie Town? The generally accepted story tells that in 1922, Clyde Norman opened a gas station here, calling it "Norman's Place." He liked to bake, so when he began selling homemade apple pies he changed his sign to read "Pie Town." Two years later, Norman Craig acquired the station and the pie-making business (Craig's wife now made the pies) and kept the sign. The pies were very popular, not only with road travelers but also with local ranchers and cowboys. In 1927, the citizens of "Pie Town" asked for a post office; local lore tells that when a postal inspector suggested a more conventional name, Craig told him, "It'll either be named Pie Town, or you can take your post office and go to hell." Craig knew best: Pie Town remains among New Mexico's most intriguing place names.

Anasazi petroglyphs on sandstone cliff face in winter, El Malpais National Conservation Area.
by William Stone.

Windmill

Adams Diggings

Adams Diggings

Segment 19B

Segments
19A & 19B
1:100,000 MAPS:
QUEMADO, MAGDALENA,
ACOMA PUEBLO, and
FENCE LAKE

| 1/4 | 1/4 | 1/2 |
SCALE: 1/2 INCH = 1 MILE

•••••• Continental Divide

───── Continental Divide Trail
       (current segment)

───── Continental Divide Trail
       (previous and next segments)

───── Access route

───── Intermittent river or stream

       Lake or pond

       Marsh or swamp

───── Primary highway

───── Secondary highway

───── Light duty road

───── Unimproved road

····· Trail

✕   Quarry or open mine pit

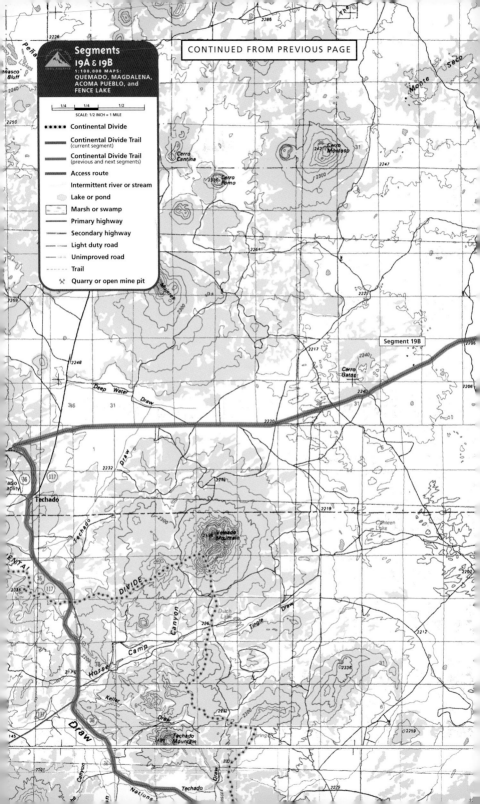

Segments
19A & 19B
1:100,000 MAPS:
QUEMADO, MAGDALENA,
ACOMA PUEBLO, and
FENCE LAKE

| 1/4 | 1/4 | 1/2 |
SCALE: 1/2 INCH = 1 MILE

•••••• Continental Divide

━━━━━ Continental Divide Trail
(current segment)

━━━━━ Continental Divide Trail
(previous and next segments)

▨▨▨▨▨ Access route

━━━━━ Intermittent river or stream

▨ Lake or pond

▭ Marsh or swamp

━━━━━ Primary highway

━━━━━ Secondary highway

━ ━ ━ Light duty road

⋯⋯⋯⋯ Unimproved road

- - - - Trail

✕ Quarry or open mine pit

Segment 19B

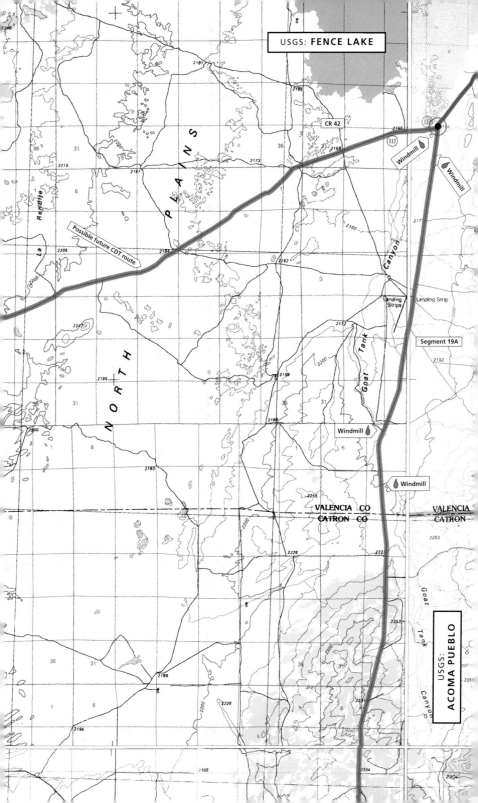

USGS: **FENCE LAKE**

CR 42

Windmill

Windmill

Possible future CDT route

Canyon

Landing Strips

Landing Strip

Segment 19A

North Plains

Goat Tank

Windmill

Windmill

VALENCIA CO
CATRON CO

VALENCIA
CATRON

Goat Tank Canyon

USGS: **ACOMA PUEBLO**

Segment 19B
Pie Town to NM 117

Showy daisy field near Pie Town.
Photo by Tom Till.

48.3 miles
Difficulty: Moderate
(would be easy except for length and paucity of water)
You may encounter: motorized vehicles

Segment 19B   **Total Elevation Gain:** 984 feet
From Mexico 384.25 miles
To Colorado 314.75 miles

CONTINENTAL DIVIDE
TRAIL ALLIANCE

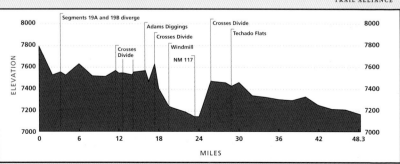

TRAIL OVERVIEW Arguably the less desirable of two alternative routes between Pie Town and NM 117 at the south end of El Malpais National Monument, this route has enjoyed the status of being the "official" Continental Divide Trail route. Its main advantage is its proximity to the actual Continental Divide, crossing it several times. The main disadvantages of this route are length, lack of water, and monotony. The alternative route, following county roads north directly from Pie Town, is also dry and monotonous, but it's a full 17 miles shorter, and thus is preferred by most thru-hikers.

Some hikers might feel this route, Segment 19B, represents an opportunity to hike along the Continental Divide, but with one small exception: The Continental Divide here is either on private land or on state land accessible only from private land. I know one landowner here whose property includes the Continental Divide, and he strongly opposes CDT hikers' trespassing on his property, primarily because earlier hikers and their dogs damaged his fences and harassed his livestock. He says, "I ain't hard to get along with," and if you asked him for permission, he might grant it. But far better opportunities exist in New Mexico to hike along the Divide.

WATER NOTES

No natural water exists along this road, but ranchers maintain wells and stock tanks. These, however, are on private land, so ask permission, or consider water drops and dry camps. At the end are two good windmills.

MOUNTAIN BIKE NOTES

This route is better for cyclists than for hikers, but most thru-bikers will still prefer the shorter eastern route.

EQUESTRIAN NOTES

Because this route requires approximately 25 miles of exposed pavement, it again is less suitable for horses than the eastern route.

SOUTHBOUND HIKERS

Going to Pie Town via this route requires hiking many long, exposed miles along NM 117. Although traffic along this highway is light, it is sometimes fast, including traffic by semis, so be careful. Although several windmills can be seen from the highway, most, if not all, are on private land; therefore, be sure to fill up at the windmill at this segment's beginning. Consider also making water caches along the route. Most land along this route is private, and many landowners are sensitive about trespassing, so respect their rights.

MAPS

USGS QUADRANGLES: Pie Town, Blue Hills, Adams Diggings, Veteado Mountain, Trail Lake, La Rendija, York Ranch, Sand Canyon

OTHER MAPS: BLM 1:100K Acoma Pueblo, Fence Lake, Quemado (because these show land ownership, they would be helpful throughout this segment)

LAND-MANAGEMENT AGENCIES

BLM/Socorro Field Office

BEGINNING ACCESS POINT

 PIE TOWN: See Beginning Access Point in Segment 19A, page 196.

ENDING ACCESS POINT

 NM 117: See Ending Access Point in Segment 19A, page 196.

SUPPLIES, SERVICES, AND ACCOMMODATIONS

PIE TOWN, described in Segment 18, page 187, is the only source of supplies and services.

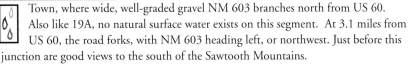

TRAIL DESCRIPTION Just like Segment 19A, this begins at the west end of Pie Town, where wide, well-graded gravel NM 603 branches north from US 60. Also like 19A, no natural surface water exists on this segment. At 3.1 miles from US 60, the road forks, with NM 603 heading left, or northwest. Just before this junction are good views to the south of the Sawtooth Mountains.

From the junction, NM 603 continues northwest through rolling hills forested with piñon-juniper. Most land here is private, with a few state parcels, and you'll pass a few ranches and residences. At about 5 miles from Pie Town you'll see again good views of the Sawtooth Mountains to the southeast. At 13.3 miles from Pie Town is a windmill, but when I tried it, its stock tank was dry. If you locate any water anywhere along this stretch, you should take advantage of it.

At approximately 11.4 miles, at N34°25'46", W108°13'48", just southeast of the low Taylor Hills, the road crosses the Continental Divide, then crosses it again 1.4 miles farther, just northwest of the Taylor Hills, N34°26'07", W108°14'35". As NM 603 heads west, then north-northwest, the road crosses the Divide again, 1.6 miles after the last crossing, at N34°26'43", W108°15'45".

Here the country becomes more broken as NM 603 heads over some low hills, still heading northwest. As you descend, at 16.6 miles from Pie Town, in an open flat, you'll reach a road junction, N34°28'11", W108°17'03".

Though no sign proclaims it, this locality is identified on maps as Adams Diggings, a reference to one of the Southwest's most fabulous and sought after lost gold mines (see Historical Notes). In the 1930s, a highway department cartographer placed a dot with this name here, within the vast, ill-defined, sparsely inhabited region within which the Lost Adams Diggings supposedly was located. A rural post office named Adams Diggings operated here from 1930 to 1945. Despite more than 100 years of looking, no one has yet found the Diggings, so presumably it's still out there, perhaps just waiting for the CDT hiker who, answering nature's call, notices the rocks underfoot glittering . . .

After 0.8 mile from Adams Diggings, when NM 603 has swung west-southwest to cross a low hogback, the road again intersects the Continental Divide, at N34°28'16",

W108°17'36". Here the road descends into a broad, rather pleasant valley of grass and rabbitbrush, flanked by low hills. As you descend, you'll see a windmill at about 0.3 mile from NM 603 to the north; when I visited, it was pumping good water into a stock tank. NM 603 remains in this broad flat as it trends northwest until, after 4.4 miles from the windmill, it joins paved NM 36, about 23.5 miles from Pie Town. *Here you walk north-northwest along the highway.* At 5.2 miles, you'll pass the abandoned log structures that once housed the homesteader community of Techado. Another 1.5 miles along NM 36 brings you to its junction with paved NM 117. Vegetation here is mostly piñon-juniper, with an occasional ponderosa pine. No natural water exists along this stretch.

From the NM 36-117 junction, NM 117 heads east, through rolling piñon-juniper-covered hills. Dirt roads branching from the highway lead to residences and ranches. NM 117 continues heading due east, gradually leaving behind the piñon-juniper for expansive short-grass plains. You'll begin to notice low hills of black rock and scruffy black rock outcrops. This is old lava, a sign that you're nearing the El Malpais volcanic area.

At N34°39'11", W108°09'3", you reach the point where the BLM Fence Lake 1:100K land status map says the CDT branches north. Ignore this. The BLM map shows the CDT coinciding with a dirt road; no such road exists. Except for a section-line fence heading north, there is nothing at the site. You could follow this or head cross-country, but the lava-cobbled soil would make for rough, dry going.

Continue east on NM 117. You'll pass a windmill to the south, but it's on private land that is posted.

A mile east of this, County Road 42 branches north. This is the most practical route to access the CDT through the Chain of Craters area and, later, NM 53 en route to Grants. Should you choose not to go this way to Grants but rather continue on NM 117, you would walk the highway 2.4 miles farther northeast to the junction with the Pie Town road. At this junction you'll see a windmill that I found pumping good water. This ends this segment, 48.3 miles from Pie Town.

HISTORICAL NOTES

Adams Diggings. The story as told around Magdalena and other mining camps in New Mexico and Arizona by the prospector Edward Adams is that he and other prospectors found a fabulously wealthy deposit of gold. While he and his partner were away from camp, locating the so-called Mother Lode, Apaches attacked the men, killing them all. Adams spent the rest of his life searching—and encouraging others to search—for the lost ore vein. People who actually knew Adams damned him as an unscrupulous liar—and a drunk to boot! He made several solo expeditions to find the mine, and no one doubts that Adams was indeed flashing gold samples around in local bars. Our not knowing where and under what circumstances he got the rich ore will forever keep the legend alive.

SEE PAGES 200–203 FOR SEGMENT 19B MAP.

Segment 20
NM 117 to Grants: El Malpais National Monument

Sunset view from Sandstone Bluffs Overlook, El Malpais National Monument. Photo by William Stone.

70.7 miles (varies with separate alternatives)
Difficulty: Varies with separate alternatives
You may encounter: **motorized vehicles**

Segment 20 **Total Elevation Gain:** varies
From Mexico 415.85 miles
To Colorado 283.15 miles

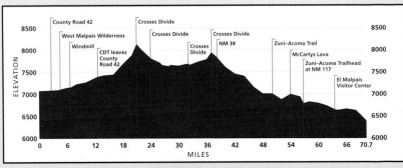

TRAIL OVERVIEW In oral traditions, the Native Americans of Acoma and Zuni Pueblos recall a time when their ancestors beheld rivers of fire flowing down the great valley east of the Zuni Mountains. Some of the lava flows in El Malpais National Monument oozed from the earth's molten core as recently as 3,000 years ago. Even today, a hiker on the McCartys Flow, the youngest of five major flows in the valley, can easily believe the lava flowed just a few years ago—so clear and fresh are the black, ropy layers, so crisp the edges of the collapsed gas chambers, so sharp the edges of the boulders. People had traversed the valley for centuries before Europeans arrived in the New World, but even today no tread appears on the young lava; to find your way across the black chaos, you must follow cairns built hundreds of years ago.

El Malpais National Monument, which the Continental Divide Trail encounters here, beguiles the visitor with its strangeness. The volcanic features—the lava flows, cinder cones, lava tubes, ice caves, and so forth—have always attracted the most attention, and for good reason. Few other places in the Lower 48 States display recent volcanism so vividly. Such recent activity holds special significance in New Mexico, where volcanism has shaped so much of the state's geography. Indeed, given the number and extent of surviving volcanic features in the state, it seems mere chance that no volcano is active now (at least, not as of this writing).

The Malpais lava flows extend about 40 miles south of Grants, filling a valley at least 5 miles wide. The youngest lava, which oozed forth from cracks and vents rather than cones, scars the valley's east and south sides. The oldest flows, along with numerous cinder cones, dominate the west and north sides. When you hike on the lava, you will confront a wilderness unlike any other.

But interesting as the volcanic features may be, other aspects of El Malpais National Monument prove at least as fascinating. Dramatic orange and tan sandstone bluffs flank the lava on the east, their origins dating back 290 million years. In their color and texture, as well as their geologic history, they contrast vividly with the lava. Prehistoric Indians carved petroglyphs of unknown meaning on rock panels on these bluffs and built small dwellings in sandstone alcoves. Indians with connections to the great Chaco Canyon civilization to the north traveled here and built a small outlier settlement.

When the Spaniards arrived in 1540, they crossed the lava and called it *el malpais,* "the bad land," a term that has since become generic for lava flows. In the ensuing centuries, the Spaniards left behind their own artifacts, including place names: Cebolla ("wild onion") Canyon, Lobo ("wolf") Canyon, La Vieja ("the old woman") to identify a weathered sandstone formation, La Ventana ("the window") for a natural sandstone arch that, at 165 feet long, is New Mexico's second longest, and, of course, El Malpais.

English-speaking settlers were relatively late in arriving here. After World War I, homesteaders drifted in and built their brave little cabins back in the canyons carved into the sandstone. Because the land was parsimonious, most homesteaders left as soon as better prospects appeared elsewhere, but the ruins of their log cabins remain.

Although the volcanic nature of much of the terrain here discourages trails, a few scenic and interesting hikes do exist, described later in the segment. If hiking on lava, wear sturdy shoes, long pants, and sunscreen; carry a walking stick.

WATER NOTES

Once again, the key to this segment is windmills. Their spacing generally is good, but the water status shouldn't be taken for granted. The driest stretches are the 7.5-mile Zuni-Acoma Trail, with no water at the beginning, middle, or end, and the cairned CDT route that leaves County Road 42 to go through the Chain of Craters Wilderness Study Area. This segment, however, has water near its beginning. The route directly along NM 117 has few but well-spaced sources, including the visitor center. Another visitor center is along NM 53 to the west.

MOUNTAIN BIKE NOTES

The rough, lava-studded soil here, even on most dirt roads, argues for seeking smoother mountain biking elsewhere. Still, you might be pleasantly surprised when you explore the Chain of Craters WSA, using its network of Forest Roads. The dirt Forest Roads of the Zuni Mountains offer outstanding mountain biking.

EQUESTRIAN NOTES

For the best horseback riding in this segment, use County Road 42. Most other routes here are conspicuously unsuited for horses because the lava damages their hooves. Anyone attempting to take a horse across the Zuni-Acoma Trail should be charged with cruelty to animals.

From County Road 42, you can find several interesting rides in the Chain of Craters WSA by using the network of Forest Roads. This area severely lacks water, however.

Another interesting ride takes you into Big Hole-in-the-Wall, the largest *kipuka*, or island surrounded by a lava sea, in El Malpais National Monument, 6,000 acres of rolling grassland broken here and there with old lava hummocks topped by ponderosa pines. To reach the trailhead, drive on County Road 42 from its south end 2.3 miles to a wilderness sign, where you take the dirt road branching right 4 miles to the trailhead. (*Note:* Avoid these roads when they're wet.) Trails are unmarked, but an old road beyond the boundary fence heads north across open cross-country for about 1 mile, then onto a lava area that hosts an open, grass-carpeted ponderosa forest. It's old lava, so not too hard on horses' feet, but stick to the road; riding cross-country here is harder than it might appear, and the topography is very confusing. After about 2 miles, you enter the Hole, where numerous tracks allow you to explore.

SOUTHBOUND HIKERS

You face the same choices going south as those hikers going north: shortest and most direct, NM 117; most varied, least on a paved road, Zuni Canyon and Chain of Craters; and myriad permutations of the two, most including the Zuni-Acoma Trail. Should your choice involve the Chain of Craters section, then be aware that you face a long stretch between reliable water sources. All the routes are parsimonious with water; the spacing is perhaps best along NM 117, but only marginally so. Zuni Canyon is least exposed to heat and wind, but also is colder, but again, only marginally so.

MAPS

USGS QUADRANGLES: Grants, Milan, Grants SE, San Rafael,
  Los Pilares, Arrosa Ranch, North Pasture, Sand Canyon, Ice Caves, Cerro Hueco,
  Ice Caves SE, Cerro Brillante, Cerro Alto, La Rendija
OTHER MAPS: BLM/National Park Service 1:100K El Malpais Recreation Guide Map
  (The CDT is not labeled on this map, but likely will be in future editions.)

LAND-MANAGEMENT AGENCIES

BLM and National Park Service: El Malpais National Monument

BEGINNING ACCESS POINT

 NM 117: See Ending Access Point in Segment 19A, page 196.

ENDING ACCESS POINT

 GRANTS: This segment arrives in Grants via NM 117. Traveling
south, you would access this segment from Grants by walking 8 miles
east on paved NM 124 to where NM 117 ends at Interstate 40. The BLM has been
negotiating with a private landowner for an easement that would avoid paved roads
by going south of the Interstate.

TRAIL DESCRIPTION: COUNTY ROAD 42

Note: This includes the route by road as well as the cross-country CDT route.

> **LENGTH:** 32.8 miles to NM 53 via the dirt road, 35.8 miles via the
>   CDT section, 43 miles to Zuni-Acoma Trailhead on NM 53.
> **DIFFICULTY:** Easy to moderate
> **ELEVATION GAIN:** 1,921 feet

This segment begins where County Road 42 heads north from NM 117, at a point
34.5 miles south of Interstate 40. County Road 42 is a moderately rough dirt road
used mostly by ranchers, hunters, piñon gatherers, and a few sightseers. It poses no
insuperable problems for most passenger cars—except during wet weather, when it
should be avoided. As a hiking route, it's straightforward, but has its subtle, understated
charms. The terrain here is relatively flat, and although the scenery usually isn't spectacular,
it's pleasant and interesting. There are few water sources along County Road 42.

  County Road 42 begins 2.4 miles west of the Pie Town Road, at N34°42'10",
W108°01'39", elevation 7,080 feet, which most thru-hikers follow to and from Pie
Town. At the NM 117–County Road 42 junction, marked with a sign, a Department
of the Interior sign reminds travelers that County Road 42 coincides with the Chain of
Craters Backcountry Byway.

SUPPLIES, SERVICES, AND ACCOMMODATIONS

At this segment's south end, no services or accommodations exist. Indeed, there are no supplies, services, or accommodations until Grants.

GRANTS, as the major stop on Interstate 40 between Albuquerque and Gallup, has numerous motels, restaurants, grocery stores, hardware stores, Laundromats, and so forth. For specialized equipment repair or replacement, you would go to Albuquerque, approximately 1.5 hours east of Grants. Since the collapse of its mining industry in the 1960s, Grants has turned to tourism and is very supportive of the CDT and its hikers.

Distance from Trail	On the CDT route	
Zip Code	87020	
Banks	Wells Fargo Bank, 201 1st Street, Mon–Thur 9–3, Fri 9–6	(800) 746-8341
	First Bank of Grants, 201 North 1st Street	(505) 287-9481
	Mon–Thur 9–6, Fri 9–6	
	Grants State Bank, 824 West Santa Fe Avenue	285-6611
Bus	TNMO, Route 66 Antiques, 1011 West Santa Fe	285-6268
Dining	Various options	
Emergency	Cibola County Sheriff	284-9476
	Grants Police	287-2984
Gear	No specialty hiking or backpacking stores, although Albuquerque is 1.5 hours east on Interstate 40; in Grants are hunting and fishing stores as well as large department stores.	
Groceries	Various options	
Information	Grants/Cibola Chamber of Commerce,	(800) 748-2142
	P.O. Box 297, Grants, NM 87020; discover@grants.org. The building at Iron and Santa Fe is open May–September, 9–5 Mon–Sat and 9–4 Sun; October–April, 9–5 Mon–Sat.	
Laundry	Various options	
Lodging	Various options	
Medical	Cibola General Hospital, 1212 Bonita Avenue	(505) 287-4446
Post Office	120 North 3rd	287-3143
Showers	Various options	

WILDERNESS ALERT
The routes here variously pass through the West Malpais Wilderness, the Cebolla Wilderness, the Chain of Craters BLM Wilderness Study Area, and El Malpais National Monument, most of which is wilderness. Please observe these wilderness guidelines: **1.** Camp out of sight, at least 200 feet from springs and drainages, on a dry, durable surface. **2.** Use a stove instead of building a fire; use existing fire rings if you do build a fire. **3.** Keep water sources pure by camping at least 200 feet from them. **4.** Bury human wastes 6 inches deep and at least 200 feet from water sources; pack out toilet paper. **5.** Dogs must be on a leash. **6.** No mountain biking. **7.** Pack out all trash; don't attempt to burn it.

From the junction, County Road 42 heads north-northeast 2 miles before heading west-northwest. At 2.3 miles, you will encounter the boundary of the West Malpais Wilderness, created in 1987 to complement El Malpais National Monument. For many of the miles ahead, you'll be hiking adjacent to the West Malpais Wilderness. If the "wilderness" designation connotes places like the Gila or Pecos country, you're in for a big disappointment. This wilderness is open grassland on dry, lava-studded soil, along with lean piñon-juniper forests (with ponderosa pines at higher elevations). It's home to pronghorns, deer, coyotes, rabbits, and even bears, but the animals you're most likely to see are cows, for grazing is among the traditional land uses allowed by the Wilderness Act of 1964. But rather than curse the cattle, remember that without them, and the windmills and stock tanks from which they drink, your hike here would be dramatically more difficult.

From the wilderness boundary, County Road 42 runs west-northwest over flat to rolling terrain, mostly a sea of grass surrounding an archipelago of volcanic outliers.

At 4.4 miles from NM 117, N34°43'58", W108°04'58", elevation 7,150 feet, look for a windmill-fed stock tank beside the road, full when I visited. Your next water, another windmill, is 6.6 miles away. County Road 42 continues northwest, rising gradually, grassland giving way to piñon-juniper at about 8 miles, with the 550-foot-high cinder cone of Cerro Brillante ("bright hill") looming ever closer. Cerro Brillante is the first of many such volcanic cones you'll encounter as you hike north, because County Road 42 marks the dividing line between the West Malpais Wilderness and the Chain of Craters WSA. As its name implies, this BLM area features numerous volcanic cones aligned in an arc around the west end of El Malpais National Monument.

Just southeast of Cerro Brillante, the CDT and County Road 42 separate, the road heading northeast while the CDT weaves its way through the cinder cones to the west. There the trail joins the Continental Divide, also winding among the craters. The BLM, working with the Continental Divide Trail Alliance and volunteer groups such as New Mexico Volunteers for the Outdoors, has been marking this route with cairns. When I was here, I didn't notice any cairns or markers, but the area is a maze of two-tracks; a person trying to approximate the CDT or attempting to find it would be able to stay oriented with the cinder cones, conspicuous landmarks here. Be mindful that in the western portions of this area, the Divide falls within the Ramah Navajo Indian Reservation, and permission is required before hiking there.

The CDT route runs on the southeast side of Cerro Brillante, departing from County Road 42 at approximately N34°45'41", W108°10'23", elevation 7,385 feet. It swings around the south and then west sides of the cinder cone as it heads across volcanic flats about 2.5 miles to pass to the east of Cerro Colorado. From there the CDT heads north 2 miles over forested volcanic jumble to pass between Cerro Chato ("cat") to the west and Cerro Chatito ("little cat") on the southeast.

From Cerro Chato, the CDT heads north, passes between two small, unnamed volcanic hills, then crosses the Divide about 1.3 miles from Cerro Chato, just south of Cerro Lobo. The CDT crosses the Divide again soon as it passes between Cerro Lobo and a southeasterly outlier.

The CDT roughly parallels the Divide as the two head generally north, the CDT to the east, until after 3.5 miles they join just south of Cerro Negro. The Divide runs over the hill's top, the CDT around to the west. They conjoin north of Cerro Negro and cross a 1.25-mile-wide grassy flat south of Cerro Leonides. Farther north 1.25 miles, the CDT and the Divide leapfrog over Cerro Americano. Another 2 miles brings the CDT to the north side of modest Cerro Comadre to again cross the Divide. From there the CDT runs east 0.8 mile to meet County Road 42 at N34°57'13", W108°08'41", elevation 7,650 feet. The huge crater to the southeast is Cerro Rendija, "split hill."

IF YOU FOLLOW COUNTY ROAD 42 INSTEAD OF THE CDT AT CERRO BRILLANTE . . .

At 11 miles from NM 117, you'll see a windmill about 0.25 mile to the north-west, N34°46'11", W108°11'13", elevation 7,490 feet. This is an excellent water source—and one of few here, so don't pass it by. The El Malpais National Monument Recreation Guide map shows several lagunas, or "lakes," along this road, but don't be deceived: These very shallow depressions hold water only after it rains or snow melts.

At 12.5 miles, County Road 42 swings north-northeast. At this point, the elevation is about 500 feet higher than at NM 117, where you began, and the vegetation has changed subtly. The grasslands have become meadows among forests of ponderosa pine and Gambel oak, as well as the ubiquitous piñon-juniper.

At 14.7 miles from NM 117, you'll see a historic homestead site, and nearby a water tank that I found to be dry but looked as though it recently had held water (N34°47'39", W108°11'52", elevation 7,480 feet). A pleasant, interesting place to camp.

At 16.2 miles, County Road 42 passes between an inhabited residence and an active stock tank.

By about 20 miles, you're approaching 7,942-foot Cerro Hueco. Two miles farther is another house with a water tank. Soon after that you reach a junction. County Road 42 heads northeast, or right. To the west rises 7,602-foot Cerro Americano. Beside the road, the depression called Laguna Americana will most likely be dry.

SOUTHBOUND HIKERS: The junction immediately below is critical if you intend to hike the CDT instead of the road. When I was last there, the junction wasn't marked, at least not conspicuously, though cairns were apparent. Use your route-finding equipment here the CDT diverges from County Road 42 just west of Cerro Rendija.

At 27.1 miles, in Section 1, N34°57'13", W108°08'42", you reach a CDT marker and a cairn, marking a route headed south. I'm sure were other markers and cairns in the vicinity, but at dusk I didn't see them.

At 28.2 miles, the road labeled 300 turns east toward the Big Tubes area—an extremely interesting side trip, 3.2 miles over a dirt road before a 0.6-mile path to the tubes.

Finally, 32.8 miles from NM 117, you reach NM 53, N35°00'22", W108°03'21", elevation 7,840 feet. As you approach this junction, the vegetation changes, ponderosa pines coming to dominate, and the numerous hills (volcanic craters) convey a sense of being in the mountains, far from the grassy plains of more than 30 miles ago. The total distance that includes the official CDT route is 35.8 miles.

TRAIL DESCRIPTION: NM 117 TO GRANTS

LENGTH: 31.8 miles to Interstate 40, 37.1 miles to Grants
DIFFICULTY: Easy
ELEVATION GAIN: 453 feet

The main advantage of the previously described County Road 42 is that it allows walkers to avoid most—but not all—of the pavement between NM 117 and Grants. If you don't object to walking along a paved road, you might consider walking NM 117, as it is the shortest (37 miles versus 43 miles) and most scenic route to Grants. Water presents a problem, though no more so than on alternative routes.

 At the NM 117–Pie Town Road junction, fill your water bottles at the windmill just to the southwest, then begin walking NM 117 north. Traffic, although light, is sometimes fast, and truckers often use this route to connect Interstate 40 and US 60. You'll notice the lava fields of El Malpais National Monument immediately to the north and west, and the sandstone cliffs of the Cebolla Wilderness appear to the east.

At 2.5 miles from the NM 117 junction, you'll notice a sign pointing to the Lava Falls, a nature trail over the lava. After about 4 miles, as you descend into the area called North Pasture, look for a windmill about a mile to the east. Continuing on NM 117 to 5.9 miles from the junction, you'll see another windmill, just off the highway to the east. This windmill, at the entrance to the Cebolla Wilderness, is a good water source.

I've always regarded this area as perhaps the most beautiful in the National Monument—broad meadows punctuated with isolated ponderosa pines, lava flows, and colorful sandstone formations. Ahead to the north rise the prow-shaped cliffs of The Narrows.

You reach the beginning of The Narrows after 10.1 miles from the junction. Here a sign marks the head of the Narrows Rim Trail, described on page 218. The pullout here has campsites, picnic tables, and toilets—but no water.

At about 11 miles, you're actually in The Narrows, marked by a sign; the highway squeezes into a narrow gap between lava on the west and vertical sandstone cliffs to the east. The cliffs are especially scenic and dramatic. The Narrows run about 3 miles. Upon exiting on the north, you immediately encounter 165-foot-long La Ventana, New Mexico's second largest natural arch. (Snake Bridge, in western New Mexico on the Navajo Indian Reservation, is the largest at 204 feet long, but it is generally inaccessible to the public.) You'll find toilets and picnic tables at the visitors' area, but no water; camping is not allowed.

About 14.5 miles from the junction is the boundary of the Acoma Indian Reservation; public access is not allowed. At 16 miles, dramatic weathered sandstone formations dominate both sides of the road; at 16.4 miles, just to the west, rises the large formation called La Vieja.

At 16.9 miles, look for the Zuni–Acoma Trail parking area next to the highway to the west. This ancient route is part of the CDT.

At 20.3 miles, look for the northern Acoma Reservation boundary. At 21.8 miles, a signed turnoff leads to the west and the Sandstone Bluffs Overlook.

A well-maintained dirt road leads after about almost 1.6 miles to a parking area: no camping allowed, no water available. You'll see spectacular views from the overlook in all directions, and you will probably enjoy scrambling over and exploring the bluffs themselves.

As you walk north from the Sandstone Bluffs Overlook turnoff, you'll see Mount Taylor ahead, a huge extinct volcano with an unmistakable conical shape. At 22.8 miles, you arrive at the BLM Ranger Station, with toilets, good cold water, and very interesting exhibits. The center is open daily from 8:30 a.m. to 4:30 p.m.

At 25 miles, you leave the monument, although the scenery remains similar: lava to the west, sandstone formations to the east. At 28.1 miles, look for a small stock pond beside the road on the east. At 31.8 miles from the beginning of this NM 117 segment, you reach Interstate 40 and a Stuckeys Restaurant and tourist center just across the overpass.

Just behind Stuckeys and heading west toward Grants runs a paved but relatively lightly-traveled road leading to Grants. To the east tower the basaltic cliffs of the Mount Taylor plateau; to the west the Zuni Mountains sketch an outline on the horizon. You'll cross the Rio San José a couple of times en route to Grants; don't get excited.

At 5.3 miles, the paved road ends at Santa Fe Street, the main street in Grants. From here it's 1.3 miles west to NM 527, or 1st Street, and the next segment's beginning.

TRAIL DESCRIPTION: ACROSS THE ZUNI-ACOMA TRAIL

LENGTH: west to east 7.5 miles
DIFFICULTY: Moderate
ELEVATION GAIN: 215 feet

The official CDT route follows the Zuni-Acoma Trail across El Malpais from west to east, connecting the cairn-route near NM 53 with NM 117. Some thru-hikers forgo walking across the lava and then pavement on NM 117 in favor of walking dirt roads through the Zuni Mountains, but the Zuni-Acoma Trail is among the CDT's most distinctive segments. NM 117, although paved, also has much to recommend it.

On the west, the Zuni-Acoma Trailhead is well-marked on NM 53, 16 miles south of Interstate 40, 1.5 miles into the park from the northern monument boundary sign. You'll find information about the trail and a parking area with a toilet at the trailhead. Regrettably, there's no water, so you must supply yourself with some before you enter the trail.

Should you remain on the CDT, you wouldn't necessarily go to the parking area but would simply continue following cairns. The total distance across the lava is

7.5 miles, but you should allow more hiking time than you normally would for that distance. The terrain has no water; the few trees, all stunted, offer little shelter; and the black lava readily absorbs heat. Be sure to wear cool, loose-fitting long pants and a long-sleeved shirt, a wide-brimmed ventilated hat, sunglasses, and sunscreen. Most hikers find a walking stick useful, as most of the hiking leads over chaotic lava.

Lava is the black blood of El Malpais National Monument—indeed, in Navajo mythology the lava flows around Grants are the congealed blood of a giant slain by the Twin War Gods—but the lava varies greatly in character according to how long ago the flow occurred and thus how much weathering it has undergone. The first lava you'll encounter on the Zuni-Acoma Trail is the monument's oldest, El Calderon Lava, so named because it came from El Calderon ("the cauldron"), a cinder cone 4 miles to the west (an interesting side trip), about 700,000 years ago. The old lava isn't very interesting; most of its more unusual forms have eroded away; because sand and soil have accumulated in low spots, sometimes only an occasional stumble over a lava chunk reminds you that you're walking across a lava field. But age does have its privileges; the soil on the older lava supports grasses, wildflowers, and a diffuse forest of junipers, piñon pines, and ponderosa pines.

At about 0.5 mile, you enter the Twin Craters Lava, which came from Twin Craters, 7 miles northwest near Bandera Crater. The boundary isn't obvious, but you might notice less vegetation, less weathering. Geologists, borrowing a Hawaiian term, call the chunky lava found here *a'a* (pronounced AH-ah). About 0.25 mile into this lava, you'll see on your right a *kipuka,* another Hawaiian term, here referring to an "island" surrounded by lava. This island, underlain by limestone, is called Encerrito ("surrounded") by the Indians of Acoma Pueblo.

As you continue west, at about 2.5 miles from the trailhead, you'll enter yet another, still younger lava flow, the Bandera Crater Lava. Bandera Crater Lava is famous for having the most extensive lava tubes in El Malpais National Monument (see El Calderon Area above). By this time you'll notice volcanic features, and lava-chunk cairns marking your route. Don't let the relatively recent appearance of these cairns deceive you; many cairns were constructed recently, but others are hundreds of years old, built by prehistoric Indians to mark their way across the malpais. The Indians also built "bridges," filling gaps in the lava with rubble.

After about another mile, you will arrive at the McCartys Lava, the monument's youngest, starkly different from the lava on which you started your hike. Only 3,000 years old, this lava sometimes looks as though it hardened only last week, its currents, sinews, and bubbles starkly visible. Indeed, the Indians of Acoma Pueblo recall in their oral traditions that their ancestors beheld rivers of fire flowing northward through the valley. The McCartys Flow is bare lava, with little or no soil. Lack of nutrients stunts what few trees exist here; this stunting effect can make it difficult to estimate distances accurately. Cracks and crevasses, collapsed gas pockets, and sinkholes surround you. Pay close attention to the cairns here, because you have no hope of following the route without them; don't leave one cairn without having sighted the next.

The McCartys Lava can be challenging, but it is by far the most interesting of any in the monument. If time and weather permit, it's a great place to dawdle and take lots of photos. The McCartys Lava is about 2 miles wide here and ends at the underlying, and much older, Laguna Lava. The boundary appears abruptly, and you should have no trouble noticing the difference. You'll still need to watch for cairns, however; I recall a family hike here where we didn't do this and we wasted about 15 minutes looking around. The route meanders through the Laguna Lava, interspersed with stretches of soft sand. This is a good opportunity to look for the tracks of El Malpais wildlife. Surprisingly for such a harsh environment, diverse wildlife abounds—deer, coyotes, foxes, bobcats, rabbits, squirrels, and mice. As late as the nineteenth century, bighorn sheep lived here; they've since vanished, victims of disease, but their horns are still found occasionally. Stakes mark the trail here, but soon lava and cairns return; the trail swings briefly south before returning eastward to end at NM 117 and the Acoma-Zuni Trailhead, with parking the only facility.

When you arrive at the trailhead, take a moment to admire the sandstone bluffs immediately to the east, and contemplate how relative geologic ages can be. The oldest lava on which you walked was 150,000 years old; the sandstone was laid down 260 *million* years ago. It is 14.9 miles from the Zuni-Acoma Trailhead to Interstate 40; into Grants is 20.2 miles.

OTHER HIKES AND RIDES: NARROWS RIM

ONE-WAY DISTANCE: 3 miles
MODE OF TRAVEL: Hiking
DIFFICULTY: Moderate

Trailhead: 19 miles on NM 117 south of the intersection with I-40. Probably the most popular hike in the Cebolla Wilderness, this easy-to-follow but rocky trail parallels the rim of the sandstone bluffs overlooking the lava flow in the section known as The Narrows. After a short but steep initial ascent, the trail climbs gradually through piñon-juniper forest to end at the overlook of La Ventana, New Mexico's second largest natural arch (a good side trip on your drive down on NM 117). The trail begins at a turnoff from NM 117, 19 miles south of the intersection with I-25 and is marked with a sign.

OTHER HIKES AND RIDES: EL CALDERON AREA

LENGTH: 3-mile loop
MODE OF TRAVEL: Hiking
DIFFICULTY: Easy

Trailhead: El Calderon Area parking. El Calderon ("the Cauldron"), with its lava tubes, sinkholes, craters, and other volcanic features, makes an excellent and easy diversion for CDT hikers, and is an outstanding day trip just by itself. To reach El Calderon Area from Grants, drive 20 miles south-southwest from Grants on NM 53 to where a sign on your left for El Malpais National Monument indicates El Calderon Area; a road leads about 0.25 mile to a parking area. If you're approaching from the west on NM 53, travel about 7 miles west of County Road 42 and look on your right for the El Calderon Area turnoff.

From the parking area, don't descend into the nearby collapsed lava tube but follow instead a well-marked trail leading after about 100 yards to Junction Cave. Before descending, make sure you have a *reliable* light source, solid footwear, long pants, and, if possible, a walking stick; the lava underfoot is extremely uneven and sharp. The tube, by no means the monument's longest, is nonetheless longer and larger than you might expect.

After exploring Junction Cave, take the gravel trail leading south toward Bat Cave, passing between dramatic double sinkholes after 0.25 mile. Another 0.5 mile brings you to Bat Cave, which has two entrances. Visitors are not allowed in Bat Cave, home to a colony of Mexican freetail bats, but during warm months, visitors can sit on the hillside above the cave entrances and watch the bats emerging in the evening.

At Bat Cave, the gravel ends. The rest of the trail is dirt footpath and dirt road. The route heads north past a lava trench and El Calderon Crater before swinging northeast back to the parking area.

OTHER HIKES AND RIDES: SANDSTONE BLUFFS

ONE-WAY DISTANCE: Less than a mile
MODE OF TRAVEL: Hiking
DIFFICULTY: Easy

Trailhead: At the scenic vista. Ten miles south of Interstate 40 on NM 117 is one of the state's most scenic vistas. Sandstone Bluffs Overlook, indicated by a sign, is 1.6 miles west of NM 117 and is well worth the drive or hike. From the bluffs you look down upon the vast river of lava that is El Malpais. Far to the west rise the Zuni Mountains; behind and to the east stand the sandstone cliffs of Cebollita Mesa; and at your feet stretch the highly contoured sandstone formations of the bluffs themselves, also demanding to be explored. There is no trailhead or trail at the bluffs. I've always simply headed north, keeping fairly close to the rim. The eroded formations are fun to explore, especially with children. A break in the rim eventually allows descent to the valley below, where a dirt track leads you along the lava's edge back to the bluffs' base. From here, simply scramble back up the cliffs to the top; it's easier than it looks. You'll find a toilet at the overlook, but no water. Camping is not allowed.

GEOLOGICAL NOTES

Though El Malpais lies in the shadow of Mount Taylor's 11,301-foot volcanic cone, any relationship geologically is several degrees of separation. By the time lava began flowing down the valley, Mount Taylor had been extinct for a million years. Of course, Mount Taylor is but an infant compared to the sandstone bluffs framing El Malpais on the east; their formation began 260 million years ago when seas began advancing and then retreating, a process that lasted until 70 million years ago. Erosion of these sedimentary layers formed the valley that channeled the lava when the first flows occurred more than 500,000 years ago.

USGS: **FENCE LAKE**

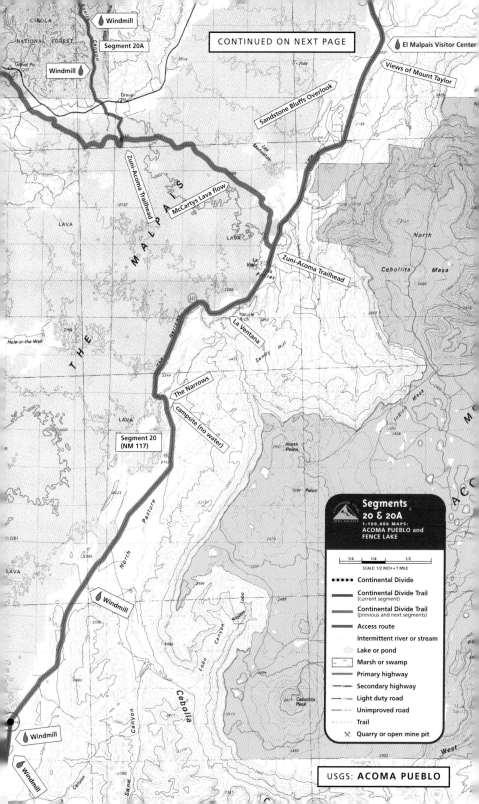

CONTINUED ON NEXT PAGE

CIBOLA

NATIONAL FOREST

Windmill

Segment 20A

Windmill

El Malpais Visitor Center

Views of Mount Taylor

Sandstone Bluffs Overlook

Zuni-Acoma Trailhead

McCartys Lava flow

THE MALPAIS

LAVA

LAVA

Zuni-Acoma Trailhead

North

Cebollita Mesa

La Ventana

Sandy Hill

The Narrows

campsite (no water)

Segment 20
(NM 117)

North Pasture

LAVA

LAVA

Windmill

North Canyon

Lobo Canyon

Cebolla Canyon

Cebollita Peak

Windmill

Windmill

Sand Canyon

Segments 20 & 20A

1:100,000 MAPS:
ACOMA PUEBLO and
FENCE LAKE

1/4   1/4   1/2

SCALE: 1/2 INCH = 1 MILE

••••• Continental Divide

━━━ Continental Divide Trail
(current segment)

━━━ Continental Divide Trail
(previous and next segments)

─── Access route

Intermittent river or stream

Lake or pond

Marsh or swamp

Primary highway

Secondary highway

Light duty road

Unimproved road

Trail

✕ Quarry or open mine pit

USGS: ACOMA PUEBLO

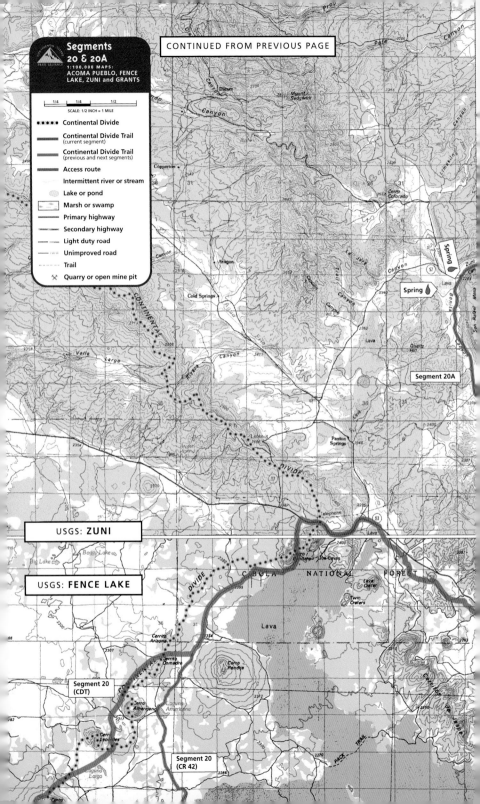

Segments 20 & 20A

1:100,000 MAPS:
ACOMA PUEBLO, FENCE
LAKE, ZUNI and GRANTS

SCALE: 1/2 INCH = 1 MILE

• • • • Continental Divide

Continental Divide Trail
(current segment)

Continental Divide Trail
(previous and next segments)

Access route

Intermittent river or stream

Lake or pond

Marsh or swamp

Primary highway

Secondary highway

Light duty road

Unimproved road

Trail

✕ Quarry or open mine pit

Segment 20A

USGS: ZUNI

USGS: FENCE LAKE

Segment 20
(CDT)

Segment 20
(CR 42)

Spring

Spring

CISOLA   NATIONAL   FOREST

Lava

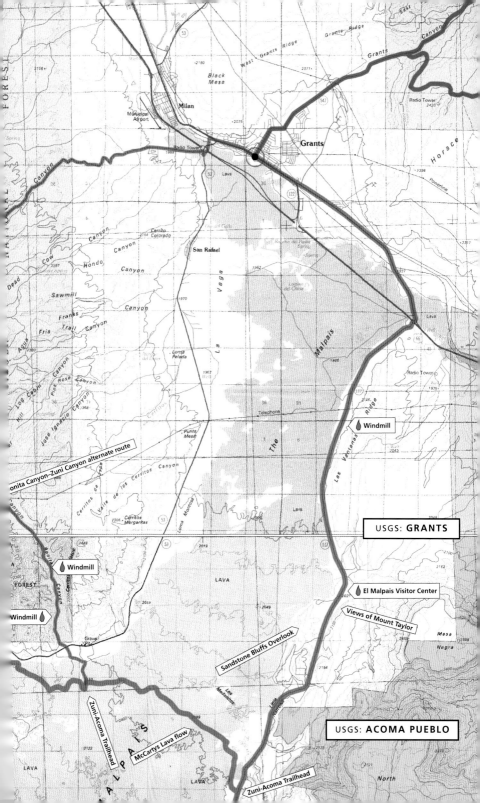

Grants

Milan

Municipal Airport

Radio Tower

Black Mesa

West Grants Ridge

Grants Ridge

East Canyon

Horace

Radio Tower

San Rafael

Rancho del Padre Spring

Laguna del Creal

La Vega

The Malpais

Las Ventanas Ridge

Radio Towers

Windmill

FOREST

Bonita Canyon–Zuni Canyon alternate route

Windmill

Windmill

FOREST

USGS: **GRANTS**

El Malpais Visitor Center

Views of Mount Taylor

Mesa Negra

Sandstone Bluffs Overlook

LAVA

USGS: **ACOMA PUEBLO**

Zuni-Acoma Trailhead

McCartys Lava flow

Zuni-Acoma Trailhead

North

Segment 20A
NM 53 to Grants: Zuni Mountains

Mount Taylor at sunset in winter, Sandstone Bluffs Overlook, El Malpais National Monument. Photo by William Stone.

25.75 miles
Difficulty: Easy
You may encounter: motorized vehicles

Segment 20A **Total Elevation Gain:** 973 feet
From Mexico 415.85 miles
To Colorado 283.15 miles

CONTINENTAL DIVIDE TRAIL ALLIANCE

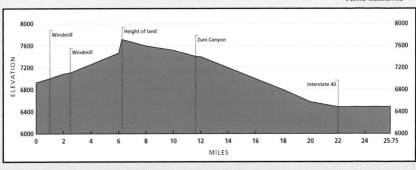

TRAIL OVERVIEW The Zuni Mountains, a small but significant range, were created when a mass of igneous rock punched up along a northwest-southeast axis through overlying sedimentary strata, the way a persistent tree root pushes up through sidewalk blocks. As mountains go, the Zunis are gentle; the highest point, Mount Sedgwick, is only 9,256 feet, certainly declassé compared with 11,301-foot Mount Taylor just to the east. For this reason, hikers mostly ignore the Zunis.

Yet people who do explore the Zunis become fond of them—and for good reasons: open ponderosa pine forests and broad grassy meadows. In the often-brown plains of western New Mexico, the Zuni Mountains are a green oasis. Campsites abound, and water is usually available. You won't find many hiking trails, but an extensive network of seldom-traveled dirt Forest Roads encourages road walking and mountain biking.

The mountains have an interesting human history. They take their name from Zuni Pueblo at the mountains' southern end. The Zuni Indians, descendants of the Ancestral Puebloans, often called Anasazis, of the Four Corners area, were the first Native Americans Coronado encountered in 1540 when he explored what is now New Mexico.

The Zunis were still here 350 years later when Anglo-Americans became active in the Zuni Mountains. Around 1900, modest and ephemeral metal mining camps sprang up; their decaying remains, at places such as Copperton and Diener, still linger in the forest. About the same time, large-scale logging commenced in the Zuni Mountains when construction of the transcontinental Atlantic & Pacific Railroad just to the north created a voracious demand for fuel and timber. Logging camps such as Breece sprouted, logging railroads snaked up canyons, and forests vanished from the mountains. Today, the loggers have gone, and the remains of their camps and railroads are just historical curiosities. The sheltering forests have returned, and the mountains once again rest, serene and beautiful.

On the Continental Divide Trail, this segment provides a scenic and pleasant alternative route from El Malpais National Monument to Grants. Unlike other routes, it avoids walking paved highways, although water sometimes is scarce. The route begins at NM 53, across the highway from the Zuni-Acoma Trailhead, and heads north over dirt Forest Road 447 through the broad, grassy valley of Bonita Canyon, bordered by open forests of ponderosa pine, piñon-juniper, and scrub oak. It meets Zuni Canyon at a small but interesting lava flow, then follows the all-weather Forest Road 49 until it meets pavement at about 4.5 miles from Grants. From NM 53 to Zuni Canyon is 12 miles, to Grants another 13.

Despite their paucity of trails, the Zuni Mountains provide several interesting day outings. The numerous and lightly traveled Forest Roads make for excellent walking, and cross-country travel is relatively easy. You'll find the areas around the old logging and mining camps, such as Copperton, Diener, and Post Office Flat, especially interesting to explore.

WATER NOTES

The two springs in the malpais at the junctions of Bonita and Zuni Canyons hold the key to this segment. The springs aren't easy to find, so check the directions carefully. A few windmills exist along Bonita Canyon, but not all of them are working. Ten-mile Zuni Canyon is dust-dry.

MOUNTAIN BIKE NOTES

 In anyone's list of New Mexico's best mountain bike rides will appear at least one in the Zuni Mountains. Here Forest Roads weave a complex pattern through gentle and scenic hill country. A favorite mountain bike route begins at the junction of Forest Road 447 and Forest Road 49 (described below). It heads around Quartz Hill, using small Forest Roads to connect 447 and 49 for a 14-mile loop. Another interesting route uses Forest Roads 480, 548, and 50 to make a 14-mile loop that includes Post Office Flat, near the site of the ghost town of Copperton. Approximately 2 miles to the southeast on Forest Road 480, you'll find the Ojo Redondo Campground.

EQUESTRIAN NOTES

Gentle terrain, sufficient corrals and water, great campsites, proximity to Albuquerque, and green meadows and open ponderosa pine forests have made the Zuni Mountains a favorite destination for backcountry horsemen. Although trails are few, the Forest Roads are seldom traveled except for Forest Road 49. The CDT itself makes a good ride, especially Bonita Canyon. Other good rides off the CDT include Paxton Springs and Copperton.

SOUTHBOUND HIKERS

 Embark upon this segment with ample water; no water exists in the 10 miles of Zuni Canyon. Two springs exist in the Malpais at the junction of Zuni and Bonita Canyons.

MAPS

USGS QUADRANGLES: Arrosa Ranch, San Rafael, Paxton Springs, Grants

OTHER MAPS: Cibola National Forest–Mount Taylor Ranger District. This map is invaluable for the Forest Roads. At least as important is the BLM/National Park Service El Malpais Recreation Guide Map.

LAND-MANAGEMENT AGENCIES

Cibola National Forest/Mount Taylor Ranger District

BEGINNING ACCESS POINT

 NM 53: Access to the segment's southern end is via NM 53, 18 miles southwest of its intersection with Interstate 40 at Grants.

ENDING ACCESS POINT

  GRANTS: Access is even better at the north end of this segment because the mouth of Zuni Canyon is less than 0.25 mile west of Interstate 40 off NM 53, at the west end of Grants.

TRAIL DESCRIPTION From the Continental Divide, marked by a sign on NM 53, travel east on this paved highway. About 0.6 mile from the Divide, you'll pass the entrance to the Ice Caves, a local attraction. The Ice Caves store, operated by the Candelaria husband-

and-wife team, sells snacks and soft drinks. For a fee, you can see the Ice Caves and Bandera Crater. I've found the Ice Caves a little underwhelming, but Bandera Crater, the largest in El Malpais National Monument, is impressive. The Ice Caves store is a good place to fill your water bottles.

From the Ice Caves entrance, hike 10.2 miles along NM 53 to the Zuni-Acoma Trailhead and the mouth of Bonita Canyon, N34°57'23", W107°56'40", elevation 6,931 feet.

Although the Zuni-Acoma Trailhead is well-marked, Forest Road 447 leading up Bonita Canyon is not; however, less than 0.5 mile from NM 53, a sign on Forest Road 447 tells you you're entering the National Forest, and soon beyond that you'll see a sign marking Forest Road 447. To the north, look for 8,664-foot Gallo Peak, a conspicuous mound of colorful red cliffs dappled with dark green piñon-juniper.

On Forest Road 447, about a mile north of NM 53, a rough and perhaps obscure track branches east and leads after 0.25 mile to a windmill, N34°58'14", W107°56'41". When I visited, this was watering two stock tanks. Hike another 1.5 miles north and look for another windmill, N34°59'30", W107°57'02", also to the east and also functioning when I was there. The San Rafael quadrangle shows a well across the valley to the east, about a mile north of the windmill, but its reliability is unknown.

About 3.25 miles farther north you'll see the next windmill, at the junction of Bonita and Ojitos Cuates (Little Twin Springs) Canyons. I found this windmill was not functioning. Forest Road 447 continues up increasingly narrow Bonita Canyon, still flanked by junipers, piñons, and ponderosa pines. Among the trees are appealing campsites, though cattle roam the area.

About 0.5 mile past the last windmill, you reach the height-of-land at 7,718 feet, N35°03'00", W107°57'35", having gained almost 800 feet in the 6.25 miles since NM 53. From here, Forest Road 447 runs gradually downhill along the east side of broad, grassy Bonita Canyon to its junction with Zuni Canyon and Forest Road 49. As you approach this junction, you'll begin to notice, less than 100 yards from the road to the west, outcrops of black, recent lava. This broken, crumbly lava is known by the Hawaiian term *a'a* (AH-ah), and although you might enjoy exploring here, be careful of your footing; jagged edges on the lava are razor sharp.

The Paxton Springs quadrangle and the Cibola National Forest–Mount Taylor Ranger District map both show Malpais Spring in the midst of this lava, at N35°05'54", W108°01'08". Actually, there are two springs in the malpais here, but both are difficult to find without directions, and the malpais is not an easy to place to explore at random. The spring shown on the maps is reached by taking the two-track dirt road that branches southwest from Forest Road 447 about 0.25 mile south of its junction with Forest Road 49.

The two-track heads toward the south end of a small, isolated hill, shown clearly on the Paxton Springs and El Malpais maps. Just after the two-track crosses a low ridge, N35°05'39", W108°01'02", a very faint two-track, not shown on the maps, heads

SUPPLIES, SERVICES, AND ACCOMMODATIONS

GRANTS, 18 miles from the trail, has a full complement of services needed by CDT users. For specialized equipment repair or replacement, Albuquerque is about 1.5 hours east on Interstate 40. For a list of facilities and services in Grants, see Segment 20, page 212.

north along the west side of the hill, swings up onto the hill's north side, then continues north down a slope toward a lava cul de sac. Here you should begin looking for a man-made notch in the lava, through which the road descends. Stand in the notch and look straight ahead; you'll notice a pressure ridge of lava less than 100 yards away. Deep in the fissure along the pressure ridge, you'll find the spring, N35°05'59", W108°01'05". The water is clear, cold, and delicious. Back at the two-track, there's a very nice campsite among some pines less than 50 yards ahead.

Although the maps label the above spring Malpais Spring, in fact Malpais Spring is the other spring. You can reach this by going to the Forest Roads 447–49 junction, heading uphill on Forest Road 49 to the historical marker documenting the temporary lumber and railroad camp here around 1920 (a few remains can still be found on the low hill just to the southwest). Continue up Forest Road 49 for 550 yards to a sign indicating the historical marker you just left. From this sign, look for a gate in the wire fence to the south. Pass through the gate, then continue south toward a wall of lava. Soon you'll find you're on the old railroad grade. Follow this less than 100 yards, looking for a manmade notch in the lava wall. Go through this notch; Malpais Spring is just downhill, marked by a stake, N35°06'03", W108°00'57". Unlike the other spring, however, its water is dense with moss, and stinging nettle grows around the spring.

Forest Road 49 through Zuni Canyon is a wide, well-graded dirt road. Scenic sedimentary sandstone cliffs flank the narrow canyon, their 400-foot height diminishing as you approach Grants. About a hundred years ago, the Zuni Mountains were heavily logged; as you hike down the canyon you can see the remains of the railroad bed once used to haul logs out, and a historical marker points out a log chute used to slide logs cut on the mesas down the cliffs to the canyon below.

After about 5.5 miles, the dirt road turns into a paved road. As you approach Grants, you'll pass through a flat, once the site of the Grants dump, now acres of rusted cans and anonymous metal; the huge and majestic 11,301-foot volcanic cone of Mount Taylor looms ahead in the distance. After passing through a residential area, the Zuni Canyon road ends at NM 53. Just to the left is Interstate 40 and the west end of Grants.

SEE PAGES 220–223 FOR SEGMENT 20A MAP.

Cabezon Peak, an ancient volcanic neck, Rio Puerco Valley (see Segment 23). Photo by William Stone.

Segment 21
Grants to Forest Road 239A: Mount Taylor

*Morning clouds blanketing
Mount Taylor, Cibola National
Forest. Photo by Tom Till.*

48.2 miles
Difficulty: Strenuous
You may encounter: motorized vehicles

Segment 21 **Total Elevation Gain:** 4,273 feet
(6,500 feet from Grants to the summit of Mount Taylor)
From Mexico 486.55 miles
To Colorado 212.45 miles

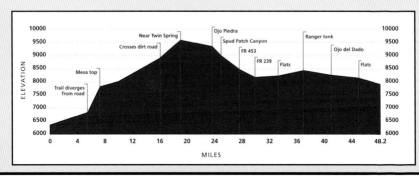

TRAIL OVERVIEW Mount Taylor is the axis around which the geography and cultures of west-central New Mexico revolve. From all directions it dominates the landscape, sitting atop a vast volcanic plateau, the patriarch of scores of lesser summits, the sire of more than 50 volcanic plugs surrounding the mountain like dwarves around a giant.

Geologically, the mountain was born with volcanism that erupted about 3.3 million years ago and lasted until about 2.5 million years ago. Many people seeing the recent lava flows along Interstate 40 near Grants and in El Malpais National Monument assume they came from Mount Taylor, but the giant volcano had long been extinct by then. In Sherry Robinson's guidebook, *El Malpais, Mount Taylor, and the Zuni Mountains,* she writes, "Taylor is actually a smallish mountain perched on a vast, 8,200-foot pedestal of mesas, which are about 2,000 feet above the surrounding area." Though no one climbing to Mount Taylor's summit, from which almost a third of New Mexico is visible, would describe it as a "smallish mountain," it is true that most people see only the mountain and not the platform on which it rests. This mesa is 47 miles long northeast to southwest and 23 miles wide. Although the volcano's hulking size makes it familiar to almost all New Mexicans, the volcanic plateau to the north and east of the mountain is conspicuously remote and uninhabited.

This is the country through which the Continental Divide Trail passes. Responsibility for the CDT around Mount Taylor rests with the Cibola National Forest–Mount Taylor Ranger District, and to the northeast the Bureau of Land Management's Rio Puerco office has responsibility. At present, several alternative CDT routes exist in this region, from dirt Forest Roads to hiking trails, and the CDT accommodates several recreational uses, including horseback riding, mountain biking, and day hiking. This segment and the elevation profile, opposite, describe the "official" off-road route— mostly developed as of winter 2000. The Forest Service advises thru-hikers simply to follow Forest Roads 239/239A as an alternate route.

Despite its massive size, Mount Taylor has surprisingly few hiking trails, though the Gooseberry Spring Trail, described on page 237, is among New Mexico's finest. Most travel here is on the complex network of dirt Forest Roads. Cross-country hiking can be pleasant in the open ponderosa forest, though it's easy to find yourself in a deep canyon flanked with vertical basalt cliffs. Water sources are small and few.

WATER NOTES

The major springs along both Forest Road 239/239A and the off-road route are reliable, though you should never forgo a chance to fill your bottles. Be sure to top off your bottles at San Mateo Spring and also Ojo de los Indios (and every place in between, if you get a chance).

MOUNTAIN BIKE NOTES

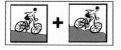

The complex and extensive network of dirt Forest Roads surrounding Mount Taylor offers outstanding mountain biking.

EQUESTRIAN NOTES

The meadows along Forest Road 239 through this segment's eastern section offer outstanding riding and good wildlife viewing. Fortunately, enough Forest Roads exist here that horses don't have to go cross-country over hidden and treacherous volcanic cobbles.

SOUTHBOUND HIKERS

 You've likely arrived at this segment tired and thirsty, so you're lucky this segment begins with a good spring, Ojo de los Indios. And within easy reach ahead is another good spring, Ojo del Dado. The walking here is as easy and pleasant as anywhere atop Mesa Chivato. Later, when you leave Forest Road 239 to ascend Forest Road 451, the hiking gets more difficult, the route-finding more challenging, but good springs continue to occur at fortuitous intervals, though you should take no source for granted and always leave a good source well-supplied.

MAPS

USGS QUADRANGLES: Grants, Lobo Springs, Mount Taylor, San Mateo, Cerro Pelon, Cerro Alesna, El Dado Mesa, Mesa Cortada

OTHER MAPS: Cibola National Forest–Mount Taylor Ranger District map. The current edition does not show the CDT, but it's still invaluable for indicating Forest Roads, which the CDT follows for much of this segment.

LAND-MANAGEMENT AGENCIES

Cibola National Forest/Mount Taylor Ranger District

BEGINNING ACCESS POINT

Smooth road to Trailhead

GRANTS: The southwestern end of this segment has exceptionally good access as Grants is a major stop on Interstate 40 and the CDT route passes through Grants and leaves via a paved road.

ALTERNATE ACCESS

Smooth road to Trailhead

FOREST ROAD 239: Graded Forest Road 456 heads north out of the village of San Mateo to climb onto the Mount Taylor volcanic plateau and join Forest Road 239 and the CDT north of Mount Taylor.

ENDING ACCESS POINT

Smooth road to Trailhead — 10 miles + Bumpy road to Trailhead — 20 miles

FOREST ROAD 239A: This segment ends at the BLM Forest Service boundary at Forest Road 239A; this road can be impassable in bad weather. There is no good access to this point from the east.

TRAIL DESCRIPTION The town of Grants marks this segment's beginning. And although it's possible to avoid going into the main part of Grants by taking NM 124 and its connecting roads, there's no good reason for doing this; walking along the main street, Santa Fe Avenue, is direct, and most thru-hikers will plan to spend at least one day here, resting and replenishing supplies after the long stretch from Pie Town and before the even longer and more isolated stretch to Cuba.

Proceed northwest along Santa Fe Avenue in Grants to where a sign indicates NM 547 heading northeast (look for a Pizza Hut restaurant at this junction). NM 547 here coincides with Roosevelt, leading after 1.5 miles to Lobo Canyon Road (look for the Lobo Canyon shopping center). From this junction, it's another mile on Lobo Canyon Road to the Cibola National Forest–Mount Taylor Ranger District offices, on your left. This would be a good place to fill water bottles and gather current information about trails and conditions.

Traffic on NM 547 through Lobo Canyon is often heavy and fast, so the Forest Service prudently removed the CDT route from it as soon as possible. You still have to walk approximately 3 miles on pavement, past the prison, to the trailhead, on the south side of the road. I didn't find The turnoff leading to the trailhead marked, but the coordinates are N35°11'26", W107°46'21"; look for posts painted red, then drive or walk about 100 feet on the graded dirt road to the parking area. Go through a pass-through; cross a small bridge to where the recently constructed trail begins slabbing up the hillside to the northeast. The sparse piñon-juniper and cholla vegetation allows great views into Lobo Canyon. Across the valley squat the basalt-capped mesas of Grants Ridge, along with tailings from 1940s pumice mines.

The trail continues slabbing east along the hillside until after 0.6 mile it bends southeast for 0.2 mile, then southwest for 0.8 mile to top out at the rim of Horace Mesa at 7,800 feet, a gain of about 1,000 feet from the trailhead. From this vantage point the views into the canyon and beyond are magnificent.

From here the CDT follows an old road east for 1.2 miles before slabbing up the side of a bench of Horace Mesa, the elevation gain this time only 140 feet. At the mesa's rim you're again treated to magnificent views. The Lobo Springs quadrangle shows this to be Acoma Indian land, but after the map was made this land was involved in a land-swap, so this now is National Forest.

Here your climbing ends for a while as the CDT heads east across the mesa's flat top, following a dirt track through open piñon-juniper forest; you'll have awesome views of Mount Taylor to the northeast. Travel east for about 3 miles until you cross the heads of two small drainages with stands of ponderosa pine, and approach Horace Mesa's eastern rim. Here the route swings northeast, climbing gradually and then more steeply just before reaching the junction, N35°12'11", W107°40'34", with the Forest Road leading 0.4 mile downhill to Big Spring, N35°11'43", W107°40'07", which the Forest Service describes as unreliable.

The CDT route crosses this junction and continues northeast uphill through increasingly frequent ponderosa pines, following an old two-track that after a mile becomes a trail. The trail jogs east briefly before again heading northeast to its junction after 0.4 mile with Forest Road 193. You'll find two stock tanks near this junction, one just to the southeast, the other to the northeast on the small drainage.

The Forest Service's plans for the CDT from here haven't yet been finalized, though both routes being considered would remove the CDT from Forest Road 193, at least in part. But until a route has been established, you're best hiking Forest Road 193 east 1 mile to where it bends sharp left, or north, at a signed junction with Forest Road 501. In less than 0.25 mile from the junction, Forest Road 193 brings you to a parking area on your left and on your right the beginning of the Gooseberry Spring Trail (not marked on the Lobo Springs quadrangle), which leads to the summit of Mount Taylor. Gooseberry Spring itself is reached by following the trail gently uphill through conifers and aspen for about 0.6 mile. At first you might just notice water trickling from a pipe, but look around until you find the spring itself, enclosed by a fence. The water here isn't abundant, and in a very dry year could be nonexistent, but otherwise it's a reliable source. There are several possible campsites nearby, though finding one not trampled by the numerous thirsty cows might be difficult. Gooseberry Spring is not labeled on the Lobo Springs quadrangle; its coordinates are N35°13'39", W107°37'23". Forest Road 193 here is not shown either, so you should consult the Cibola National Forest-Mount Taylor Ranger District map.

Despite the obvious appeal of the Gooseberry Spring Trail to reach the summit of Mount Taylor and beyond, the Forest Service has not chosen this for the CDT in deference to the Native American tribes, especially the Acoma, who have said the CDT would intrude upon their sacred mountain. Still, hikers have used the Gooseberry Spring Trail for decades, and should you choose this alternate route, you'll be treated to one of New Mexico's most spectacular hikes. It's described on page 237.

The CDT from Gooseberry Spring has not yet been determined. One possibility under consideration was to create a trail just east of Forest Road 193 that would pass through aspens as it paralleled the Forest Road. This trail would go north about 1 mile, roughly following contour lines, to cross the Lobo Canyon drainage and ascend to its north side, where it would intersect an old road at approximately N35°14'03", W107°38'14". At present you can attempt to reach this junction from Forest Road 193 soon after it crosses Lobo Canyon, or you can continue east on Forest Road 193 past Lobo Canyon to pick up the road in Section 26 of the Forest Service map. This goes past reliable Twin Spring, N35°14'46", W107°38'27" to connect after about 2.5 miles with Forest Road 453. Here the CDT makes use of the toilet and water facilities of the Mount Taylor Winter Quadrathlon (see page 238).

From here follow an old road through ponderosa pine forest as it leads to George Tank, N35°16′29″, W107°37′22″, a fairly reliable water source. Here several Forest Roads intersect. From here, the Forest Service's CDT route is again tentative. It would follow a Forest Road northeast from George Tank 0.8 mile then begin following an east-west drainage on the southwest side of Cerro Venado. In the cooler canyons and valleys here you encounter stands of Douglas fir. Just south of Cerro, at 9,150 feet, the route tops out at a small col, descends briefly, then begins climbing again along the southwest slopes of a drainage to reach Ojo Piedra ("Rock Spring"), N35°16′26″, W107°35′47″, a very reliable water source. Were you to follow this drainage north 0.6 mile, steeply downhill over densely timbered slopes, you would reach reliable San Mateo Spring, N35°16′49″, W107°35′56″, and, about 100 yards farther, Forest Road 239.

A decision is required of you at Ojo Piedra. Should you choose at Ojo Piedra not to follow Forest Road 239 quite yet, you would continue to Manuel Spring and Forest Road 451, which you would follow 0.5 mile into Spud Patch Canyon. The canyon here is scenic and interesting, with numerous abrupt formations of granite, an anomaly in this volcanic plateau. You descend Spud Patch Canyon, heading north through ponderosa pine and Douglas fir for 0.8 mile to where a Forest Road crosses the canyon at N35°17′21″, W107°34′59″. The road climbs a small drainage east out of Spud Patch Canyon before descending north-northeast through the forest to reach another small canyon after about 1 mile. It crosses this, then continues its steady descent north to reach Forest Road 453 at 1.5 miles. Water in all these drainages is problematic, and ahead the water situation is even worse, so if you encounter water, take advantage of it. Follow Forest Road 453 north to its junction with Forest Road 239.

From its junction with Forest Road 453, the proposed CDT route will continue northeast, passing by American Tank N35°19′19″, W107°34′21″, after 0.2 mile, then continuing to descend gradually through ponderosa pine and piñon-juniper forest 1.5 miles to Antelope Tank, N35°20′25″, W107°33′59.″ From here, the proposed CDT route continues cross-country northeast 0.4 mile to join Forest Road 239 near the head of the eastern prong of American Canyon, N35°20′46″, W107°33′45″.

Upon joining Forest Road 239 at the head of American Canyon's eastern branch, the CDT route becomes straightforward: It follows Forest Road 239 and Forest Road 239A until it becomes BLM Road 1103, which continues northeast over relatively flat Mesa Chivato. It continues following this road until finally it plunges off the mesa's eastern escarpment and into the valley of the Rio Puerco. Along this stretch, vehicular traffic on Forest Road 239 lessens dramatically from what it was near Grants and Mount Taylor; the road itself becomes narrower and rougher; and the Forest Service feels, correctly, that constructing a trail to avoid this long stretch of seldom-used road would not constitute the best use of limited funds. Ponderosa and piñon pines, juniper, and Gambel oak dominate the forest here, though broad grassy flats intersperse the landscape. Water is scarce along this stretch, though a few widely spaced springs and tanks do exist.

The Forest Road 239 option. Should you at Ojo Piedra choose to walk Forest Road 239, which is gravel but wide, graded, and well-traveled, San Mateo Spring would be a good place to begin. The spring is reliable, and the water delicious. Stock up here, as the next water, if any, won't be as plentiful or as appealing. From San Mateo Spring, Forest Road 239 slabs up the east side of San Mateo Canyon before topping out at the junction with Forest Road 451. If you wanted to avoid the steep timbered slopes on the descent from Ojo Piedra to San Mateo Spring, you could walk an old road north and northeast from Ojo Piedra, contouring along the east side of San Mateo Canyon until you reach Manuel Spring, N35°16'52", W107°35'34", also a reliable water source. Just north of Manuel Spring, you reach the junction of Forest Road 451, which you would follow downhill 0.4 mile to join Forest Road 239.

From the Forest Road 451-239 junction, Forest Road 239 descends north for 5 long, dry, monotonous miles to its junction with Forest Road 456. Forest Road 239 here turns sharp southeast, descends to cross the grassy valley of Colorado Canyon, then ascends to the junction with Forest Road 453, which heads south. Forest Road 239 continues east, descending into American Canyon, a pleasant place but with no reliable water, though you might find some in wet seasons. Forest Road 239 continues east for a mile to another branch of American Canyon, where the Forest Service-designated CDT route joins it.

From the American Canyon head, Forest Road 239 heads generally northeast, crossing Antelope Flats, curving around a small mountain, then arriving at San Miguel Canyon after 1.9 miles. From San Miguel Canyon, elevation 8,100 feet, Forest Road 239 begins a gradual ascent through broken, semi-open country to arrive after 5.2 miles at Ranger Tank, N35°25'01", W107°29'19", elevation 8,460 feet, at the junction of Forest Road 198 and Forest Road 202. You will likely find water here, though cattle may have made it unappealing. You'll find somewhat better water 3.8 miles farther as Forest Road 239 now begins a gradual descent to arrive at Ojo del Dado, N35°26'52", W107°26'25", elevation 8,250 feet. The spring is on the north side of the road, in a little box canyon just beneath some rock ledges. It too is used by cattle. The name Ojo del Dado, "spring of the die" (as in dice), is said to take its name from the El Dado Stage Stop, where a station keeper, legend has it, proposed that passengers shake dice for drinks. Local lore says the dice were loaded.

From Ojo del Dado, your next reliable water is Ojo de los Indios, about 7 miles away. Forest Road 239 heads east 0.4 mile to a junction where Forest Road 239 splits, with Forest Road 239A, the CDT route, turning north-northeast, passing between two volcanic hills and beginning a long gradual descent through meadow and forest for about 5 miles, then descending more steeply through forest before entering meadows again and swinging north. In a little more than 0.5 mile, just before crossing a small drainage, at N35°31'19", W107°22'59", look for a post. Here an unmarked but clear two-track heads northwest and after 0.3 mile overlooks Los Indios Canyon. Increasingly rough switchbacks snake down the canyon wall. At the bottom, follow the drainage upstream about 0.1 mile to two concrete tanks, at least one of which is fed by a flowing pipe. Ojo de los Indios, "spring of the Indians," is a very reliable water source, with water conspicuously more desirable than most sources along the route.

OTHER HIKES AND RIDES: GOOSEBERRY SPRING TRAIL TO MT. TAYLOR SUMMIT

APPROXIMATE ONE-WAY DISTANCE: 3.2 miles
MODE OF TRAVEL: Hiking and biking
DIFFICULTY: Moderate to strenuous/technical for biking

Lobo Canyon Road Trailhead: The Gooseberry Spring Trail, No. 77, to the top of Mount Taylor is one of New Mexico's classic day hikes, and deservedly so. The trailhead is reached from Grants by taking paved NM 547, also known as the Lobo Canyon Road, approximately 12 miles from Grants. Where NM 547 ends and dirt Forest Road 239 continues, graded dirt Forest Road 193 heads southeast until at 5.1 miles it reaches an unmarked parking area on the right. From here the Gooseberry Spring Trail heads east through aspens and conifers. Gooseberry Spring is reached after about 0.5 mile; it's not marked, and you'll have to leave the trail briefly and head uphill to your left to find it, but it's a pleasant spot; a fence surrounds the spring (see page 234 for location).

From here the trail begins ascending through conifers, but it soon leaves the forest to climb gradually but steadily through a grassy meadow, where overlooking a valley it swings north. You'll have spectacular views from here to the summit; look for elk in the valleys and meadows as you hike. The trail continues through open high-elevation grassland, with switchbacks avoiding steep gradients, until at about 3 miles from the trailhead, and at an elevation of 11,301 feet, you're at the summit. Breathtaking!

OTHER HIKES AND RIDES: FOREST ROAD 193 TO NM 547

APPROXIMATE ONE-WAY DISTANCE: 21 miles
MODE OF TRAVEL: Biking
DIFFICULTY: Moderate to strenuous

Forest Road 193 at NM 547: An appealing loop ride coinciding with the CDT uses Forest Road 193. This graded dirt road heads east from paved NM 547 about 7 miles from Grants. Forest Road 193 winds up past a picnic area as it ascends the volcanic plateau, passing through pleasant ponderosa pine forest. After about 11 miles of steady gradual climbing, you reach the junction with Forest Road 501; Forest Road 193 turns north and after less than 0.25 mile you reach the parking area and head of the Gooseberry Spring Trail, the most scenic route to Mount Taylor's summit. Gooseberry Spring is about 0.5 mile from the parking area just off the trail. From here Forest Road 193 is more level and rolling as it heads northwest 5.1 miles to join Forest Road 239. From here it's 4 miles mostly downhill on paved NM 547 to complete the loop.

OTHER HIKES AND RIDES: MOUNT TAYLOR WINTER QUADRATHLON

APPROXIMATE ONE-WAY DISTANCE: 22 miles
MODE OF TRAVEL: Biking, running, snowshoeing, cross-country skiing
DIFFICULTY: Strenuous

Each February, endurance athletes from throughout the West and Southwest assemble in Grants to compete in a unique event: a 44-mile, 6,500-foot-elevation-gain round-trip to the 11,301-foot summit of Mount Taylor and back, traveling first by bicycle, then running, then cross-country skiing, and finally snowshoeing. Some athletes do it as members of two- and four-person teams, but many do it solo, an achievement carrying the cachet of true endurance. Contact the Grants/Cibola Chamber of Commerce for details, Segment 20, page 212.

HISTORICAL NOTES

Piñon nuts: food of the gods. The piñon-juniper association is the most widespread forest type in New Mexico—for which countless generations have been grateful. That's because the piñon pine, *Pinus edulis,* produces in its cones nuts high in energy and nutrition, and delicious. They've been a staple of Native American diets for millennia; they provided sustenance to Hispanic settlers, and now they're sold as a delicacy to tourists.

Some years are better than others for piñon harvest, and no one has figured out quite why. Even in good years, some areas produce nuts and others don't. Finally, often you crack a nut only to find a dry husk inside. Still, the nuts are common enough that it's worth checking some trees in October. The nuts, nestled among the cone's scales, are small and brown. Crack them open to reveal the creamy white meat inside. Piñon nuts generally are roasted before the meat is extracted, but even raw they're delicious. You'll spend a lot of time to obtain just a few nuts, and you'll get your hands smeared with pine sap. But there are worse ways to spend an evening in the outdoors.

Note: To avoid the remote danger of rodent-borne disease, harvest from cones on the tree rather than on the ground.

HISTORICAL NOTES

Mount Taylor. All the Native American peoples living within Mount Taylor's compass consider the mountain sacred. From their ancient mesa-top pueblo called Sky City, the residents of Acoma Pueblo look north toward the huge cone and tell tourists of when almost 400 years ago their men carried huge ponderosa pine logs from the mountain's slopes to make beams that still support the seventeenth-century mission church; the men slept beneath the logs' weight lest the logs touch the ground and be profaned. Acoma tribal elders tell children the mountain is the Rainmaker of the North.

At Zuni Pueblo far to the southwest of Mount Taylor, the tribe's lore masters speak of the Lightning Hole, a pit still extant on the mountain's summit. Should the hole become blocked, they believe, drought will ensue. Zunis once made summer pilgrimages to the summit to keep it open.

Viewing Mount Taylor from the west and northwest, Navajos explain one of its ceremonial names, Turquoise Mountain, by telling how the peak was fastened from the sky to the earth with a great flint knife decorated with turquoise. They tell of the mountain's being the home of Turquoise Boy and Yellow Corn Girl. Of the Navajos' four sacred mountains, Mount Taylor is the Mountain of the South.

Early Spanish-speaking explorers and settlers called the mountain *Cebolleta,* "little onion," for the little wild onions (genus *Allium*), a name still used in Hispanic villages around the mountain. Their oral history recalls battles with Navajos at places like Seboyeta, on Mount Taylor's south side.

The name Mount Taylor was given in September 1849 by Lt. James H. Simpson, a member of Lt. Col. John Washington's military expedition into Navajo country. Simpson called it "one of the finest mountain peaks I have seen in this country," and in his journal he wrote: "This peak I have, in honor of the President of the United States, called Mount Taylor. Erecting itself high above the plain below, an object of vision at a remote distance, standing within the domain which has been so recently the theater of his sagacity and prowess, it exists, not inappropriately, an ever-enduring monument to his patriotism and integrity."

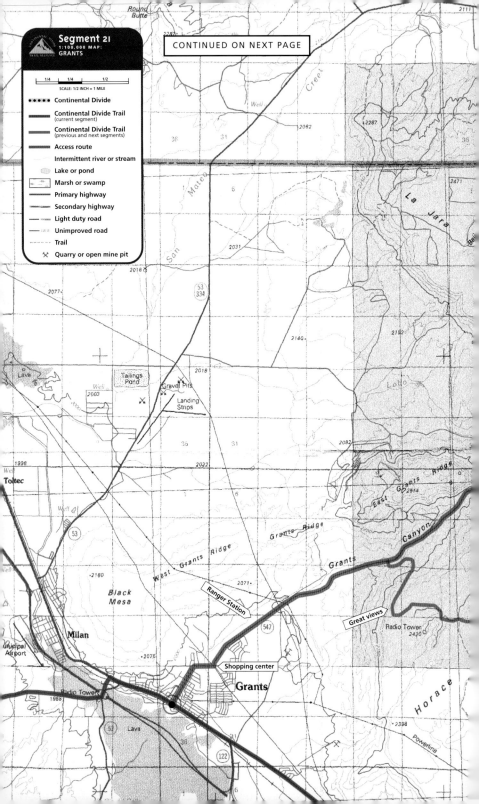

CONTINUED ON NEXT PAGE

Segment 21
1:100,000 MAP:
GRANTS

SCALE: 1/2 INCH = 1 MILE

| | 1/4 | 1/4 | 1/2 |

●●●●● **Continental Divide**

━━━ **Continental Divide Trail** (current segment)

━━━ **Continental Divide Trail** (previous and next segments)

━━━ **Access route**

Intermittent river or stream

Lake or pond

Marsh or swamp

Primary highway

Secondary highway

Light duty road

Unimproved road

Trail

✕ **Quarry or open mine pit**

Round Butte

Creek

2082

2287

2111

La Jara

2471

San Mateo

6

2031

2016

2077

53
334

2140

2152

Lava

Well
2003

Tailings Pond

Gravel Pits

2018

Landing Strips

36

31

2082

Lobo

Grants Ridge

2514

East Grants Ridge

Canyon

1996

2022

Toltec

Well

53

2180

Black Mesa

West Grants Ridge

Grants Ridge

2071

Ranger Station

Grants

Great views

Radio Tower
2420

Milan

Municipal Airport

2075

Radio Tower

1988

Shopping center

Grants

53

Lava

36

Horace

2398

122

Powerline

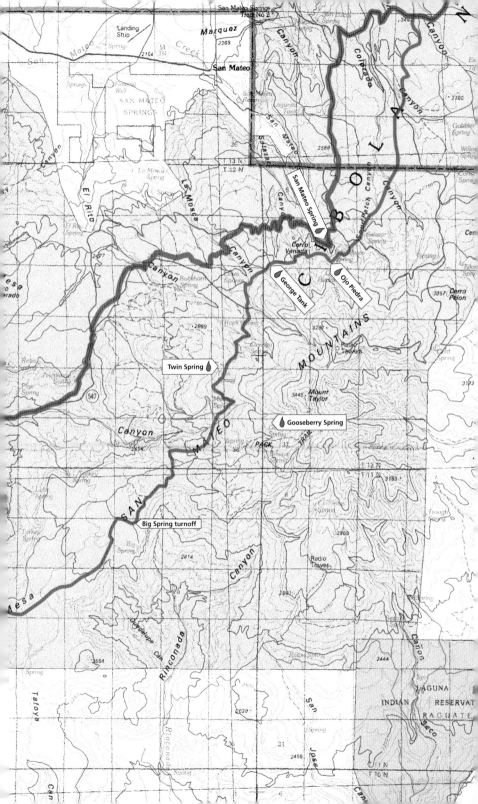

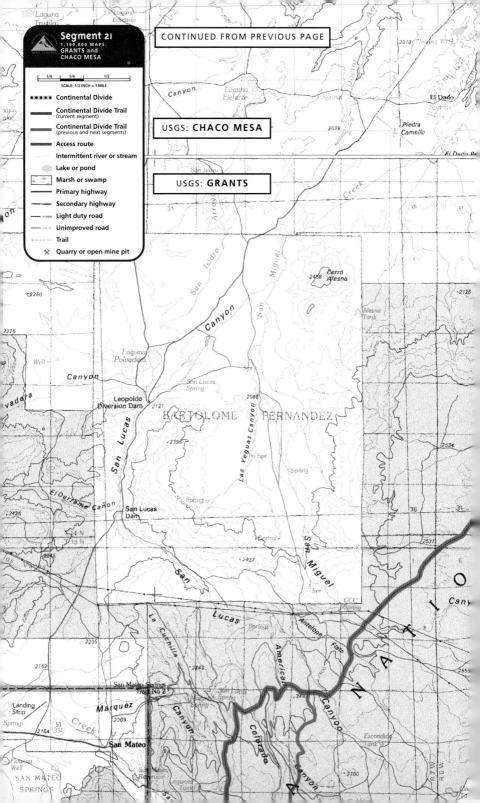

Segment 21
1:100,000 MAPS:
GRANTS and
CHACO MESA

| 1/4 | 1/4 | 1/2 |

SCALE: 1/2 INCH = 1 MILE

•••••• Continental Divide

▬▬▬▬ Continental Divide Trail
(current segment)

▬▬▬▬ Continental Divide Trail
(previous and next segments)

▬▬▬▬ Access route

Intermittent river or stream

Lake or pond

Marsh or swamp

Primary highway

Secondary highway

Light duty road

Unimproved road

Trail

✕ Quarry or open mine pit

USGS: **CHACO MESA**

USGS: **GRANTS**

El Dado

Piedra
Camello

El Dado

Laguna
Elefante

Canyon

Spring

2028

Flowing Well 2018

Doctor Arroyo

2125

Creek

Cerro
Alesna 2458

Alesna
Tank

2250

2225

Laguna
Polvadera

Well

Canyon

San Isidro

Canyon

San Miguel

31

38

San Lucas
Spring

BARTOLOME FERNANDEZ

Leopoldo
Diversion Dam

2121

2088

2534

2396

Las Veguas Canyon

Spring

2426

El Derrame Canon

San Lucas Dam

San Lucas

Spring

Spring

Spring

San Miguel

2531

14 N
13 N

2205

San Lucas

La Cuchilla

Lucas

Springs

Antelope Flats

CCC
Spring

6

Canyon

NATIO

Cany

2437

Spr

2205

2162

American Canyon

2443

2559

San Mateo Springs
Trail No 2

San Lucas
Spring

2493

Escondida
Tank

Marquez

2209

Creek

53
334

Colorado Canyon

2700

Landing
Strip

Springs

2164

San Mateo

San Mateo Reservoir

Laguna
Tank

R 7 W
R 6 W

SAN MATEO
SPRINGS

Flowing
Well

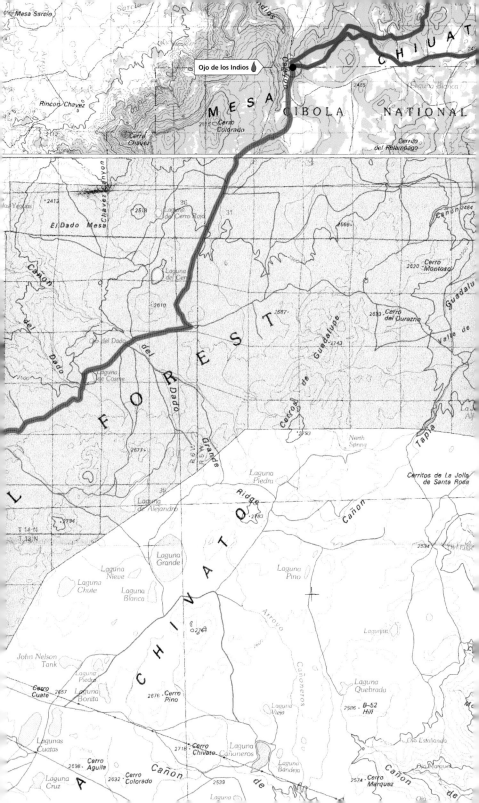

Segment 22
BLM 1103 (FR 239A) to Mesa Chivato
Escarpment: Ignacio Chavez

Tower kiva at Kin Ya'a, Chaco Culture National Historical Park. Photo by Tom Till.

8.9 miles
Difficulty: Easy
You may encounter: motorized vehicles

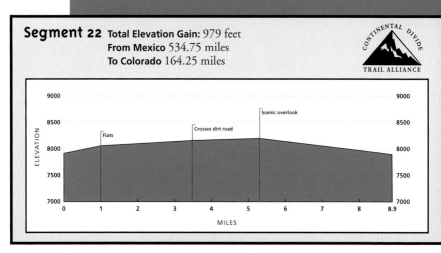

Segment 22 Total Elevation Gain: 979 feet
From Mexico 534.75 miles
To Colorado 164.25 miles

CONTINENTAL DIVIDE TRAIL ALLIANCE

TRAIL OVERVIEW This vast, sprawling mass of volcanic upland is known to local land managers as "The IC." This stands for Ignacio Chavez, recipient of a land grant made in 1768 by the Spanish government to encourage communities in this area. The attempt failed. Even the hardy Hispanic settlers mustered no enthusiasm for the harsh environment atop the volcanic plateau known as Mesa Chivato ("kid goat"). At an elevation of around 8,000 feet, with thin soil studded with lava cobbles and boulders, snowbound in the winter and parsimonious in the summer, the plateau was a great place to cut firewood, to gather piñon nuts, to hunt elk, but not to establish a village and practice subsistence agriculture. Besides, the region was frequented by Navajos, whose raids were the curse of such isolated Hispanic settlements.

In the nineteenth century, a stage route went through here, connecting Santa Fe with Fort Wingate; however, no settlements resulted, and nothing remains but a few place names such as Ojo del Dado (see page 236).

Today, the IC is scarcely less remote than it was in 1768. Except during hunting season, few people come here. The Bureau of Land Management, which acquired the former land grant in 1937, has designated the area the 33,264-acre Ignacio Chavez Wilderness Study Area; and the area does indeed richly deserve wilderness protection. A vast forest of piñon and ponderosa pines, oaks, and scattered Douglas firs caps the plateau; expansive grassy meadows provide valuable winter forage for elk. The area is especially rich in birds—warblers, chickadees, juncos, swallows, nuthatches, flycatchers, and woodpeckers, as well as such raptors as kestrels, sharp-shinned hawks, red-tailed hawks, turkey vultures, and golden eagles.

The lava flows from Mount Taylor that created the plateau resulted in a landscape generally lacking in relief features, though a few deep canyons penetrate the uplands. The volcanic geology also meant that most precipitation would be readily absorbed and surface water would be rare.

The hiking here is easy, sometimes almost monotonously so, as the route simply follows or parallels the main dirt road through the area. Forest Road 239 becomes Forest Road 239A, which at the Forest Service–BLM boundary becomes BLM Road 1103. It's all the same main road, despite the changes in numbering. Still, you should pay attention at junctions and the road does become progressively rougher as it approaches the mesa's eastern escarpment.

For hikers weary of the road, the New Mexico Mountain Club, in cooperation with the BLM, has created an off-road route, marked with cairns and signs, which roughly parallels the road. This recently designated route has the advantages of being slightly more direct and affording better access to scenic viewpoints along the northern escarpment. Water is scarce along both the road and trail, through a few springs and stock tanks exist.

The BLM, however, accepted a proposal from Charlie McDonald of the New Mexico Mountain Club to create a route here that would take the CDT off the road, and, after much work by volunteers, that route has been brushed and marked. This guide describes both the road and off-road routes.

The vast, generally featureless character of this segment, along with its remoteness, makes it an unlikely destination for day-hikers.

WATER NOTES

Water obtained from either Ojo de los Indios at one end or Ojo Frio at the other should get you through this short segment. In between and near the route are several fairly reliable stock tanks.

MOUNTAIN BIKE NOTES

The area is slightly more appealing to mountain-bikers because of the extensive network of Forest Roads here, though persons with support vehicles should be aware that BLM 1103 is gated and closed for much of the year. As of this writing, the gate is open from April 1 to June 30 and September 16 to November 14; you should call the BLM/Albuquerque Field Office, (505) 761-8700, for the gate's current status.

EQUESTRIAN NOTES

Sprawling grassy meadows, gently rolling terrain, sparse but adequate water, and ponderosa pine forests, along with occasional corrals, make Mesa Chivato well-suited for horse travel. Indeed, Back Country Horsemen of New Mexico–Northwest Chapter has adopted this segment. In air miles, this segment isn't far from Albuquerque, but the travel time is much more than the map would suggest.

SOUTHBOUND HIKERS

Ojo de los Indios near this segment's southern end is an outstanding water source. Your next likely water source heading south is 7 miles away, at Ojo del Dado.

MAPS

USGS QUADRANGLES: Mesa Cortada, Cerro Parido
OTHER MAPS: Cibola National Forest–Mount Taylor Ranger District,
  BLM 1:100K Chaco Mesa

LAND-MANAGEMENT AGENCIES

BLM/Albuquerque Field Office

BEGINNING ACCESS POINT

BLM 1103 (FOREST ROAD 239A): This is the continuation of the main road through this region. It began in Grants with paved NM 547, which later became dirt Forest Road 239, then Forest Road 239A, which becomes BLM 1103.

ENDING ACCESS POINT

MESA CHIVATO ESCARPMENT: See Beginning Access Point in Segment 23, page 255.

SUPPLIES, SERVICES, AND ACCOMMODATIONS

GRANTS, described in Segment 20, page 212, is the only source of supplies and services.

TRAIL DESCRIPTION: (CDT) Begin this segment by topping off your water bottles at Ojo de los Indios, an excellent water source, well worth the half-mile hike to it. For those using the road, your next water is Ned Tank (yecch!), 9 miles away, and Ojo Frio is 11.2 miles.

From the track leading to Ojo de los Indios, Forest Road 239A heads due north. After 0.25 mile, at the Cibola National Forest boundary, Forest Road 239A (now BLM 1103) turns abruptly east, but the CDT heads north another 0.1 mile through the El Banquito Road gate. Here the CDT heads generally northeast.

It parallels BLM 1103 for 1.9 miles until it returns to the road at the head of Azabache Canyon. From this point, the CDT trends eastward; after descending a short slope, it passes just south of Heifer Tank, although Ojo de los Indios (2.5 miles away) would be a preferable water source. The CDT here follows a ranch road for a short way as it passes across the head of Azabache Canyon. After climbing out of Azabache Canyon onto a forested flat, the trail follows an abandoned ranch road to the rim of the northern escarpment of Mesa Chivato 5.25 miles from the National Forest boundary. You'll want to pause here to enjoy the views that are truly spectacular. From the rim, you can follow the ranch road south 0.8 mile to Seco Tank, a potential emergency water source that despite its name—*seco* means "dry"—usually has some water. Another emergency source is Toruno Spring, N35°33'56", W107°18'48", down on the escarpment, a very steep 1,200-foot round-trip.

This CDT segment continues paralleling the rim as the route heads east, then northeast through flat meadows and short sections of forest to end at the mesa's eastern escarpment, 8.9 miles from the segment's beginning, at N35°34'31", W107°15'48", 7,900 feet. The route here has been brushed and marked. There's no water here, but 1.5 miles south is Ned Tank, a pleasant campsite, even if the water must be heavily treated.

About half a mile before the escarpment, a spur trail branches north to lead after 0.8 mile to the cliffs just south of Bear Mouth. It's an easy and interesting side trip.

TRAIL DESCRIPTION: (BLM 1103) From the Ojo de los Indios turnoff, BLM 1103, a continuation of Forest Road 239A, heads gently downhill 0.25 mile to a junction. The road here turns abruptly east, paralleling the National Forest boundary as it heads uphill. From here, the CDT is on BLM land. This land, the former Ignacio Chavez Land Grant, now includes the BLM Ignacio Chavez Special Management Area, within which are the BLM Ignacio Chavez and Chamisa WSAs. Except during hunting season, few people come here, and the area deserves wilderness status. From Ojo de los Indios, it's approximately 9 miles to your next water source, Ned Tank. You'll walk through gentle country, a collage of open grasslands and piñon-juniper, ponderosa pine, and Gambel oak forest. Campsites are abundant, though water is not.

After about 4.4 miles from the National Forest boundary, you'll reach a conspicuous junction in an open meadow, but Forest Road 239A, now BLM 1103, continues as the main road as it swings northeast and then east to reach Ned Tank, N35°33'25", W107°15'35".

Ned Tank is a stock pond in a meadow just south of the road. It usually contains water, but cows trample its banks and almost certainly have polluted the water; you might find cleaner pools nearby. If Ned Tank disappoints you, you could search for Barrel Spring, approximately 1.5 miles farther along the road. A sign on the road marks the nearby spring, but no trail leads to it, and most people (including me) who have searched for it have failed to find it; the map shows its coordinates to be N35°34'17", W107°15'03". A surer and cleaner source of water is Ojo Frio, about 4.25 miles away down the road, near Hunters Camp at the bottom of the trail leading down the escarpment, described in the next segment.

Ned Tank is a pleasant place to camp, beside the meadow and beneath ponderosa pines. From this point, the road plunges off the escarpment into the valley of the Rio Puerco, and the character of the CDT changes dramatically.

OTHER HIKES AND RIDES: BEAR MOUTH OVERLOOK

APPROXIMATE ONE-WAY DISTANCE: 2 miles
MODE OF TRAVEL: Hiking
DIFFICULTY: Easy

Ned Tank atop Mesa Chivato: From where BLM 1103 reaches the eastern rim of Mesa Chivato, just north of Ned Tank, it's an easy walk cross-country or along two-tracks to a point, N35°34'57", W107°15'54", overlooking the dramatic formation called Bear Mouth. From where this CDT segment ends at the mesa's rim, it's 0.5 mile north along the rim to the overlook.

SCALE: 7/8 INCH = 1 MILE

7/16   7/16

Continental Divide
Continental Divide Trail
(current segment)
Continental Divide Trail
(previous and next segments)
Access route
River or stream
Lake or pond
Marsh or swamp
Primary highway
Secondary highway
Light duty road
Unimproved road
Trail
Quarry or open mine pit

Bear Mouth overlook

Ned Tank

Seco Tank

Scenic overlook

MC KINLEY CO
SANDOVAL CO

CHIUATO

BLM 1103

Ojo de los Indios

NATIONAL FOREST

MESA

Segment 23
Mesa Chivato Escarpment to Cuba: Rio Puerco Valley

Cabezon Peak, flowing wash, and storm clouds at sunset, Rio Puerco area. Photo by William Stone.

46.1 miles
Difficulty: Strenuous
You may encounter: motorized vehicles

TRAIL OVERVIEW The Rio Puerco defines this segment, and though the Continental Divide Trail here doesn't cross or follow the Puerco, the river's numerous tributaries have shaped the complex topography in this vast drainage basin. The term "river" is used in the New Mexico sense and should not be confused with what most people think of as a river. For most of the year, the Rio Puerco is a shallow, meandering stream that carries more silt than water (*puerco* means "muddy"). The river is noted primarily for the deep, destructive arroyos it has cut; geologists blame this on overgrazing and a period of unfortunately timed torrents. Despite all this, the Rio Puerco is among the major drainages in north-central New Mexico, and this region, now all but abandoned by humans, once was a populated agricultural area. The diffuse village of San Luis has survived, but the villages of Guadalupe and Casa Salazar are abandoned, though the people who once lived here still call the villages home and maintain their houses. Most of the land here is administered by the Bureau of Land Management, including several BLM Wilderness Study Areas, but the area also has numerous private inholdings, and the BLM urges visitors to respect locked gates and private property. Ranching continues throughout the area. Local people tend to be suspicious of outsiders, and it's worth the time to introduce yourself and establish friendly relations.

Most casual New Mexico hikers are ignorant of the Rio Puerco Valley; it certainly has received none of the publicity of, say, the Pecos or the Jemez regions; no guidebooks exist to it; there are no designated trails (except for the CDT) or trailheads; and the roads are dirt, some very rough. Long-term New Mexico hikers, however, recognize the Puerco country as an outstanding area for hiking and exploration, one that never fails to surprise and delight. For this reason, the New Mexico Mountain Club has adopted this CDT segment and has been responsible for laying out and marking the route.

The Rio Puerco Valley is very interesting geologically—and starkly dramatic: high, cliff-bound mesas and *cuestas* with polychrome sandstone cliffs, as well as dark basaltic volcanic plugs looking like tree stumps from an age of giants. Cabezon Peak ("big head"), rising 2,160 feet above the surrounding terrain, is the most conspicuous. Cabezon Peak, however, is but one of at least 50 such necks around Mount Taylor, most in the Rio Puerco Valley. They have names such as Cerro Cuate ("twin"), Cerro de Guadalupe, and Cerro de Santa Clara. The CDT, as it descends from Mesa Chivato heading north, offers spectacular views of the volcanic necks in the valley below. Once in the valley, the CDT passes just to the west and north of Cerro Cuate, one of the largest and most dramatic volcanic necks.

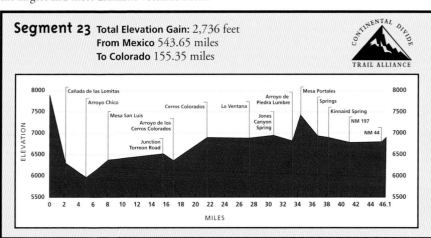

Segment 23 Total Elevation Gain: 2,736 feet
From Mexico 543.65 miles
To Colorado 155.35 miles

CONTINENTAL DIVIDE
TRAIL ALLIANCE

The CDT here is along a route laid out by the New Mexico Mountain Club, led by member Charlie McDonald, in cooperation with the BLM and work parties organized through the Mountain Club and the Continental Divide Trail Alliance. This segment, when joined with the preceding two segments, Mount Taylor (Segment 21) and Ignacio Chavez (Segment 22), rivals the Black Range as being the state's longest section with no community nearby, not even a tiny one. Pie Town would seem downright metropolitan.

The route in the south is mostly cross-country, though the open terrain makes for relatively easy hiking. The route is marked with cairns or other trail markers. The New Mexico Mountain Club route ranks among the CDT's most scenic and interesting segments.

In the north, the BLM has selected an interim route on dirt roads until surveys can determine an off-road route that will avoid fragile archaeological sites. But even hiking along the road you'll likely find artifacts from earlier settlements, from prehistoric times to the homesteader era. Admire these relics—then leave them. Present-day Native Americans have earned the respect of archaeologists because though the Native Americans—Navajos and Puebloans—use this area, they don't disturb the remains of those who have gone before. CDT hikers should strive to earn the same respect.

Vegetation here is sparse, mostly piñon-juniper, scrub oak, sagebrush, and high-desert grassland, with occasional ponderosa pine stands. But whether following cairns, walking roads, or hiking cross-country, you should be well-equipped with map, compass, and a Global Positioning System unit, if you have one, as the topography can be complex and confusing.

Water is scarce here. And when scanning the map for sources, ignore the myriad blue lines; they signify intermittent water courses that rarely see flowing water. Most water here comes from springs, BLM well heads, or stock tanks. But if you accept that all these sources must be treated—cattle graze throughout the area—you should be able to find water at reasonable intervals.

After all, prehistoric Indians were able to survive here. The Indians who lived here were Ancestral Puebloans, relatives of the people who created the great civilization at Chaco Canyon and elsewhere on the Colorado Plateau around A.D. 900–1350. Why they abandoned the area is still debated, but the likelihood is great that descendants of the Rio Puerco Valley people now are living at the pueblos of Zia and Santa Ana and perhaps Jemez. They left behind numerous artifacts—ruined dwellings, pottery shards, flint scatters, and rock art. Examine the artifacts you'll likely encounter, wonder at them—and then leave them.

The Puebloans were succeeded by Navajos, who arrived around 1600 and whose ruined dwellings still are found in the area. With Spanish colonization, several large land grants were made, and Hispanic homesteaders moved into the area, where their abandoned dwellings also remain.

Today the Rio Puerco Valley is all but uninhabited. Ranching and oil and gas operations take place here, but for the most part the land is open and wild, so much so that no fewer than five WSAs are here: Cabezon Peak, Ignacio Chavez, Empedrado,

Chamisa, and La Leña. The New Mexico Wilderness Alliance has proposed a wilderness that comprises 82,347 acres.

DAY HIKES **CDT: Rio Puerco Valley.** Only a few people regard the Rio Puerco Valley as a hiking destination, yet hikers who do come here say it offers some of the finest hiking in central New Mexico. This includes stretches of the CDT.

Among the most scenic and easily accessible of these stretches is reached by driving NM 44/US 550 northwest from San Ysidro approximately 18 miles to a green sign pointing to San Luiz (should be San Luis). Here the paved Torreon Road heads west, then southwest, then northwest at 10.4 miles. After 4 miles on the Torreon Road, at the top of a hill, the pavement ends at a cattle guard. Follow the main dirt road 0.6 mile northwest to a junction where a sign points toward Highway 197, Torreon Wash, La Ventana, and the Piedra Lumbre Road. Park near here, walk the dirt road downhill southeast 0.15 mile to a large CDT cairn on your right. Across the small valley is a gravel operation. *Note:* Plans exist to pave the dirt road all the way to Torreon, which would change the configuration of this junction.

From here, the CDT cairns head west, up onto a bench along the San Luis Mesa's south rim. The trail remains near the rim, affording spectacular views of Cabezon Peak and the other volcanic necks of the Rio Puerco Valley. The hiking is easy and interesting. After about 2.5 miles you descend a long-abandoned road down to the plain, but the hiking is no less interesting as you keep near the mesa's base, passing hoodoos, weathered sandstone formations, petrified wood scatters, and more. After about 2 miles, you come to the dirt road in La Cañada Santiago. Spotting a car would make an outstanding shuttle hike; to reach this, drive about 4.5 miles north on the sometimes rough dirt La Cañada Santiago Road, looking for cairns marking the CDT route. The coordinates of the intersection are N35°40'53", W107°10'30".

Cabezon Peak. Most hikers in the Rio Puerco Valley come to climb the huge volcanic plug called Cabezon Peak. To reach it, drive 19 miles northwest from the village of San Ysidro on NM 44/US 550—you'll see Cabezon Peak to the west—to a sign indicating San Luis is west via a paved County Road. The pavement ends at 10.4 miles. Twelve miles from NM 44/US 550, when you're north of the peak, you reach a road fork marked with a post reading BLM 1114. Take the left (south) fork in the road, cross a bridge, then continue until a rough dirt road—consider walking this—heads east 1 mile to the peak. From here a crude, unmarked trail heads south then southeast to the summit route. Still unmarked, this ascends a steep talus slope, climbs a chute onto a ledge, then scrambles over rocks, eventually to reach the summit. No technical climbing is required, but beware of loose rock and test holds. Don't hike when snow and ice are present, and look for indications that you're on the standard route; don't climb anything you can't climb down. Avoid this area if thunderstorms threaten.

WATER NOTES

Water is scarce along this route, especially as the interim BLM route along dirt roads in the north bypasses important springs. Careful planning, however, will allow access to other springs and wells, some installed by the BLM. Also, numerous stock ponds of varying reliability are along the route. Still, the area is exposed and often hot, and some thru-hikers have experienced dehydration here.

MOUNTAIN BIKE NOTES

 The Rio Puerco Valley offers exciting possibilities for mountain biking. Even the paved 10.4-mile stretch from NM 44/US 550 through the village of San Luis is very lightly traveled, and beyond this is a maze of dirt roads and two-tracks used only by ranchers and the occasional BLM employee. There are not really any trails here; the CDT route is too new to have tread yet.

One challenging but appealing ride goes around Cabezon Peak, the dominant landmark in the Rio Puerco Valley. To reach this, drive on NM 44/US 550 northwest from Bernalillo, through the village of San Ysidro. At approximately 19 miles on NM 44/US 550 from San Ysidro, a paved road branches left to San Luis (the green sign reads, incorrectly, San Luiz). Follow the pavement 10.4 miles through San Luis to where the pavement ends. Continue southwest on the main road, now dirt, another 2.6 miles to where the road forks, at a post marked BLM 1114. Park here and begin riding the left fork. Almost immediately, you'll descend to cross the Rio Puerco on a bridge, then climb to ride south. You'll pass several junctions, but keep veering left. After more than 7 miles, you'll pass a corral on your left, and less than a mile later you'll begin heading east, to join BLM Road 1113, the Ridge Road. You'll follow this northwest, back to where you started, having circled Cabezon Peak.

EQUESTRIAN NOTES

This is great horse country; just ask the members of the Back Country Horsemen of New Mexico–Northwest Chapter, who have spent many hours working on the CDT here. The complex of dirt roads and cross-country routes offers a myriad of multi-length possibilities.

SOUTHBOUND HIKERS

 Do not underestimate the length and remoteness of the segments ahead. Together, the Rio Puerco, Mesa Chivato, and Mount Taylor segments total 85 miles, and only the very beginning and end are on paved road. Cuba is the last town you'll visit for 85 miles, so consider arranging for food caches along the route.

MAPS

USGS QUADRANGLES: Cerro Parido, Cabezon Peak, Guadalupe, Arroyo Empedrado, San Luis, Headcut Reservoir, Mesa Portales, San Pablo, Cuba
OTHER MAPS: BLM 1:100K Chaco Mesa, Los Alamos

LAND-MANAGEMENT AGENCIES

BLM/Albuquerque Field Office

BEGINNING ACCESS POINT

MESA CHIVATO ESCARPMENT: The only practical access to the segment's south end is from NM 44/US 550. From there, a paved road leads through the diffuse community of San Luis. The Torreon Road heads northwest at 10.4 miles, where the main graded gravel-dirt road continues west. At 6 miles from the pavement's end, the road is due north of Cerro Cuate, a huge, stark volcanic formation. Soon the road heads south and descends into the deep valley, crossing Arroyo Chico at 10 miles from the pavement. The graded road then climbs somewhat steeply to reach Hunters Camp after 2 miles. From here the dirt road, now rougher, climbs the obvious escarpment to the west, arriving at the top about 3.3 miles from Hunters Camp. From the escarpment's top, going cross-country about a mile over relatively level ground will bring you to the east-west CDT.

ALTERNATE ACCESS

DIRT ROAD: Ten miles south of Cuba, a well-traveled dirt road crosses the Rio Puerco via a bridge, then heads west to provide access to the roads and features around La Ventana Mesa.

ENDING ACCESS POINT

CUBA: This important supply point on the CDT is accessible via NM 44/US 550, the major highway through northwestern New Mexico.

SUPPLIES, SERVICES, AND ACCOMMODATIONS

CUBA is the nearest community where supplies, services, and accommodations are available. See Segment 24, page 267.

WILDERNESS ALERT

The routes here variously pass through the West Malpais Wilderness, the Cebolla Wilderness, the Chain of Craters BLM Wilderness Study Area, and El Malpais National Monument, most of which is wilderness. Please observe these wilderness guidelines: **1.** Camp out of sight, at least 200 feet from springs and drainages, on a dry, durable surface. **2.** Use a stove instead of building a fire; use existing fire rings if you do build a fire. **3.** Keep water sources pure by camping at least 200 feet from them. **4.** Bury human wastes 6 inches deep and at least 200 feet from water sources; pack out toilet paper. **5.** Dogs must be on a leash. **6.** No mountain biking. **7.** Pack out all trash; don't attempt to burn it.

TRAIL DESCRIPTION A steep 1,700-foot plunge down the eastern escarpment of Mesa Chivato begins this segment. The trailhead is at N35°34'31", W107°15'48", 7,900 feet, 1.2 miles north of Ned Tank, the only likely water source near the rim. Ned Tank is a low spot in a meadow where water collects; it's fairly reliable but definitely polluted by the cattle that muddy its banks and foul its water. Unless you really need water, you'd do better to wait for Ojo Frio on the CDT, near Hunters Camp. To reach the trailhead from Ned Tank, follow a faint cattle path north from where the road tops out; this path is unmarked except for a cairn near its beginning.

 SOUTHBOUND HIKERS: Before beginning the segments atop Mesa Chivato, top off your water bottles at either Ojo Frio or Ned Tank. From the mesa's edge, the next water to the south is Ojo de los Indios, about 9 miles away.

Charlie McDonald selected this route because it's direct; the basalt cliffs allow but a few access points. The route also is steep, rough, and rocky, with relief of 1,600 feet in about 2 miles, though the views of the Rio Puerco Valley are spectacular. By the time this book is published, the trail likely will be fully marked with cairns, which as of this writing mark only the trail's lower and middle portions. The CDT follows what likely was a route used to drive livestock up and down; an old brush fence is near the top, and remnants of a cattle trail can still be seen on the benches. Now elk are the route's main users.

SOUTHBOUND HIKERS: In planning your day's hiking here, be mindful that climbing the escarpment will be much more demanding of time and energy than might appear. For those who prefer easier hiking, the dirt road from Hunters Camp to Ned Tank is a convenient alternative.

From the mesa top, the trail plunges abruptly through volcanic scree and boulders, between ponderosa pines and piñon-juniper. In less than 0.5 mile it reaches the first of several benches, at about N35°34'31", W107°15'22". The route then descends steeply again, following a ridge downhill. It climbs over a fence at Section 27, then continues downhill as the ridge becomes gentler, more rounded. After about 2 miles from the top, it leaves the ridge to cross the dry (usually) streambed of Cañada de las Lomitas (Canyon of the Little Hills) at N35°35'16", W107°14'09". Here the CDT continues heading northeast, marked by cairns, though these might be difficult to see in the tall grass. After 0.6 mile, the CDT, marked by large cairns, intersects a wide, graded dirt road. This road marks the boundary between the BLM's Ignacio Chavez WSA, which you've been in since the National Forest atop the mesa, and the BLM Empedrado WSA.

Cairns parallel the road as it heads north. Just 100 yards from where the trail meets the road is the turnoff to Ojo Frio, marked by a sign. The spring is 0.25 mile away. A circular tank collects the water, which is indeed cold, as the name suggests, and, according to Charlie McDonald, "excellent tasting." From the spring, a trail follows the faint remains of a road south-southeast uphill about 0.5 mile to Hunters Camp beside the road. No facilities are here.

From Ojo Frio, the CDT runs north 0.75 mile, on the northwest side of Cerro del Ojo Frio. It crosses again Cañada de las Lomitas, one of many dry washes the CDT crosses during this segment. Another 1.75 miles brings you to an even larger wash, Arroyo Chico. Unless this major tributary of the Rio Puerco is in flood, you should have no trouble crossing this, except for getting sand in your boots. But be wary in flood times, and watch out for quicksand then. There's usually more sand than water here, but you probably can find some water (though it's likely to be salty). The CDT goes into the arroyo and climbs out to the east via a dirt ramp. A gated fence is at the ramp's top.

From Arroyo Chico, the CDT runs cross-country over relatively level grassland. At 1.3 miles from Arroyo Chico, in the southwest corner of Section 7, the CDT intersects a dirt road; here the CDT goes from the Empedrado WSA into the La Leña WSA. After 2.5 miles from Arroyo Chico, the CDT climbs a ridge conveniently situated between two arroyos for 0.6 mile to reach San Luis Mesa's top. After about a mile, you'll see a tank at about N35°39'33", W107°11'14", 0.25 mile west of the CDT, but it's not a reliable source. About 1.5 miles from here, in Section 32, is Laguna de la Leña, a stock tank, 0.5 mile east of the CDT at N35°39'58", W107°10'26". After 1.6 miles of relatively level grasslands atop San Luis Mesa, the CDT arrives at the base of some colorful sandstone cliffs. It parallels them until after 2.5 miles across the mesa's top it arrives at a dirt road, N35°40'10", W107°10'25", 6,400 feet. This is an interesting and scenic stretch. Look on the ground beneath the cliffs for small pieces of petrified wood. The route is well-marked with cairns.

The cairns continue on the road's east side. The route follows the cliff's base for 3 miles, then along a ridge for 2.8 miles before reaching another road. The hiking is easy, and the terrain and scenery are exceptionally intriguing: strange rock formations known as "hoodoos," scatterings of petrified wood, a level bench atop the cliffs, awesome views of Cabezon to the south. Only a waterfall would improve it! This delightful stretch ends at yet another dirt road, the Torreon Road junction.

S **SOUTHBOUND HIKERS:** At this road junction, resist the temptation to follow the dirt road leading southwest, the direction you're heading. The off-road CDT is just as easy—and far more interesting.

This is a major road junction. As Charlie McDonald explains: "There is a lot of development concentrated in this area. It includes several roads, an electrical transmission line, gas pipeline rights-of-way, a pipeline compressor station, and a microwave tower." The route also is a heavily traveled route between Albuquerque and Torreon.

From the junction, the CDT stays just south of the well-traveled dirt road heading east, going up a small hill. At 0.5 mile, at N35°42'32", W107°06'13", the CDT leaves the road to head east. It drops down the mesa's rim, then heads northeast to arrive after 1.6 miles from the major junction at another dirt road, in the valley of Arroyo de los Cerros Colorados. There are several water developments in the area: ponds on both sides of the arroyo, as well as windmills (most not functioning) and water tanks.

The best water source is the least conspicuous—a pipe with a spigot that projects from the center of a piece of vertical culvert. It is just west of the Arroyo de los Cerros Colorados and about 50 yards south of the CDT, across a small gully. Raise the spigot's handle to obtain clear, cold water. It is part of a system built by the BLM and now maintained by ranchers to distribute water for livestock.

From the arroyo, the CDT follows dirt roads to climb onto the mesa to the east, but near the top two diverge, the CDT, marked by cairns, heading northeast, then north. At 1.2 miles from the arroyo, the CDT joins a dirt road, which it follows

1 mile north to a road junction at N35°43'31", W107°04'33". Just east of this junction is a pond. Here the CDT goes its own way northeast, intersecting dirt roads as it heads toward three distinctive hills; from the east, they are Cerros Colorados, 7,051 feet; Deadman Peaks, 6,987 feet; and Cerro Colorado, 6,986 feet. The CDT approaches the gap between Cerro Colorado and Deadman Peaks, where it joins the road. The interim BLM route follows this road until it reaches NM 44.

North of Deadman Peaks, the dirt road, not labeled on the ground but easy to recognize as the main road, runs northeast for a mile before turning north and going gently downhill. You'll pass several earthen dams intended to catch runoff; water availability at these dams depends on recent rainfall. The first reliable water is at a windmill and stock pond approximately 3.5 miles north of Deadman Peaks, coordinates N35°47'29", W107°04'29". On a hillside near the stock pond are the stone ruins of a homesteader dwelling, one of many scattered throughout the area.

From the windmill, the road is fairly level as it enters the broad valley of Arroyo Piedra Lumbre. Two miles from the windmill you reach Headcut Reservoir. Don't let the name mislead you; chances of the "reservoir" having water are slim. The BLM proposes to install a water facility along the road to accommodate CDT hikers during the interim period in which non-road alternatives are studied.

From Headcut Reservoir, the CDT follows the Piedra Lumbre Road generally north-northeast through the broad valley for 4.1 miles until a "T." Here, up on the valley's northern flank, the CDT heads due east. After 1.2 miles, at 6,913 feet, coordinates N35°52'17", W107°00'48", the road and the CDT begin a long descent through a valley filled with aromatic sagebrush, flanked by hills and small cliffs vegetated with piñon-juniper. Soon you'll see to the east, across the Rio Puerco Valley, the pink granite of the Sierra Nacimiento and, lower, the oranges and tans of sandstone formations. You'll also see ahead the cars and trucks on NM 44, your destination. At 2.75 miles, immediately after crossing the awesomely deep, steep arroyo carved by the Rio Puerco (appropriately, "muddy river"), you reach the highway, N35°52'40", W106°58'19", 6,585 feet.

SOUTHBOUND HIKERS: The bridge over the Rio Puerco arroyo is not labeled. If you miss this bridge, you don't leave the highway again until 3.5 miles farther south, where a dirt road leads to the cluster of structures named La Ventana.

Caution: Once on NM 44/US 550, you must follow the highway 10 miles north to Cuba. Construction crews have converted this road from two to four lanes. And as much as I generally dislike bigger roads replacing smaller roads, I welcome this upgrade. This road terrifies me; my family has been touched by two fatal accidents on NM 44/US 550. Traffic often is heavy, fast, and drunk. Near misses are common. So *please* use caution when walking along this highway.

Ten miles brings you to Cuba. Just as you enter the village from the south, the Santa Fe National Forest–Cuba Ranger District office is just to the east; this office has responsibility for the southern portion of the next segment, in the San Pedro Parks; inquire there for current conditions. Numerous motels and restaurants are along the highway as it passes through the village.

CONTINUED ON NEXT PAGE

Bear Mouth overlook

Hunters Camp

Ojo Frio

Arroyo Chico (water likely)

Torreon Road junction

Spigot and spring

Pond

MESA

SAN LUIS

Blanco

Cañon de Alamo

Cabezon

San Luis

Bosque Grande Mesa

Angostura Hills

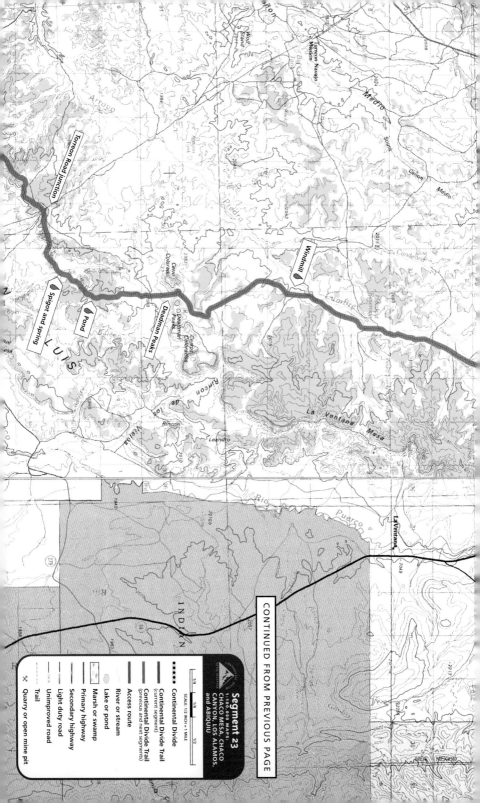

CONTINUED FROM PREVIOUS PAGE

Torreon Road Junction

Spigot and spring

Pond

Deadman Peaks

Windmill

La Ventana

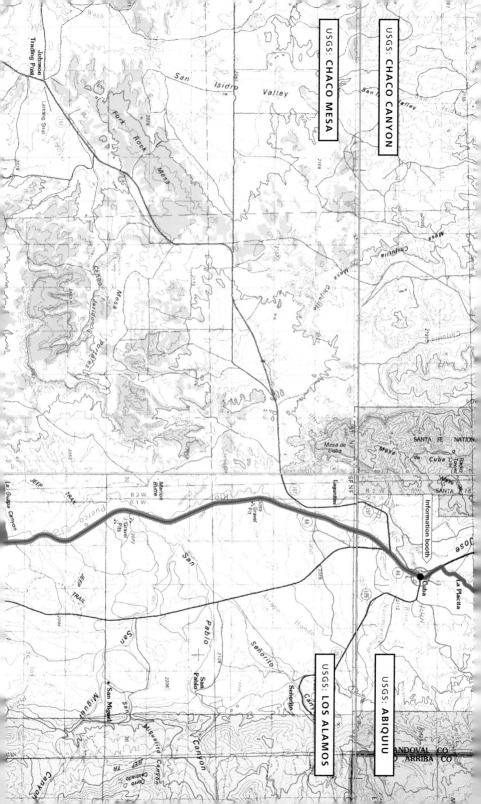

USGS: CHACO CANYON

USGS: CHACO MESA

USGS: LOS ALAMOS

USGS: ABIQUIU

Segment 24
Cuba to NM 96: San Pedro Parks Wilderness

Green grasses and afternoon clouds, San Pedro Parks Wilderness, Santa Fe National Forest. Photo by Tom Till.

26 miles
Difficulty: Moderate

You may encounter: hikers, equestrians, and motorized vehicles

Segment 24 **Total Elevation Gain:** 3,904 feet
From Mexico 589.75 miles
To Colorado 109.25 miles

CONTINENTAL DIVIDE
TRAIL ALLIANCE

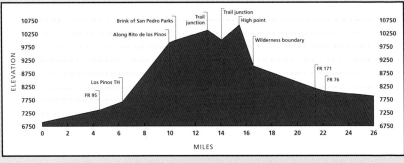

TRAIL OVERVIEW A green oasis is how the San Pedro Parks Wilderness in this segment will seem after the arid, brown Rio Puerco country. The San Pedro Parks is the fourth of five wilderness areas the Continental Divide Trail traverses as it wends its way between Mexico and Colorado. But although "wilderness" connotes remote, rugged terrain, this wilderness gently welcomes. The CDT is well-marked, and though you'll have to climb to enter the parks, once there you'll discover beautiful grassy meadows interspersed with forest, gentle rolling terrain, abundant water, and inviting campsites. The area lends itself well to day hikes or easy backpack trips. Trout are small but numerous in the diminutive streams. Indeed, the greatest regret in hiking this area is leaving it so soon.

The wilderness here owes much of its pleasant character to geology and location. The San Pedro Parks lie atop the small mountain range called the Sierra Nacimiento, (Spanish for "birth mountains," probably because in these mountains the Rio Puerco that flows near Cuba is born, as well as several other important streams). The Sierra Nacimiento abuts the more extensive Jemez Mountains to the east. But where the Jemez Mountains represent relatively recent volcanic deposits, easily eroded and highly permeable to water, the Sierra Nacimiento is underlain by ancient Precambrian granite, which resists weathering and blocks water absorption. Because the high, abrupt Sierra Nacimiento is the first mountain group that storm systems encounter as they move east on the prevailing westerlies, plenty of unabsorbed moisture accumulates.

Thus precipitation collects in the broad basins and meadows of the Sierra Nacimiento parks (in the West, a term referring to broad, open grasslands surrounded by mountains and forests) and eventually moves laterally to fill the many streams that originate here. Because the granite keeps water near the surface, much of the San Pedro Parks area is boggy, but it's a small price to pay for the beautiful meadows, the lush vegetation, and the plenitude of streams.

You'll most likely camp at the edge of one of these meadows, and perhaps you'll find an inconspicuous spot at twilight to sit and watch for wildlife emerging from the forest; I've done this and have been rewarded by seeing a young buck deer, with antlers in velvet, and several elk. Your chances of seeing elk are especially good. The rich habitat here supports numerous other species: black bear, coyote, fox, bobcat, mountain lion, blue grouse, squirrel, and beaver. On one trip, I met a woman who had just seen a black bear—on Oso ("bear") Creek!

And cows. In the San Pedro Parks Wilderness you're all but certain to encounter cows—sometimes lots of cows. Upon seeing the cow flops and attendant flies, fouled water, and trampled trails and vegetation, you'll likely be tempted to complain bitterly about the cows and the management policies that have allowed them to roam the wilderness. But before you do so, consider the perspective of the local people who own the cattle. The National Forests here that now belong to all of us once were their lands, in the form of land grants that predated the American annexation of New Mexico in 1846. Part of the 1848 Treaty of Guadalupe Hidalgo that ended the Mexican-American War stipulated that land grants be honored, and although legal chicanery and title confusion resulted in the absorption of many land grants into National Forests, land managers still have tried to respect the spirit of the treaty—especially as the 1964 Wilderness Act allowed certain traditional uses of the land, including grazing. Some grazing leases here go back five generations. If the cattle grazing here had been part of your family's life for five generations, how would you feel?

Dense conifer forests, primarily Engelmann spruce and Douglas fir, coexist with the wilderness parks in patchwork-quilt fashion. Deciduous trees are rare, and even the normally ubiquitous aspens are relatively uncommon, testament to the long-term stability of this ecosystem.

Wildflowers abound in this fertile and diverse environment. On one three-day Fourth of July trip, I recorded 35 species in bloom—and saw many, many more I couldn't identify. Shooting stars blazed along streams; shrubby cinquefoil dotted the short-grass meadows; a few wild iris lingered, perhaps a week past their prime; and the tiny yellow umbrellas of mountain parsley dappled the short-grass meadows.

The flowering season is brief in the 10,000-foot-high San Pedro Parks Wilderness. Snow lingers late, into May and often into June. Then around mid-July, the monsoon season begins. Early in the afternoon, moisture that's flowed into the region from the Gulf of Mexico rises to condense into towering thunderheads that erupt into thunderstorms whose ferocity can be formidable. With nightfall, the clouds dissipate, and the morning dawns moist and clear—until the afternoon. There's some variability to this cycle, but you definitely should be aware of it if you hike in mid-to-late summer. As September arrives, the pattern weakens, then disappears, and the fall hiking season begins. This is a time of warm, clear days, of turquoise skies and brilliantly colored foliage—the scattered San Pedro Parks aspen turn a shimmering gold—and crisply cold nights. Ask New Mexico hikers to name their favorite hiking season, and the majority will say the fall.

A CDT hiker traveling from the south crosses the San Pedro Parks Wilderness from east to west. The climb into the wilderness from the Los Pinos trailhead is relentlessly and sometimes steeply uphill, though it is shaded and water is available along the stream. Once in the parks, the CDT traverses the meadows and forests heading east before abruptly heading north, following a gradual forested trail downhill to exit the wilderness at the northern boundary. From there the CDT follows Forest Roads downhill through a pleasant ponderosa forest to join NM 96.

The San Pedro Parks Wilderness offers outstanding day hiking—cool, green, scenic, lots of wildlife, well-marked trails, and gentle gradients, though usually some climbing is required to reach the parks. The extensive trail network allows numerous loop hikes. Treat all water before drinking it, and be wary of afternoon thunderstorms. In the winter, the San Pedro Parks Wilderness offers some of northern New Mexico's finest ski touring, most centered around San Gregorio Reservoir.

WATER NOTES

At last! Here is a segment bountiful with water from end to end. Use wantonly, luxuriously, and enjoy! (But treat it first.)

MOUNTAIN BIKE NOTES

 Although the San Pedro Parks Wilderness, like all wildernesses, is closed to mountain bikes, a network of Forest Roads that make for outstanding riding surround the wilderness (see page 270).

EQUESTRIAN NOTES

This CDT segment represents perhaps the best country for horses and pack animals in New Mexico—not just on the CDT. Trails are, for the most part, easy and rolling; you'll find abundant water, idyllic campsites, lush meadows, proximity to Albuquerque and Santa Fe, corrals at trailheads—equestrians are as fond of the San Pedro Wilderness as hikers and backpackers. Indeed, generations of New Mexicans have made horses the traditional means of travel in the San Pedro Parks, and local ranchers, as well as recreationists, still use horses. You'll find corrals at the Los Pinos Trailhead, as well as at the San Gregorio Reservoir Trailhead and parking area. The Resumidero Campground on the northeast provides plenty of room for horses.

SOUTHBOUND HIKERS

  Water is abundant in the San Pedro Parks, but check your supplies at the Rio Cecelia, from whence you ascend to the wilderness boundary and then to the parks.

MAPS

USGS QUADRANGLES: Cuba, Nacimiento Peak, Gallina

OTHER MAPS: Santa Fe National Forest (best small-scale map for showing forest roads), San Pedro Parks Wilderness–Visitors Travel Guide and Map (best small-scale source of trail information). Although the USGS quadrangles show more detail, they are considerably out of date. The Nacimiento Peak quad, which covers most of the wilderness, has not been updated since 1963, a year before formal wilderness designation.

LAND-MANAGEMENT AGENCIES

Santa Fe National Forest/Cuba Ranger District; Carson National Forest/Coyote Ranger District

BEGINNING ACCESS POINT

  CUBA: The CDT on the south intersects the village of Cuba, and the CDT route to the San Pedro Parks begins at the northwest end of Cuba.

ALTERNATE ACCESS

  SAN GREGORIO RESERVOIR TRAILHEAD: This route allows access to the CDT from the south. At the Visitor Center at the northern end of Cuba, take NM 126 right. Follow this paved road approximately 11 miles. Just as NM 126 begins to descend, Forest Road 70 branches left and after 2.8 miles arrives at San Gregorio Reservoir Trailhead.

ENDING ACCESS POINT

NM 96: Reaching the Rio Capulin Trailhead at the northern San Pedro Parks Wilderness boundary requires some careful map reading and a high-clearance 4WD vehicle. From NM 96 east of Gallina, where Forest Road 103 and Forest Road 76 branch on the south side of the highway, take Forest Road 76 right for 3 miles to the junction with Forest Road 171 at the junction with the Rio Cecelia. These are well-graded dirt roads. Go 1 mile south on Forest Road 171 to N36°11'27", W106°47'40", where the CDT heads southwest 1.7 miles to the Wilderness boundary. You can also drive from Forest Road 171 to the Wilderness boundary by taking Forest Road 1162 right. This road is rough and suitable only for high-clearance 4WD vehicles.

TRAIL DESCRIPTION

The CDT route to the San Pedro Parks Wilderness begins at the northwest end of Cuba. Just as NM 44/US 550 begins leaving the village heading northwest, 0.6 mile from the Visitor Center, just past Mile Marker 65 and a sign for the San Pedro Parks Wilderness, Los Pinos County Road branches north-northeast. This road is paved for 3.6 miles before becoming good dirt and is a pleasant walk or drive through a diffusely settled rural valley, flanked by sandstone bluffs. When the pavement ends, walk another 0.4 mile to where Forest Road 95 branches right at N36°04'45", W106°56'18" at a sign saying the Los Pinos Trailhead is 3 miles (4 miles is more accurate). This road is narrower than the earlier road but poses no problems for vehicles—except following wet weather, when it can get muddy and slippery. *Note:* Forest Road 95 does not appear on the 1963 Cuba quadrangle.

The trailhead for the Los Pinos Trail, No. 46, N36°06'12", W106°54'13", elevation 8,198 feet, has ample parking and even a corral for equestrians and hikers using pack animals; here also you'll see the first signs denoting that this is the CDT. The trail begins by entering a thicket of Gambel oak interspersed with ponderosa pine, but before a mile it leaves the oak as it enters and begins climbing the moister, greener canyon of the Rito de los Pinos ("creek of the pines"). The trail's gradients are gentle, especially in the canyon's lower reaches, and it is generally well-maintained and easy to follow, with no confusing side trails. The canyon is a delight, particularly after the CDT's drier, browner sections; it evokes images of a rain forest, with green velvety moss softening boulders and gracing rotting logs, pale green old man's beard lichen dripping from Douglas fir branches, and a dense forest canopy of huge trees. When I hiked the San Pedro Parks segment of the CDT with outdoor photographer Tom Till, this was his favorite section.

The trail becomes steeper as it ascends the canyon until after 3.1 miles and a 2,000-foot elevation gain, the Los Pinos Trail tops out at the edge of the San Pedro Parks and the junction with the Anastacio Trail, No. 435, N36°05'56", W106°51'45", elevation 10,196 feet. This is a beautiful place, and here, flanking the Rio Puerco and Rito Anastacio drainages, stretch the broad, lush meadows so characteristic of the San Pedro Parks. In these meadows you're most likely to initially encounter the cattle ubiquitous in the Wilderness. They're a reminder to treat *all* water here. From the trail junction post, you can find a great campsite by following the Anastacio Trail downhill and crossing a small meadow to reach a small knoll, about 100 yards from the post.

SUPPLIES, SERVICES, AND ACCOMMODATIONS

CUBA is a small but growing town on NM 44/US 550, the main route into northwestern New Mexico, and thus sees heavy freight and passenger traffic. Cuba has an array of basic services and is the major supply point to the northeastern part of the Navajo Nation.

Distance from Trail The designated CDT route runs through Cuba; distance to hiking trailhead, 8 miles

Zip Code	87013	
Bank	Wells Fargo Bank, 6381 South Main	(505) 289-3433
	(lobby hours 9–6 Mon–Thur, 9–6 Fri)	
Bus	None	
Dining	Several options; El Bruno's at the north end of town has a reputation for good New Mexican dinners	
Emergency	State Police: located on NM 44/US 550 in Cuba	289-3443
	Local police	289-3911
Gear	Basic hunting and fishing supplies can be found at ABM Sporting Goods and Richard's True Value Hardware Stores on NM 44/US 550	
Groceries	Several medium-sized grocery stores	
Information	Cuba Region Visitor Center, P.O. Box 56, Cuba, NM 87103 (located at the junction of NM 44/US 550 and NM 126)	289-3808
Laundry	A Laundromat is located on NM 44/US 550 in Cuba	
Lodging	Cuban Lodge Motel, at south end of town, P.O. Box 1538, Cuba, NM 87013 (welcomes CDT hikers and will help with packages)	289-3269
	Del Prado Motel	289-3475
	Frontier Motel, at north end of town, P.O. Box 338, Cuba, NM 87013 (All motels are on NM 44/US 550 in Cuba.)	289-3474
	Circle A Ranch, near the CDT–Los Pinos Trailhead Box 2142, Cuba, NM 87013 (rustic but delightful accommodations)	289-3350
Medical	Cuba Health Center, 6349 NM 44/US 550	289-3291
Post Office	On NM 44/US 550	289-3498
	(lobby open 6:30–5:30 Mon–Fri; will hold general delivery 30 days)	
Showers	None	

GALLINA, a diffuse Hispanic community along NM 96, is at this segment's northern end. Supplies and services are meager, accommodations nonexistent. For emergency and medical information, see Cuba (above) or Coyote (Segment 25, page 279); there is a sparsely stocked Mini Mart, open seven days a week, on NM 96 in the village.

Distance from Trail 4 miles
   Zip Code 87017

Back at the trail junction post, the CDT is indicated on the sign; it continues to coincide with the Los Pinos Trail. (*Note:* Although it's still Trail 46, the Los Pinos Trail, it now is following the drainage of the Rio Puerco.) The trail descends briefly to join the valley of the Rio Puerco before continuing its gradual 2.6-mile ascent along the creek to San Pedro Park. It's a pleasant hike, not nearly as steep as the Los Pinos Trail you just ascended to reach the parks. Rich, verdant meadows often flank the creek. Several tributary canyons enter the Los Pinos valley, but the Los Pinos Trail is easy to follow as it climbs about 230 feet in 2.6 miles to terminate at its junction, N36°07'05", W106°49'59", 10,396 feet, with the San José Trail, No. 33, and the Vacas Trail, No. 51, near the northwestern edge of San Pedro Park, probably the wilderness's largest and most impressive park. Appealing campsites are easy to find in the forests around the park, and the Rio Puerco, which flows through the park's lush grass, provides water. A watcher at the park's edge at dawn or dusk would likely see elk emerge to graze.

At San Pedro Park, the CDT follows the Vacas Trail. Within the San Pedro Parks Wilderness, and especially in the meadows and marshes, the trail is not easy to discern and therefore it's marked with stakes, many with the CDT symbol stamped on them. Southeast of the Los Pinos Trail's end, one of these stakes indicates the Vacas Trail. If this stake isn't present or the trail is obscure (likely in the thick grass), take a bearing from the Los Pinos–San José-Vacas Trail junction post for south-southeast. The Vacas Trail skirts the San Pedro Park's southeast side, passing another impressive meadow as it proceeds gently downhill to a junction (after 0.9 mile) with the Peñas Negras Trail, No. 32, N36°06'29", W106°49'23", elevation 10,393 feet.

At this junction you'll see a signpost. The Vacas Trail continues south to junction with the Anastacio Trail after 2.4 miles. A visible but unsigned trail continues north along the Rio de las Vacas. Take the Peñas Negras Trail east across the meadow. A CDT stake points the way, but again, if the stake isn't present, look for a modest rock outcrop southeast across the meadow; just beyond it is a small drainage. Here you'll find the Peñas Negras Trail, N36°06'27", W106°49'09", which parallels the drainage gently uphill east for 0.6 mile to its junction with the Rio Capulin Trail, No. 31, N36°06'26", W106°48'56", elevation 10,396 feet.

Here, the CDT, still marked by stakes, follows the Rio Capulin Trail directly north. (*Note:* On the 1963 Gallina quadrangle, the Rio Capulin Trail is labeled the San Pedro Parks Trail.) The terrain rolls gently here, and Engelmann spruce stands punctuate flower-filled grasslands. To the east lies the green basin called Vega del Oso, "meadow of the bear." Continue north on the Rio Capulin Trail for about 2.3 miles; the trail then begins a descent from the parks, entering increasingly dense conifer forest as it heads down a gradual ridge. After 3.8 miles from the Peñas Negras Trail, the parks are well behind you by the time you reach the junction with the Red Rock Trail, No. 30. From here it's another 1.6 miles to the wilderness boundary and the trailhead (N36°10'22", W106°48'43"). You'll find campsites here; there's no obvious water, but Forest Service personnel say that Santana Spring (not shown on the Gallina quadrangle but at approximately N36°10'43", W106°48'33") has water.

The 1963 Gallina quadrangle shows a trail heading northeast downhill about 1.7 miles to a spring and Forest Road 171, near the Rio Cecelia. The Forest Service intends this trail to become the official CDT route. This route should be shorter and preferable to following Forest Road 1160 for 3 miles, and easy to follow. The coordinates for the destination junction are N36°11'27", W106°47'40". The area near the Rio Cecelia is a pleasant place, with good campsites beneath tall ponderosa pines near grassy meadows and the tiny creek. The map shows a spring at this junction, but the Forest Service says it's hard to find, and indeed in twice looking I've yet to find it. Don't waste your time; water is readily available in the Rio Cecelia.

 Follow Forest Road 171 northwest to its junction with Forest Road 76 and the confluence of the Rio Cecelia and the Rio Capulin, both reliable water sources. Heading northeast, then southeast on Forest Road 76 for 2.6 miles, brings you to Forest Road 103 and almost immediately to paved NM 96 and the end of this segment.

WILDERNESS ALERT

Wilderness preservation in the San Pedro Parks began in 1931 when the area was designated a primitive area by the chief of the Forest Service. In 1941 the Secretary of Agriculture reclassified it as a Wild Area, with 41,132 acres. It became a formal Wilderness in 1964, with the passage of the Wilderness Act. Because traditional uses of the land continue here, and because recreational use is relatively high, please observe these wilderness guidelines:

1. Camp out of sight, at least 200 feet from springs and drainages, on a dry, durable surface.
2. Use a stove instead of building a fire; use existing fire rings if you do build a fire.
3. Keep water sources pure by camping at least 200 feet from them.
4. Bury human wastes 6 inches deep and at least 200 feet from water sources; pack out toilet paper.
5. Hobble or picket all livestock at least 200 feet from streams.
6. Dogs must be on a leash.
7. No mountain biking.
8. Pack out all trash; don't attempt to burn it.

OTHER HIKES AND RIDES: VACAS TRAIL TO THE RITO ANASTACIO

APPROXIMATE ONE-WAY DISTANCE: 5.5 miles
MODE OF TRAVEL: Hiking
DIFFICULTY: Easy to moderate

The Vacas Trail, No. 51: See Alternate Access for this segment, page 265.
This popular route into the San Pedro Parks Wilderness is readily accessible, scenic, and avoids the steep climbs of other entry routes. The Vacas Trail heads north, and after slightly less than a mile of gentle ascent through spruce-fir and aspen forest arrives at San Gregorio Reservoir, popular with local fishermen. The Vacas Trail continues to head north around the east side of the lake, then bends east to join Clear Creek. The trail parallels the stream, soon entering an area of aspen groves and meadows. After almost 2 miles from the lake, the Vacas Trail leaves Clear Creek to pass through more forest, aspen groves, and meadows to arrive after 4.3 miles from the lake at the Rio de las Vacas ("river of the cows") and the intersection with the Las Palomas Trail, No. 50. Just 0.2 mile farther lies the terminus of the Anastacio Trail, No. 345.

OTHER HIKES AND RIDES: PALOMAS TRAIL TO THE RITO ANASTACIO

APPROXIMATE ONE-WAY DISTANCE: 4 miles
MODE OF TRAVEL: Hiking
DIFFICULTY: Easy to moderate

The Palomas Trail, No. 50: Reach this relatively easy route into the San Pedro Parks by driving 7.1 miles past the San Gregorio Lake trailhead to the Palomas parking area and trailhead, on your left. The trail ascends a ridge before a short, steep descent to the Rio de Las Perchas at 1.4 miles. The Palomas Trail continues northwest after skirting a small meadow and following a small drainage uphill. After about 0.5 mile, it reaches the 10,000-foot elevation—and easy walking. After 2.4 miles from the Rio de las Perchas, running through pleasant forest and green-velvet meadows, the trail arrives at the Vacas Trail, No. 51. Follow this 0.2 mile north to its junction with the Anastacio Trail, No. 435.

OTHER HIKES AND RIDES: FOREST ROAD 70

APPROXIMATE ONE-WAY DISTANCE: 7.1 miles
MODE OF TRAVEL: Biking
DIFFICULTY: Easy

Trailhead: San Gregorio Reservoir parking area. You will reach the route from Cuba by taking NM 126 to where the pavement ends and good dirt Forest Road 70 branches left. After 2.8 miles, you'll see the parking area and trailhead for San Gregorio Reservoir and the Vacas Trail, No. 51.

   A pleasant and relatively easy out-and-back ride on the south is the 7.1-mile stretch of Forest Road 70 between the San Gregorio Reservoir trailhead and campground and the Palomas Trailhead.

HISTORICAL NOTES

Place Names. People often are perplexed by the name Cuba, wondering what connection it has with the Caribbean island. The answer is none. *Cuba* here is a Spanish word referring to a "water trough, tank," or possibly "sink, draw." The community earlier had been called Nacimiento, a reference to the Sierra Nacimiento, the mountain range immediately northeast on whose 10,000-foot-high plateau lies the San Pedro Parks Wilderness. The Spanish name *Nacimiento* means "birth," but it also can mean "origin," and here it refers to this high area's role as the headwaters of the Rio Puerco, one of north-central New Mexico's major drainages. (Actually, another Rio Puerco heads in the San Pedro Parks Wilderness; it flows east, then north. Although initially larger than the former, it is less significant.)

The village of Gallina lies at this segment's northern end. Your Spanish dictionary will tell you that this means "chicken, hen," but in New Mexico it is more likely a contraction of *gallina de la tierra,* or "wild turkey," and indeed this area is rich habitat for wild turkeys.

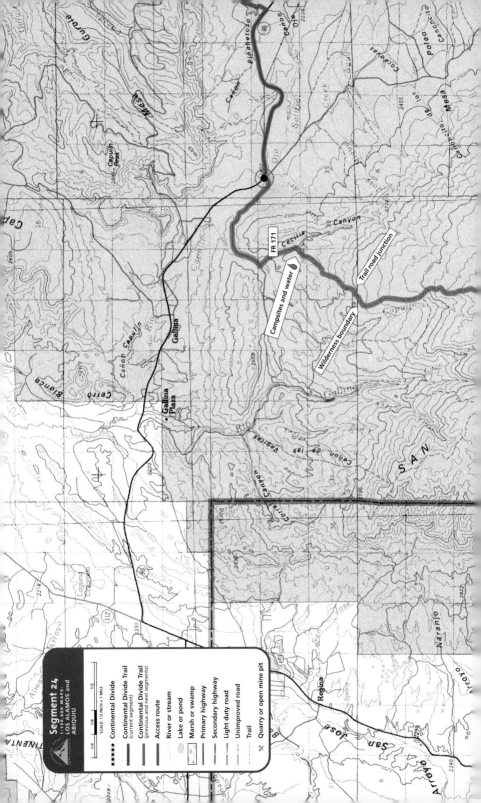

Segment 24
1:100,000 MAPS:
LOS ALAMOS and
ABIQUIU

SCALE: 1/2 INCH = 1 MILE

1/8   1/4   1/2

••••• Continental Divide

—— Continental Divide Trail
(current segment)

—— Continental Divide Trail
(previous and next segments)

---- Access route

—— River or stream

⬤ Lake or pond

🟦 Marsh or swamp

—— Primary highway

—— Secondary highway

---- Light duty road

---- Unimproved road

····· Trail

✕ Quarry or open mine pit

Campsites and water

FR 171

Trail road junction

Wilderness boundary

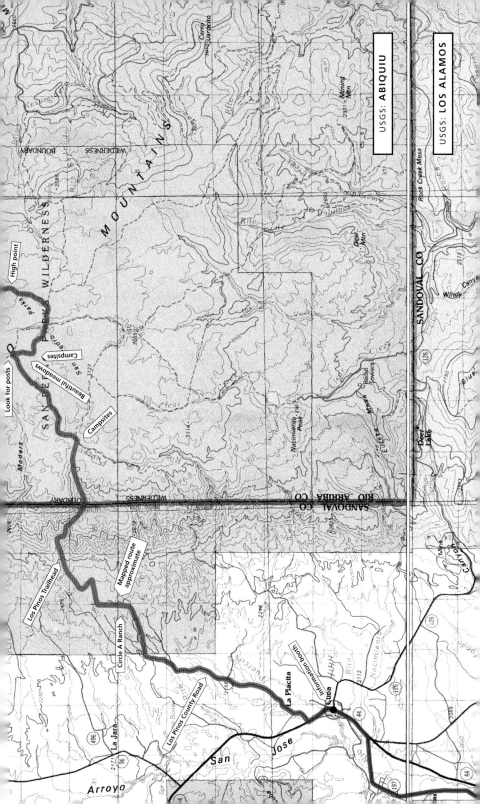

USGS: ABIQUIU

USGS: LOS ALAMOS

High point

Look for posts

Campsites

Beautiful meadows

Campsites

Los Pinos Trailhead

Mapped route approximate

Circle A Ranch

La Placita

Information booth

Los Pinos County Road

SANDOVAL CO
RIO ARRIBA CO

SANDOVAL CO

Cuba

La Jara

San Jose

Arroyo

SAN PEDRO PARKS WILDERNESS

MOUNTAINS

WILDERNESS BOUNDARY

WILDERNESS BOUNDARY

Segment 25
NM 96 to Skull Bridge: Mesa del Camino

*Sunrise over the Rio Chama,
Chama River Canyon
Wilderness, Santa Fe
National Forest.
Photo by Tom Till.*

20.2 miles

Difficulty: Moderate to Strenuous

You may encounter: motorized vehicles

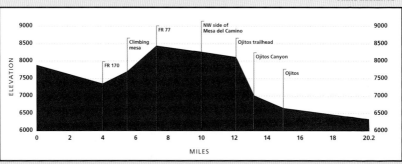

Segment 25 Total Elevation Gain: 1,730 feet
From Mexico 615.75 miles
To Colorado 83.25 miles

CONTINENTAL DIVIDE
TRAIL ALLIANCE

Elevation profile labels:
FR 170
Climbing mesa
FR 77
NW side of Mesa del Camino
Ojitos trailhead
Ojitos Canyon
Ojitos

ELEVATION — MILES

TRAIL OVERVIEW Painters and photographers made this area famous—and vice versa. This Continental Divide Trail segment traverses the distinctive and spectacular scenery "discovered" around 1915 by Ernest Blumenschein, Bert Geer Phillips, E. Martin Hennings, Oscar E. Berninghaus, and others of the famed Taos Society of Artists. It's the landscape that appeared so often in paintings Georgia O'Keeffe made from her home in nearby Abiquiu.

The prevailing contemporary culture is Hispanic, with settlements here dating from the 1800s. The villages are small and diffuse, the people struggling to preserve their rural resource-based lifestyle and values in the face of a changing economy and the tides of modern influences. No contemporary Native American groups currently live here, though the region was within the traditional territories of Jicarilla Apaches, Navajos, and Tewa-speaking pueblos. Still earlier people of the so-called Gallina Culture lived here, from about A.D. 1000 to 1300. Little is known about these people, as no contemporary culture traces its ancestry to them. Archaeological sites throughout the area provide evidence—burned timbers, human remains, and others—that suggest the culture died violently.

Dirt roads comprise much of this segment, though the segment ends with a good hiking trail. Water, although not abundant, is generally available, and the prevailing forest of ponderosa and piñon pine, Gambel oak, and juniper makes for sheltered and shaded walking and camping.

Only one hiking trail has been designated in this area, the Ojitos Trail, No. 298, described on page 278. South to north thru-hikers follow this trail downhill from Mesa del Camino 6 miles to the Rio Chama. The trail makes an excellent though challenging day hike beginning at Skull Bridge on the Rio Chama, a 12-mile round-trip. A friend of mine who did this as a day hike beginning on Mesa del Camino recommends strongly against this because you finish with a steep uphill ascent. Hiking this one-way requires spotting a vehicle at both ends, a long and often difficult drive. It would be a great hike for a key-exchange, if you can find friends willing to do the uphill hike.

WATER NOTES

 After the San Pedro Parks in Segment 24, it's back to dry. The water nearest the beginning is either the Rio Cecelia or the Rio Capulin, about 2.5 miles from this segment's beginning. Water is available at the Coyote Ranger Station, and at Fuertes Spring atop the mesa. That should get you into Ojitos Canyon, a likely source, or the nearby Ojitos, soon before the Chama.

MOUNTAIN BIKE NOTES

 Although hiking trails in this area are limited, mountain-bike routes abound through an extensive network of dirt Forest Roads that run atop the mesas between NM 96 and the Rio Chama. Access to this area is via Forest Road 77 at the east end of Gallina. Local people sometimes remove Forest Service signs, so look for the blue county road sign with yellow lettering. The good dirt road heads toward the very scenic red-and-yellow cliffs to the north, passing the interesting white Santo Niño church after about 0.25 mile. The road ascends somewhat steeply toward the mesa's top, then winds along its top past pleasant valleys until, at 10 miles from NM 96, it reaches the junction with Forest Road 468. This road, part of the CDT, leads to the Ojitos Trail, but for mountain-bikers it offers a great loop ride as it curves around Mesa del Camino. Using the Santa Fe National Forest map, you easily could identify other loop rides atop the mesas.

At this segment's north end runs Forest Road 151, whose eastern end lies 8 miles from the bridge at US 84 just north of the Ghost Ranch Museum and Visitor Center, operated by the Carson National Forest. The open, rolling terrain along this Forest Road beggars even normal northern New Mexico hyperbole. This gravel road is suitable for all vehicles—except when it's wet; then it should be avoided. From Skull Bridge north on Forest Road 151, you'll travel 3.5 scenic rolling miles to a Forest Service campground; just a mile farther is the Christ of the Desert Monastery, which offers limited meals and lodgings to visitors (as well as spiritual rest, contemplation, and a reminder that being in the wilderness is about more than logging miles).

The extensive Forest Roads atop the mesa also are excellent for mountain biking, though the CDT itself is rather steep and rocky, except on top. These Forest Roads connect springs, meadows, and campsites. Once you reach the mesa top, the gradients are generally easy. Look for Forest Roads that take you toward the mesa's eastern edge; the views of the Rio Chama valley are awesome.

EQUESTRIAN NOTES

This segment offers outstanding horseback riding (except, of course, for the stretch along paved NM 96). Indeed, the 1997 reconnaissance of this segment during Uniting Along the Divide was done by Back Country Horsemen of New Mexico–Santa Fe Chapter, with veteran horsepacker Eldon Reyer as its leader. Most equestrian parties would start at Skull Bridge over the Rio Chama and ride east onto Mesa del Camino. To the right of the trail, about a mile from the bridge, look for a stock watering tank; other water suitable for horses is found at Los Ojitos and in Ojitos Canyon. On Mesa del Camino you'll find water at Fuertes Spring, along with good campsites and pasturage.

SOUTHBOUND HIKERS

Springs and possible creek water in Ojitos Canyon will be your last reliable water when you begin the steep climb out of the canyon until you reach NM 96; should you decide to camp atop Mesa del Camino, however, you could obtain good water at Fuertes Spring (see page 277).

MAPS

USGS QUADRANGLES: Arroyo del Agua, Gallina, Laguna Peak
OTHER MAPS: Santa Fe National Forest, BLM 1:100K Abiquiu

LAND-MANAGEMENT AGENCIES

Santa Fe National Forest/Coyote Ranger District

BEGINNING ACCESS POINT

NM 96: This segment begins with a 4-mile walk along NM 96 to Forest Road 170, east of the Ending Access Point in Segment 24, page 266.

ENDING ACCESS POINT

SKULL BRIDGE: From US 84, Forest Road 151 heads west and then northwest along the Rio Chama for 9.1 miles to Skull Bridge and this segment's end. The bridge is closed to vehicular traffic. You can access this point only along the dirt road coinciding with the CDT.

TRAIL DESCRIPTION

A walk along the highway begins this segment. From where Forest Roads 76 and 103 join NM 96, N36°12'02", W106°46'14", elevation 7,881 feet, the CDT route as designated by the Forest Service runs east along paved NM 96 for 4 miles to Forest Road 170. NM 96, although a major route, doesn't receive a lot of traffic and leads the hiker through pleasant ponderosa pine forest. Forest Road 170 may be marked with a Forest Service sign; because local people often remove these signs as part of their general antipathy toward the Forest Service, you may have to look instead for a blue sign with yellow lettering saying Rio Arriba County 424; I found a corral-like structure about 75 yards from the highway; the longitude for the junction is W106°42'40", elevation 7,370 feet. Before beginning your hike, continue east on NM 96 2.3 miles farther to the Santa Fe National Forest–Coyote Ranger District offices for

the most current information about trail conditions. This also would be a good place to replenish water, as there's no other reliable water until you reach the top of Mesa del Camino, 5 miles and 1,200 feet later.

Forest Road 170 is the old wagon road that local people in the 1900s used to ascend Mesa del Camino and Mesa Alta. Scenic cream-and-ochre sandstone cliffs guard this mesa. The first mile of Forest Road 170 ascends rather gradually, crossing two drainages as it approaches the mesa. The road then becomes steadily rougher and steeper as it begins wiggling its way up the escarpment. As you hike you might pause to notice Cerro Pedernal to the southeast. The chisel-shaped profile of this 9,862-foot peak has been a conspicuous and important landmark in northern New Mexico for as long as people have lived here. Its Spanish name means "Flint Mountain," a reference to its obsidian, which indigenous peoples prized highly. The mountain's summit houses Native American and Hispanic shrines.

At about 3.6 miles from NM 96, Forest Road 170 finally begins to level out, crossing a small intermittent drainage as it enters a broad, grassy valley just before joining Forest Road 77 N36°14'00", W106°41'30", elevation 8,420 feet. Near the junction of Forest Roads 170 and 77 would make a good place to camp—if it had water. (In wet times the small drainage you just crossed might have some.) The nearest reliable water is

about a mile away, reached by following Forest Road 468 northeast and downhill along pleasant Cañada de las Fuertes to Fuertes Spring, N36°14'26", W106°40'46", elevation 8,300 feet. Look for the spring, which runs into a trough, on the road's north side; it's marked by a sign and is easy to find. You'll find good campsites nearby.

WILDERNESS ALERT

The trailhead at Mesa del Camino to Skull Bridge on the Rio Chama is within the 50,300-acre Chama River Canyon Wilderness, designated in 1988 to complement the adjacent Chama Wild and Scenic River, also designated in 1988. Please observe these wilderness guidelines:

1. Camp out of sight, at least 200 feet from springs and drainages, on a dry, durable surface.
2. Use a stove instead of building a fire; use existing fire rings if you do build a fire.
3. Keep water sources pure by camping at least 200 feet from them.
4. Bury human wastes 6 inches deep and at least 200 feet from water sources; pack out toilet paper.
5. Dogs must be on a leash.
6. No mountain biking.
7. Pack out all trash; don't attempt to burn it.

To continue on the CDT from the Forest Roads 170-77 junction, walk east on Forest Road 77 for 0.7 mile to where Forest Road 468 branches north, N36°13'45", W106°42'05". (The Arroyo del Agua map, prepared in 1953, shows a trail running up to and along the top of Mesa del Camino, and no road or trail along Cañada Camino.) As Forest Road 468 heads north it parallels a grassy meadow along the Cañada del Camino flanked by ponderosa pines, a pleasant camping place but lacking permanent water. At 0.8 mile, the road crosses the drainage from west to east to slab upward about 80 feet; it then follows the mesa's contours northeast at about 8,500 feet. After about 1.7 miles, Forest Road 468 returns to the drainage and the junction with several smaller Forest Roads. Water is likely available here in Cañada Camino. Forest Road 468 soon leaves the drainage again for the side of the mesa. After another 2 miles, you reach the head of the Ojitos Trail, where the trail and the CDT are marked with signs, N36°16'44", W106°40'01", elevation 8,110 feet.

The Ojitos Trail, No. 298, immediately begins its descent from the mesa, dropping about 1,100 feet in 1.2 miles, using switchbacks over the steepest sections. In less than 0.5 mile, the trail reaches the Chama River Canyon Wilderness boundary, where the slopes become steeper. The trail levels out in the narrow valley of Ojitos Canyon, where you'll likely find water in the stream as it meanders through mixed conifers beneath spectacular sandstone cliffs. About 0.5 mile downstream from where you joined the stream, you'll find small but good campsites. After 2.3 miles downstream from where you joined the canyon, look for the reliable Ojitos ("Little Springs") from which the valley and the trail take their names, N36°18'35", W106°39'37", elevation 6,707 feet.

SUPPLIES, SERVICES, AND ACCOMMODATIONS

CUBA. See Segment 24, page 267.

COYOTE: At 11.2 miles east of the Forest Road 76–NM 96 junction is the Hispanic village of Coyote, another diffuse Hispanic community that has slightly more to offer than Gallina (that's not saying much). It also has a post office, and the Coyote Crossing store, open seven days a week, with a Laundromat and a store well-stocked with groceries and hardware. No overnight accommodations are available in either community.

Distance from Trail	11.2 miles east of the Forest Road 76–NM 96 junction, 7.2 miles east of the Forest Road 170–NM 96 junction
Zip Code	87012
Bank	None
Bus	None
Dining	None
Emergency	State Police: see Cuba, page 267.
Groceries	Coyote Crossing Store on NM 96
Gear	None
Information	None
Laundry	Coyote Crossing Store
Lodging	None
Medical	Health Centers of Northern New Mexico (505) 638-5487
Post Office	638-9182
Showers	None

At the springs, Ojitos Canyon becomes broader and flatter, and from here it's easy walking for 3 miles, through piñon pines and sagebrush (two of the Southwest's best scents). The trail follows CDT posts every 0.1 to 0.2 mile, to the Rio Chama and Skull Bridge. (Ignore the ominous connotation of the name; it was supposedly the surname of a local rancher.) Cross the bridge, gated to prevent vehicular use, to Forest Road 151 to end this segment, N36°19'48", W106°37'28", elevation 6,330 feet. There are numerous good informal campsites, mostly used by boaters just in the spring, all along the Rio Chama here.

At about 4.5 miles west and north along the dirt road, you'll find an excellent Forest Service campground. About a mile beyond that, look for Christ of the Desert Monastery, which offers limited lodgings and meals for a fee. Contact: Monastery of Christ of the Desert, P.O. Box 270, Abiquiu, NM 87510-0270; www.christdesert.org

OTHER HIKES AND RIDES: FOREST ROAD 468 AROUND MESA DEL CAMINO
APPROXIMATE TOTAL LOOP DISTANCE: 10 miles
MODE OF TRAVEL: Biking or walking
DIFFICULTY: Easy to moderate

Forest Road 468: This relatively recent Forest Road makes a large loop around Mesa del Camino, staying just beneath the cliffs. The road does include some hills, especially in Cañon de las Fuertes, but in general it stays near the 8,000-foot contour line. Water is available at Fuertes Spring. The junction of Forest Roads 468 and 77 makes a good place to begin. Just east of this junction, maps show a jeep road heading to the top of Mesa del Camino. The top is basically flat, and the views from almost anywhere along the rim are spectacular.

Amanita muscara mushrooms, Cruces Basin Wilderness, Carson National Forest. Photo by Tom Till.

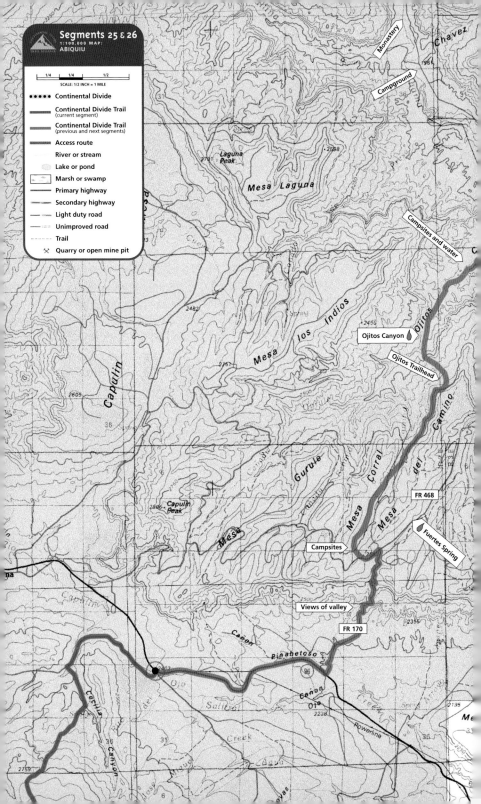

Segment 26
Skull Bridge to US 84: Rio Chama

Ghost Ranch Butte at sunset,
Ghost Ranch. Photo by Tom Till.

10.7 miles
Difficulty: Easy
You may encounter: motorized vehicles

Segment 26 **Total Elevation Gain:** 506 feet
From Mexico 635.95 miles
To Colorado 63.05 miles

CONTINENTAL DIVIDE
TRAIL ALLIANCE

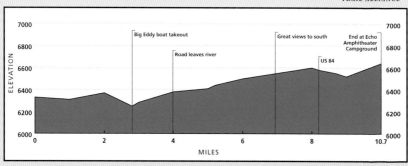

Elevation profile labels:
- Big Eddy boat takeout
- Road leaves river
- Great views to south
- US 84
- End at Echo Amphitheater Campground

ELEVATION (7000, 6800, 6600, 6400, 6200, 6000)
MILES (0, 2, 4, 6, 8, 10.7)

TRAIL OVERVIEW Short, easy, and very scenic summarize this segment, whose beauty is not to be prejudiced by the Continental Divide Trail's consisting entirely of a dirt road. The first few miles head along the Rio Chama, in the Chama River Canyon Wilderness. Sandstone cliffs in layers of red, orange, and buff flank the river. The Rio Chama ranks among New Mexico's most important rivers, and unlike so many pseudo rivers in the state, the Chama is a true river by anyone's definition. If you're here in the spring, when Colorado's high country sends its meltwater south, you'll enjoy watching kayakers, rafters, and canoeists floating through the scenic canyon. You might want to hang out a while at the Big Eddy boat takeout as you're hiking toward US 84.

As you're heading northeast up the gradual slopes of the open plains abutting Mesa de los Viejos, "Mesa of the Old Men," to the north, you'll be rewarded by some of the most picturesque views in all New Mexico. To the southeast you'll see the polychrome cliffs and canyons of Ghost Ranch; to the south lie the Abiquiu Reservoir and surrounding plains; to the southwest rise the high northern peaks of the Jemez Mountains, dominated by chisel-shaped Cerro Pedernal. The landforms and vistas here have attracted painters and photographers for generations.

Hiking trails are few here. The best known is the Ojitos Trail, which coincides with the CDT in the previous segment. The Rim Vista Trail is described on page 287. But for persons who don't mind walking lightly traveled dirt roads, Forest Road 151 along the Rio Chama is exceptionally scenic and interesting.

WATER NOTES

The only water source here is the river itself, so be sure to treat the water. Then it's not far to US 84 and the Ranger Station.

MOUNTAIN BIKE NOTES

The only real mountain bike route here is Forest Road 151—but it's outstanding. It offers easy terrain, numerous pullouts along the river, water at the Forest Service campground, and an interesting destination at Christ in the Desert Monastery.

EQUESTRIAN NOTES

Forest Road 151 is as appropriate for equestrians as it is for hikers and mountain-bikers. Equestrians might also want to take the short ride across Skull Bridge to Ojitos.

SOUTHBOUND HIKERS

Although much of this short segment runs along the Rio Chama, you might still consider carrying an overnight supply of water. Beyond the Chama, you'll find the next water at Los Ojitos, 3 miles into the next segment, a fairly easy stretch from US 84.

MAPS

USGS QUADRANGLES: Echo Amphitheater
OTHER MAPS: Santa Fe National Forest

LAND-MANAGEMENT AGENCIES

Ghost Ranch Living Museum/Carson National Forest

BEGINNING ACCESS POINT

SKULL BRIDGE: See Ending Access Point in Segment 25, page 277

ENDING ACCESS POINT

US 84: This segment ends at Echo Amphitheater, a scenic recreation area on US 84 north of Abiquiu.

SUPPLIES, SERVICES, AND ACCOMMODATIONS

ABIQUIU, an ancient settlement site inhabited first by Tewa Indians and later by Hispanic settlers, gained fame as the longtime home of painter Georgia O'Keeffe. Because of this, Abiquiu attracts numerous visitors, not always to the delight of the local people. Abiquiu is small, and its services very limited. Should you need more than the most basic supplies, you would go to Española or Santa Fe.

Distance from Trail	17.75 miles	
Zip Code	87510	
Bank	None	
Bus	None	
Dining	None	
Emergency	Rio Arriba County Sheriff	(505) 753-3320
Gear	None	
Groceries	Bodes General Merchandise Store	685-4422
Information	Ghost Ranch Museum	685-4312
Laundry	None	
Lodging	Ghost Ranch Conference Center	685-4333 or 685-4334
Medical	Las Clinicas del Norte, medical clinic	685-4479
Post Office	87510	685-4460
Showers	None	

GHOST RANCH: Although Ghost Ranch, operated by the Presbyterian Church as a conference center, doesn't sell supplies, they do rent rooms and campsites, have showers, and perhaps they even hold mail or caches. The setting, about 4 miles from the Forest Road 151–US 84 junction, is idyllic and more. Contact: Ghost Ranch Conference Center, Abiquiu 87510; (505) 685-4333 or (505) 685-4334.

TRAIL DESCRIPTION From Skull Bridge, N36°19'48", W106°37'28", elevation 6,330, turn east-southeast along dirt Forest Road 151. You'll stay on this road—indeed, you can't really get off—until you've reached US 84, 10 miles away. The terrain is mostly level as the road runs beside the river.

After about 4 miles, Forest Road 151 leaves the river and its valley to climb about 150 feet to the plains overlooking Abiquiu Reservoir. Here Forest Road 151 runs straight northeast, along the boundary between the Carson National Forest and the Piedra Lumbre Land Grant. It ascends gradually as it parallels the escarpment of Mesa de los Viejos, ("old men"), to the north. After about 2 miles, Forest Road 151 makes a slight jog north, heads over a modest divide, then drops after about a mile to US 84.

From there it's a 1.6-mile walk north along scenic US 84 to Echo Amphitheater and its Carson National Forest campgrounds. From the Forest Road 151–US 84 junction, it's a 1-mile walk south on US 84 to the Ghost Ranch Living Museum and the Carson National Forest Ranger Station there. *Note:* Forest Road 151 is wonderful—when it's dry. But when wet, it has a well-deserved reputation as one of the state's worst muddy roads—and New Mexico has a lot of horrible muddy roads. People camped along the Chama have been trapped by rainstorms that turned the road into mud. I once attempted a CDT reconnaissance during a wet period; I got less than 0.25 mile before I beat a retreat in my 4WD Toyota.

WILDERNESS ALERT

The Chama River Canyon Wilderness was designated in 1988 to complement the adjacent Chama Wild and Scenic River, also designated in 1988. The 50,300-acre Wilderness and the 24.6-mile stretch of river, running between El Vado Reservoir and Abiquiu Reservoir, are two components of a collage of public lands collectively called the Rio Chama Corridor, administered by several federal agencies that include the Santa Fe and Carson National Forests, the Bureau of Land Management, and the U.S. Army Corps of Engineers. Adjacent to the northern boundary of the Chama River Canyon Wilderness is the 11,985-acre Rio Chama Wilderness Study Area, administered as Wilderness by the BLM.

OTHER HIKES: RIM VISTA TRAIL

APPROXIMATE ONE-WAY LENGTH: 2.3 miles
MODE OF TRAVEL: Hiking
DIFFICULTY: Easy to moderate

Off Forest Road 151, 0.7 mile from its junction with US 84, a little two-track leads 0.5 mile to the Rim Vista Trail. This easy-to-moderate 2.3-mile hike to the rim of the mesa to the north takes but three hours or less, yet the vista from the rim of this part of the Rio Chama Valley is, well . . . the word "spectacular" seems somehow inadequate.

HISTORICAL NOTES

Why is it called Ghost Ranch? When Arthur Newton Pack, founder of the conference center, arrived in 1933, his guide to the property told him it had been called *Rancho de los Brujos,* "Ranch of the Witches," because it was supposed to have been haunted by evil sprits. "The name came to be freely translated as Ghost Ranch," said Pack. Some cottonwoods on the property were reputed to have served as gallows for local cattle thieves. The canyon was settled near the end of the 19th century by the Archuleta family, who built a stockade of cedar poles that came to be known as the Ghost House. A girl brought up in this house said she always believed the canyon was inhabited by evil spirits, or *brujos,* including "Earth Babies," 6 feet tall with red hair.

Georgia O'Keeffe and other local artists. O'Keeffe is but one of many well-known painters and photographers inspired by the landscape here, including Edward Weston, Eliot Porter, Thomas Moran, and Ernest Blumenschein. The main difference between these artists and most people who come here is that the artists spent time with the landscape, allowed their eyes to open to see the subtleties, details, and ceaseless cycle of change. So be grateful you're traveling through here at a slower pace; if ever there was a place to just let your eye and mind wander while you walk, this is it.

Cerro Pedernal. This chisel-shaped 9,862-foot peak, conspicuous from Forest Road 151, was well-known to ancient people both for its appearance and even more for its composition. Its name is Spanish and means "flint mountain"; Bernardo Miera y Pacheco on his map of 1779 labeled it Serra Pedernal and even drew its distinctive flat top. The nearby abandoned pueblo of Tsiping took its name from this peak; the Tewa name means "flaking stone mountain." More recently, Cerro Pedernal was made famous through the paintings of Georgia O'Keeffe, who saw the peak from her home in Abiquiu.

SEE PAGES 282–283 FOR SEGMENT 26 MAP

Prickly pear blooms in the desert grasslands. Photo by Andrew Ward.

Segment 27
US 84 to Chama: The Tierra Amarilla

Ghost Ranch buttes and badlands,
Ghost Ranch. Photo by Tom Till.

44 miles
Difficulty: Moderate
You may encounter: motorized vehicles

TRAIL OVERVIEW *Note:* Because of the unresolved status of former land grant property in northern New Mexico, local people, the Continental Divide Trail Alliance, and the Forest Service are in a long, complex, and delicate process of education and negotiation. While this deliberation continues, the "official" CDT route—the subject of this book—

follows along highways. Hikers always are free to investigate other ways to get from the Rio Chama to the Colorado border—taking care not to trespass on private land. Please check with the Forest Service for information about alternatives to the "official" route.

THE TIERRA AMARILLA. Often abbreviated TA, the term Tierra Amarilla represents not only a town but also a region, a cause, and a symbol. In 1967, much of the nation heard about Tierra Amarilla when land rights activist Reies López Tijerina staged an armed takeover of the county courthouse. Leading a movement called Alíanza Federal de los Mercedes, "Federal Alliance for Land Grants," Tijerina charged that grantees' heirs became unjustly dispossessed when titles to the lands passed to the U.S. government and private owners through fraudulent means.

The takeover led to a shootout in which a deputy sheriff was wounded. The New Mexico National Guard were summoned, bringing tanks and helicopters. Tijerina was arrested and jailed, but he later was found innocent of charges arising from the incident. Since then, Tijerina's personal influence has waned, but others have assumed his cause. Local Hispanic peoples are extremely sensitive about the status of the lands not only within the Tierra Amarilla Land Grant but also in the nearby Carson National Forest, as it was largely from land grant property that the forest was created.

So intense and current is this issue that New Mexico's congressional delegation successfully promoted legislation in the 207th Congress to study the land grant issue. No other action has been taken at this time.

For day hikes in this region, the Brazos Cliffs and the Brazos Box offer an exciting side trip from the end of NM 512 , east of the village of Brazos.

WATER NOTES

 As this segment is currently along the highway, water here is relatively easy to obtain in communities and facilities along the road.

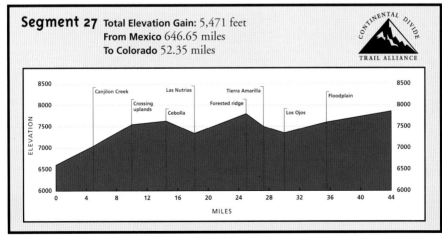

Segment 27 Total Elevation Gain: 5,471 feet
From Mexico 646.65 miles
To Colorado 52.35 miles

MOUNTAIN BIKE NOTES

 Although the CDT runs along heavily traveled US 84, the surrounding roads, such as NM 512 along the Rio Brazos and NM 95 and 112 leading to El Vado Reservoir and Heron Lake and associated state parks, offer appealing mountain biking.

EQUESTRIAN NOTES

The CDT is patently unsuited for horse travel, but numerous outdoor recreation resorts offer facilities and suggestions for trail rides.

SOUTHBOUND HIKERS

A very long walk along a highway lies ahead of you. Fortunately, the miles go rather quickly, the scenery is pleasant and interesting, limited supplies and certainly water are readily available, and some of New Mexico's most spectacular landscapes await you.

MAPS

USGS QUADRANGLES: Echo Amphitheater, Alire, Canjilon, Cebolla, Las Nutrias, Tierra Amarilla, Brazos, Chama

OTHER MAPS: Carson National Forest (best small-scale coverage of this area), New Mexico Road & Recreation Atlas, New Mexico State Highway

LAND-MANAGEMENT AGENCIES

Carson National Forest/Canjilon Ranger District

BEGINNING ACCESS POINT

 US 84: 18.5 miles north of Abiquiu.

ALTERNATE ACCESS

 US 64: US 64 intersects US 84 at Tierra Amarilla, about two-thirds of the way north between Echo Amphitheater and Chama.

 NM 17: NM 17 heads over Cumbres Pass (to Chama from the north), to coincide with the CDT.

ENDING ACCESS POINT

 CHAMA: This segment ends at Chama, the junction of US 64, US 84, and NM 17.

TRAIL DESCRIPTION The second-longest CDT segment in New Mexico will have this book's simplest trail description: Just follow US 84 to Chama.

That's the official route right now. The reason is land grants, specifically the Tierra Amarilla Land Grant (see page 291). Local officials and leaders have stated opposition to the CDT's going across present or former land grants. They feel,

SUPPLIES, SERVICES, AND ACCOMMODATIONS

CHAMA aspires to become a major outdoor recreation center for northern New Mexico. Considering that northern New Mexico now has only one other such center—Taos— it's hardly an impossible dream; Chama certainly has the natural resources. The Rio Chama and nearby Rio Brazos are trout celebrities. The Rio Chama canyon is known for classic southwestern rafting and kayaking—whitewater and laid-back flatwater—red canyon walls, and turquoise skies. New Mexico's best, and certainly most reliable, cross-country skiing is here, as well as some of New Mexico's best big-game hunting. And now the village is the last stop in New Mexico on the CDT. Despite all this, however, Chama remains very much a northern New Mexico village, so CDT hikers should not expect the same array of services as in comparable villages in, say, Colorado.

Distance from Trail	On the trail	
Zip Code	87520	
Bank	Sunwest Bank, 541 Terrace Avenue	(505) 756-2111
Bus	None	
Dining	Viva Vera's Mexican Kitchen, 2202 Hwy. 17 (at the "Y")	756-2557
Emergency	Marshall's office	756-2319
	State Police	756-2343 or 753-2777
Gear	Dark Timber, 2242 Main Street	756-2300
Groceries	Chama Valley Supermarket,	756-2545
	US 84 and NM 17 (at the "Y")	
Information	Chama Chamber of Commerce,	(800) 477-0149
	499 Main Street, Cumbres Mall	
	P.O. Box 30, Chama, NM 87520	
Laundry	Speed Queen Laundry, Pine Street	756-2479
Lodging	Branding Iron Motel, 1511 West Main Street	756-2156
	River Bend Lodge, Route 1	756-2264
Medical	Health Services of Northern New Mexico,	756-2143
	211 North Pine, 87520	
	Ambulance	588-7252
Post Office	199 West 5th, 87520	756-2240
Showers	Twin Rivers RV Park and Campground	756-2264
Other	Cumbres & Toltec Scenic Railroad,	756-2151
	500 Terrace Avenue, 87520	

TIERRA AMARILLA: Despite being the seat of Rio Arriba County, Tierra Amarilla has relatively few services. Basic supplies such as groceries are available.

BRAZOS: Corkins Lodge on the Rio Brazos, (505) 588-7261, caters to outdoor recreationists, especially trout fishermen. It is reached by taking NM 512 east from the village for 7 miles.

HERON LAKE AND EL VADO RESERVOIR: Although not on the CDT, these lakes and associated state parks and recreation facilities could be of interest to CDT travelers.

Camping	Heron Store and Restaurant, NM 95	(505) 588-7436
	El Vado Lake Campground, NM 112	588-7255

understandably, that a federal project such as the CDT would diminish their claims to their traditional lands.

The Continental Divide Trail Alliance and the Carson National Forest have been sensitive to local concerns, and have met with local leaders and officials to promote greater mutual understanding. With the passage of the legislation, this is an especially precarious time for federal initiatives, such as the CDT, on former land grants. Assuredly, compromises eventually will be struck, and the CDT will be seen not as a threat but as an asset. But for now, we all must be patient and realize that the best we can do now to promote the CDT here is to be respectful, responsible, and friendly.

In the meantime, the "official" CDT runs along US 64 to Chama. To be sure, nothing prevents you from hiking trails and roads in the National Forest. Though the status of former land grants is under study by Congress, as of now these are public lands, and you're entitled to use them. The Forest Service can advise you of trail and dirt road options. As one Forest Service official put it, "There's nothing to prevent people from hiking here; just don't call it the CDT."

Along US 84, the distances can be read from the state highway map. From NM 96 to Cebolla, 21 miles; Cebolla to Tierra Amarilla, 13 miles; from Tierra Amarilla to Brazos, 3 miles; Brazos to Chama, 11.5 miles.

You can't get lost.

Here's a summary of the route:

At the Echo Canyon–US 84 junction, elevation 6,603 feet, US 84 goes northnorthwest along the Arroyo Seco until at 1.9 miles it swings north, then at 4.2 miles north-northeast to parallel Canjilon Creek. The highway goes along the creek for 1.2 miles until at 5.4 miles from Echo Amphitheater, below the southern tip of a mesa, Canjilon Creek heads northeast while US 84 enters a narrow canyon heading north-northeast. It stays in the canyon for 1.8 miles, until at 6.2 miles the country opens up at 7,200 feet. The highway stays on the west side of a small drainage, climbing gradually until the Canjilon turnoff, elevation 7,469 feet (11.8 miles from Echo Amphitheater).

To the village from US 84 is 3.6 miles. Hispanics were at least trading and trapping in this area as early as the late eighteenth century. Like many villages here, Canjilon still has some flavor of a wilderness outpost. Its support services are limited, but the Carson National Forest–Canjilon Ranger Station is here.

From the Canjilon turnoff on US 84 to Cebolla, 7,630 feet, is 4.2 miles, 17.5 to Tierra Amarilla. The country here is more open and rolling and remains thus through Las Nutrias. The highway here crosses the Rio las Nutrias, "Beavers River."

From Las Nutrias, the highway is level to climbing gently until at 7.5 miles it goes through a narrow divide, climbs to 7,850 feet, then descends to the broad plain of Tierra Amarilla and the Rito de Tierra Amarilla. Basic supplies are available in Tierra Amarilla, seat of Rio Arriba County. This area, including the villages of Los Ojos, Los Brazos, and La Puente, are the heart of the Tierra Amarilla, and many buildings date from the area's permanent settlement, around 1860.

At Tierra Amarilla, US 64 joins US 84 from the east, and the two highways coincide through Chama. At about 3.5 miles north of Tierra Amarilla, US 64-84 crosses the Rio Brazos just before the village of Brazos, elevation 7,370 feet. Here the highway stays along the east side of the floodplain of the Rio Chama en route to Chama. **Conspicuous to the east of the village of Brazos** are the Brazos Cliffs. Sheer cliffs of Precambrian quartzite, they mark the abrupt boundary between the 7,500-foot agricultural lands of the Rio Chama Valley and the 10,000-foot Brazos high country. The cliffs are popular with rock climbers; the Brazos Box is an awesome rift in the dark rock. Brazos Falls is the highest waterfall in New Mexico. Trout fishing here is renowned.

From Brazos to Chama along US 64–84 is 11.5 miles, straight north along the Rio Chama. The countryside is cool and scenic. Some of New Mexico's finest trout waters are here, and in the nearby forests some of the state's finest elk hunting.

At Chama, US 64–84 heads west, but here the CDT goes into the village on NM 17.

HISTORICAL NOTES

More place names. The two dominant names in this part of New Mexico both are based on color. *Chama* most likely derives from the Tewa *tzama,* "red," a reference to the river's color. And *Tierra Amarilla* is merely the Spanish version of the Tewa and Navajo names, all meaning "yellow earth," for yellowish clay deposits. The Tewas had pueblos throughout the area along the river, one named something like Chama. Navajos, Jicarilla Apaches, and Utes, among other tribes, saw the area as their hunting, trading, and raiding territory.

Thus Hispanic settlement of this area came rather late, despite being just upriver from New Mexico's oldest Hispanic settlement, San Gabriel, at the confluence of the Rio Grande and Rio Chama, near San Juan Pueblo.

As *The Place Names of New Mexico* explains: "In the early days, the term *Tierra Amarilla* referred to the entire region, from Canjilon north to the Colorado border, west to the Jicarilla Apache Reservation, and east to Tres Piedras; the grant made in 1832 to Manuel Martínez and others was called the *Tierra Amarilla Grant.* Indian danger retarded Hispanic settlement of the area, and when Hispanics established a village here about 1862, they called it *Las Nutrias,* "the beavers," likely for beavers living along the *Rito de Tierra Amarilla,* which flows through the village, though the post office here has always been called Tierra Amarilla. In 1880, the state legislature moved the Rio Arriba County seat to here and at the same time formally changed the village's name to Tierra Amarilla."

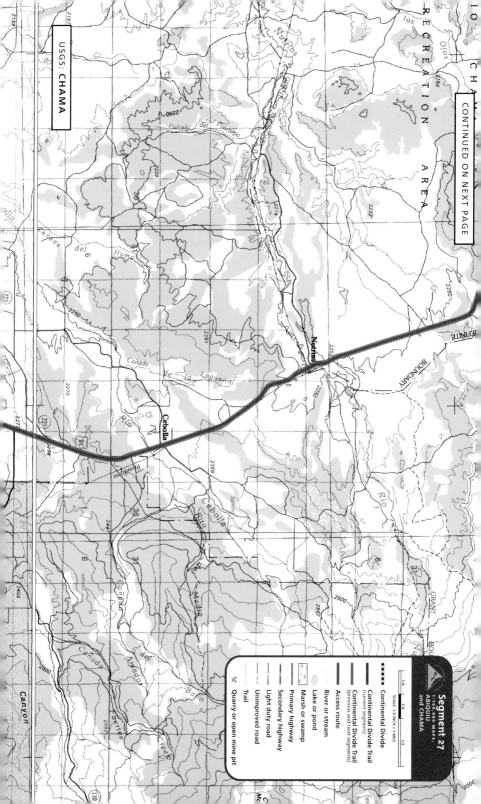

Segment 27

ABIQUIU MAPS
and CHAMA

SCALE 1/2 INCH = 1 MILE

1/4   1/4   1/2

• • • • • Continental Divide

Continental Divide Trail
(current segment)

Continental Divide Trail
(previous and next segments)

Access route

River or stream

Lake or pond

Marsh or swamp

Primary highway

Secondary highway

Light duty road

Unimproved road

Trail

×   Quarry or open mine pit

CONTINUED FROM PREVIOUS PAGE

Segment 28
Chama to Cumbres Pass

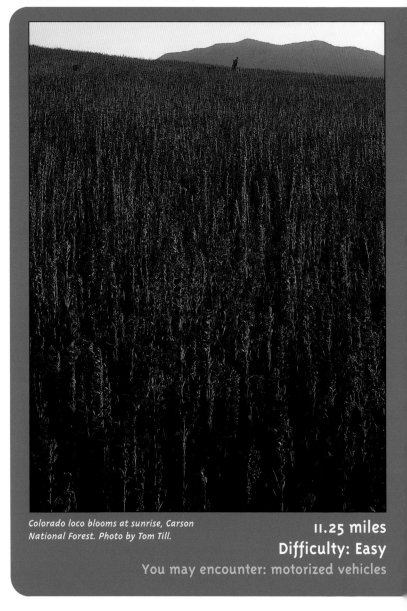

Colorado loco blooms at sunrise, Carson National Forest. Photo by Tom Till.

11.25 miles
Difficulty: Easy
You may encounter: motorized vehicles

TRAIL OVERVIEW *Note:* Because of the unresolved status of former land grant property in northern New Mexico, local people, the Continental Divide Trail Alliance, and the Forest Service are in a long, complex, and delicate process of education and negotiation. While this deliberation continues, the "official" CDT route—the subject of this book—follows along highways. Hikers always are free to investigate other ways to get from the Rio Chama to the Colorado border—taking care not to trespass on private land. Please check with the Forest Service for information about alternatives to the "official" route.

THIS, THE FINAL CDT SEGMENT in New Mexico, is in ironic contrast to the first segment. There the CDT, traversing country filled with roads and few trails, headed cross-country; in this segment, with abundant trails and dirt roads, the CDT follows a paved highway.

The primary reason is the Tierra Amarilla Land Grant. The generations-old and continuing sensitivity over this huge area is described in the previous segment; but the result is that the CDT in New Mexico ends as it began—on a road.

It is an attractive road. By the time you've walked it to Cumbres Pass, you'll already have a sense of being in Colorado. The desert is behind you. The forests ahead are spruce, fir, and aspen; water is plentiful. It looks like elk country—and it's also good habitat for deer, bear, and mountain lion. Highway traffic is relatively light; approaching Colorado feels good. Appropriately, you'll reach your goal at Cumbres Pass, *cumbre* being Spanish for "top," "peak," "summit," "acme," and "best."

Despite a paucity of designated and maintained trails, there's limited but scenically spectacular hiking here. There are several trails close to where County Road 445 meets the Colorado border.

WATER NOTES

The highway that currently is also the CDT route goes along Wolf Creek, as well as passing by houses and other possible sources.

MOUNTAIN BIKE NOTES

The routes described below for equestrians also are great for mountain biking. Forest Road 445 is especially beautiful in the fall.

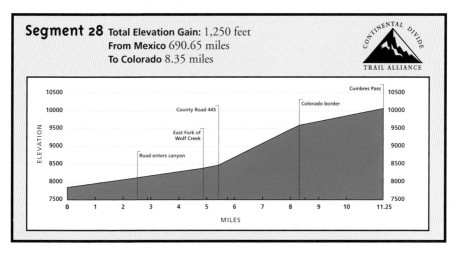

Segment 28 Total Elevation Gain: 1,250 feet
From Mexico 690.65 miles
To Colorado 8.35 miles

CONTINENTAL DIVIDE TRAIL ALLIANCE

EQUESTRIAN NOTES

Some of New Mexico's finest horseback riding is around Chama. The official CDT route runs along the highway, but surrounding the highway is a network of Forest Roads traversing spectacular wild country. You'll find especially appealing riding along County Road 445 as it parallels the Rio Chama into Colorado. Just outside the village of Chama on the north is the Edward Sargent State Wildlife Area, whose 10-mile access road provides excellent riding—a great place to watch birds and see elk.

SOUTHBOUND HIKERS

Your first segment in New Mexico is along a paved road. At least as of this writing. Alternatives to this are actively being pursued. And as highways go, this one is far more appealing than most, and not just because it's downhill.

MAPS

USGS QUADRANGLES: Chama, West Fork Rio Brazos
OTHER MAPS: Carson National Forest

LAND-MANAGEMENT AGENCIES

Carson National Forest/Canjilon Ranger District

BEGINNING ACCESS POINT

 CHAMA: US 64/84, a major highway, provides access to Chama from the west and south. From the north, access is via NM 17, the CDT route.

ENDING ACCESS POINT

 CUMBRES PASS: This segment's end is reached from the north; from Antonito, Colorado, located on US 285, take CO 17 west to the pass. A parking area is about 0.1 mile west of the summit on the highway's south side.

SUPPLIES, SERVICES, AND ACCOMMODATIONS

CHAMA, described in Segment 27, page 293, is an appealing vacation spot, and should you want to rendezvous with people for your final New Mexico segment, this would be a good place. Hikers wanting to give their feet a respite can revel in taking a 128-mile round-trip train ride between Chama and Antonito, Colorado. The Cumbres & Toltec Scenic Railroad is the nation's longest surviving narrow-gauge line. Your passenger car is pulled by an old-time steam engine that draws water from old wooden water tanks; it travels through scenery that's lost none of its beauty since the railroad was built around 1880.

TRAIL DESCRIPTION Starting at the train station in Chama, NM 17 heads north through the village, then swings east to cross the Rio Chama at 0.8 mile; soon thereafter, it crosses the tracks of the Cumbres & Toltec Scenic Railroad. The highway heads northeast across broad, open country, climbing gradually until, at 2.5 miles from the train station, it enters a narrow canyon whose bottom it shares with the railroad. The canyon is about 1.7 miles long, and the road climbs 100 feet. When the canyon ends and the terrain opens, at 8,200 feet, the railroad passes the locality of Lobato. Here the railroad makes a loop to gain elevation while the road continues northeast and climbs steeply as it crosses Wolf Creek.

Arriving at Wolf Creek, you'll notice on the hillside to the west the cabins and structures of Lobo Lodge. Heading uphill and west from NM 17 here is County Road 445, a maintained dirt connecting the Wolf Creek valley with that of the Rio Chama. The junction is N36°57'41" W106°31'38", elevation 8,450 feet. At 3.3 miles from NM 17, County Road 445 reaches the Colorado border (see page 304).

NM 17 continues along the mountainside above Wolf Creek for 1.5 miles before heading uphill to cross the railroad at about 7.5 miles from the train station. It levels out briefly at 8,900 feet, on the northeast side of a 9,090-foot mountain, then climbs rather steeply for about a mile to run parallel above the railroad to the Colorado border, N36°59'36" W106°29'57", elevation 9,100 feet.

From the border, you can follow a trail for 1.5 miles to Cumbres Pass, or you can continue on the highway as it climbs almost 1,000 feet to the top. A green highway sign labels the pass. You will pass beneath a railroad trestle, after which you'll see a sign on the road's right side; this reads "CDTNST" and points to the trail turnoff on the left (southwest). Nearby is a post proclaiming "Cont Div Tr 813." If you're unclear about the trail, look for a post reading "813" about 20 yards from the road.

This is a pleasant spot to end your New Mexico trek and begin your Colorado journey. The hills here are rolling, with grassy meadows interspersed with stands of spruce, fir, and aspen. Water is available at several places here, including the station of the Cumbres & Toltec Scenic Railroad, a historic narrow-gauge rail road still offering seasonal passenger service between Chama and Antonito.

Congratulations—and good hiking!

OTHER HIKES AND RIDES: COUNTY ROAD 445 TO THE COLORADO BORDER

APPROXIMATE ONE-WAY DISTANCE: 3.3 miles

MODE OF TRAVEL: Hiking, horseback riding, mountain biking, cross-country skiing

DIFFICULTY: Easy to moderate

This is a stunningly beautiful area, especially popular among trout fishermen— a maze of streams and beaver ponds, with lots of campsites. County Road 445 is not plowed in the winter, which makes it one of New Mexico's premier cross-country ski routes. Near the Colorado border, the roads dwindle and hiking trails wind through aspen groves and meadows.

From NM 17, County Road 445 runs west uphill for 0.5 mile, crosses a ridge before swinging north, then descends gently along the hillside to reach the Chama floodplain after 2 miles and at about 8,400 feet; from here, the road stays in the flood plain to the Colorado border.

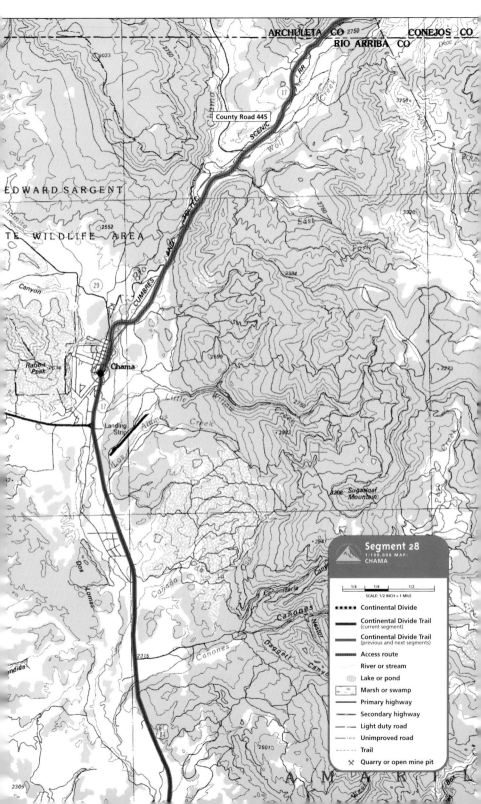

ARCHULETA CO 2750   CONEJOS CO
RIO ARRIBA CO

County Road 445

EDWARD SARGENT

TE WILDLIFE AREA

Canyon

Rabon Peak

Chama

Landing Strip

Little William Creek

Sugarloaf Mountain

Appendix A: Land-Management Agencies in New Mexico

BUREAU OF LAND MANAGEMENT

Albuquerque Field Office
Rio Puerco Resource Area
435 Montano Road NE
Albuquerque, NM 87107
(505) 761-8700

Farmington Field Office
1235 La Plata Highway
Farmington, NM 87401
(505) 327-5344

Las Cruces Field Office
1800 Marquess Street
Las Cruces, NM 88005
(505) 528-8228

Socorro Field Office
198 Neel Avenue NW
Socorro, NM 87801
(505) 835-0412

Taos Field Office
224 Cruz Alta Road
Taos, NM 87571
(505) 758-8851

U.S. FOREST SERVICE

Southwestern Region
517 Gold Avenue SW
Albuquerque, NM 87102
(505) 842-3292
(Information/Maps/Locator)

GILA NATIONAL FOREST

3005 East Camino del Bosque
Silver City, NM 88061
(505) 388-8201

Black Range Ranger District
P.O. Box 431
1804 Date Street
Truth or Consequences, NM 87901
(505) 894-6677

Wilderness Ranger District at Mimbres Station
Route 11, Box 50
Mimbres, NM 88049
(505) 536-2250

Quemado Ranger District
Box 159
Quemado, NM 87829
(505) 773-4678

APACHE NATIONAL FOREST

Most of this is in Arizona. The New Mexico portions are administered by the Gila National Forest through the Quemado Ranger District.

CIBOLA NATIONAL FOREST

2113 Osuna Rd. NE
Albuquerque, NM 87113
(505) 346-2650

Mount Taylor Ranger District
1800 Lobo Canyon Road
Grants, NM 87020
(505) 287-8833

SANTA FE NATIONAL FOREST

1474 Rodeo Road
Santa Fe, NM 87502
(505) 438-7840

Cuba Ranger District
P.O. Box 130
Cuba, NM 87103
(505) 289-3264

Coyote Ranger District
P.O. Box 160
Coyote, NM 87012
(505) 638-5547

CARSON NATIONAL FOREST

208 Cruz Alta Road
Taos, NM 87571
(505) 758-6200

Ghost Ranch Living Museum
Highway 84
Abiquiu, NM 87510
(505) 685-4312

Canjilon Ranger District
P.O. Box 488
Canjilon, NM 87515
(505) 684-2486

NATIONAL PARK SERVICE

El Malpais National Monument
P.O. Box 939
Grants, NM 87020
(505) 285-4641

Appendix B: Equipment Checklist

I've seen as many equipment lists as I've seen guidebooks (and that's a lot!). Rather than burden you with yet another basic equipment list, which you can pick up in any outdoor store, I'll describe the method I use.

I work from a computer (though that's not necessary), and on it I keep a running checklist of equipment I've found necessary and useful. The list constantly is evolving as I discard items and add new ones; I recently added duct tape, for example. When I want to go for a backpack trip I simply print out the list and then cross off items as I put them in my pack or my car. With some items on the list I'll say, "Nah, I don't think I'll need that," but at least the list has forced me to consider them. If you do this conscientiously for several trips, you'll quickly have your own personalized list of essential items.

Because New Mexico poses some unique challenges for hikers unfamiliar with the Southwest, I'll list here a few items that might otherwise be overlooked:

Rain gear (yes, it's a semiarid environment, but it does rain—and sometimes in torrents)
Sun protection hat, sunscreen, dark glasses
Tweezers (lots of stickers and cacti here)
A lightweight ground cloth (lots of sharp stuff on the ground here)
Water filter and treatment tablets (you'll drink from a lot of stock tanks in New Mexico)
A really good compass and/or Global Positioning System unit, along with map ruler for determining latitude-longitude coordinates (much of the Continental Divide Trail here is cross-country over confusing topography)

BOB'S CURRENT BACKPACKING-TRIP CHECKLIST

(*Note:* Bob does *not* take all these items on any given trip. In fact, he's discovering just how many he can do without. Bob's reasonably fit, but he's not a gorilla! This list is only to give you grist for your own list.)

TO TAKE:

- Pack and pack fly
- Water bottles for sides of pack
- Tent, with rain flies
- Sleeping bag
- Pillow
- Ground cloth
- Garbage bags
- Inflatable pad, stuff sack, and repair kit
- Stove
- Fuel in fuel bottle
- Flashlights and batteries
- Tent lantern
- Trowel for toilet
- Waterproof matches and/or a disposable lighter
- Cookset

Sponge & scrub pads	Matches
Knife	Can opener
Plates	Mugs

- Food
- Water/water bottles
- Water filter or iodine tablets (and vitamin C tablets)
- Boots
- Toilet paper
- Multi-tool knife
- Binoculars
- Camera and film

- Whistles
- Clothing (no cotton anywhere, except in underwear)
  - Socks (liners and outers, two of each)
  - Underwear
  - T-shirts/turtlenecks
  - Long pants/shorts
  - Sweater/sweatshirt
  - Jacket
  - Mittens/gloves
  - Hat (day and night)
  - Bandannas (at least two)
  - Rain gear
- Global Positioning System (GPS) unit
- Cell phone
- Zippered plastic bags
- Compressed roll of duct tape
- Compass
- Maps and guides

Topo maps	Highway map
USFS maps	Wildflowers
Birds	Stars

- Notebook and pens
- Sunscreen
- Insect repellent (rarely needed)
- Extra glasses (and/or contact lenses)
- Watch
- Sewing kit
- Nylon cord
- Walking stick
- Extra car key
- Money and credit cards
- Reservations/tickets, etc.
- Pertinent phone numbers and addresses
- Car registration/insurance/driver's license
- Toiletries
  - Toothpaste and toothbrushes
  - Soap
  - Unbreakable mirror
  - Comb
- Towels/washcloths
- First-aid kit/medical

Aspirin	Ibuprofen
Band-Aids	Moleskin
First-aid cream	Antacid pills
Anti-diarrheal	Safety pins
Laxative	Dental floss

Appendix C: Map Sources

HOLMAN'S, INC.
6201 Jefferson Street NE
Albuquerque, NM 87109
(505) 343-0007

MAPLINK
Map Distributors
30 La Patera Lane #5
Santa Barbara, CA 93117
(800) 962-1394

NEW MEXICO EARTH SCIENCE INFORMATION CENTER (USGS PRODUCTS)
Earth Data Analysis Center (EDAC)
Bandelier West, Room 111
University of New Mexico
Albuquerque, NM 87131-6031
(505) 277-3622 Ext. 230

UNITED STATES BUREAU OF LAND MANAGEMENT (BLM)
Bureau of Land Management
Albuquerque District Office
Rio Puerco Resource Area
435 Montaño Road NE
Albuquerque, NM 87107
(505) 761-8700

UNITED STATES FOREST SERVICE
Southwestern Region
517 Gold Avenue SW
Albuquerque, NM 87102
(505) 842-3292

UNITED STATES GEOLOGICAL SURVEY
Denver Federal Center
P.O. Box 25286
Lakewood, CO 80255
(303) 202-4700

Appendix D: Map Lists

The *New Mexico Road & Recreation Atlas,* published by Benchmark Maps and Maplink (see above), provides the best overall coverage for New Mexico. Maps of the National Forests, including Wilderness Areas, are available either from the individual Forest or from the U.S. Forest Service's Southwestern Region Office in Albuquerque.

Following is a comprehensive list of the 1:24K and 1:100K USGS maps covering the Continental Divide Trail route in New Mexico. For much of the route, it is not necessary to obtain full 1:24K coverage as the 1:100K maps are fully adequate—and much lighter.

USGS 1:100,000 BLM MAPS:
Abiquiu
Acoma Pueblo
Animas
Chaco Mesa
Chama
Fence Lake
Hatch
Lordsburg
Los Alamos
Quemado
San Mateo
    Mountains
Silver City
Truth or
    Consequences
Tularosa Mountains
Zuni

USGS 1:24,000 QUADRANGLES:
Adams Diggings
Alegres Mountain
Alire
Allie Canyon
Arrosa Ranch
Arroyo del Agua
Arroyo Empedrado
Bell Peak
Big Hatchet Peak
Blue Hills
Bonine Canyon
Bonner Canyon
Brazos
Brockman
Burro Peak
C Bar Ranch
Cabezon Peak
Cabin Wells
Canjilon
Cerro Alesna
Cerro Alto

Cerro Brillante
Cerro Parida
Cerro Pelon
Chama
Collins Park
Cox Peak
Cuba
Echo Amphitheater
El Dado Mesa
Gallina
Grants
Grants SE
Guadalupe
Hachita Peak
Hatchet Ranch
Headcut Reservoir
Ice Caves
Ice Caves SE
John Kerr Peak
La Rendija
Laguna Peak
Las Nutrias
Lobo Springs
Lookout Mountain
Los Pilares
Mangas Mountain
Mesa Cortada
Mesa Portales
Milan
Mojonera Canyon
Mount Taylor
Nacimiento Peak
Ninetysix Ranch
North Pasture
North Star Mesa
O Bar O Canyon

Paddys Hole
Pelona Mountain
Pie Town
Playas Peak
Rail Mountain
Reading Mountain
Red Flats
Reeds Peak
Salvation Peak
San Luis
San Mateo
San Pablo
San Rafael
Sand Canyon
Sawmill Peak
Separ
Sheridan Canyon
Silver City
Third Canyon
Tierra Amarilla
Trail Lake
Tres Lagunas
Tularosa Canyon
Twin Sisters
Tyrone
U Bar Ridge
Veteado Mountain
Wahoo Peak
Wallace Mesa
Werney Hill
West Fork Rio
    Brazos
West Pitchfork
    Canyon
Wind Mountain
York Ranch

Appendix E: Conservation and Trail Advocacy Groups

**ADVENTURE CYCLING
ASSOCIATION**
P.O. Box 8308
Missoula, MT 59807
(406) 721-1776

AMERICAN HIKING SOCIETY
1422 Fenwick Lane
Silver Spring, MD 20910
(301) 565-6704
E-mail: ahshiker@aol.com

**AMERICAN LONG DISTANCE
HIKERS ASSOCIATION–WEST
(ALDHAW)**
P.O. Box 651
Vancouver, WA 98666-0651

**BACK COUNTRY HORSEMEN
OF AMERICA**
P.O. Box 1367
Graham, WA 98338-1367
www.backcountryhorse.com

**BACK COUNTRY HORSEMEN
OF NEW MEXICO**
P.O. Box 37005
Albuquerque, NM
87176-7005
(505) 853-1033

**BACK COUNTRY HORSEMEN
OF NEW MEXICO–NORTHWEST
CHAPTER**
P.O. Box 2774
Corrales, NM 87048
(505) 898-8450 or
(505) 898-1093

**CONTINENTAL DIVIDE TRAIL
ALLIANCE**
P.O. Box 628
Pine, CO 80470
(303) 838-3760
(888) 909-CDTA
E-mail: CDNST@aol.com
www.cdtrail.org

**CONTINENTAL DIVIDE TRAIL
SOCIETY**
3704 North Charles Street,
#604
Baltimore, MD 21218-2300
(410) 235-9610
E-mail: cdtsociety@aol.com

FOREST GUARDIANS
1411 Second Street SW
Santa Fe, NM 87505
(505) 988-9126
E-mail: swwild@
fguardians.org
www.fguardians.org

**INTERNATIONAL MOUNTAIN
BIKE ASSOCIATION**
P.O. Box 7578
Boulder, CO 80306-7578
(303) 545-9011
E-mail: info@imba.com
www.imba.com

LEAVE NO TRACE
P.O. Box 997
Boulder, CO 80306
(303) 442-8222
(800) 332-4100
www.lnt.org

NEW MEXICO MOUNTAIN CLUB
P.O. Box 4151
University Station
Albuquerque, NM 87196

**NEW MEXICO WILDERNESS
ALLIANCE**
P.O. Box 13116
Albuquerque, NM 87192
(505) 255-5966 Ext. 106
E-mail: nmwa@earthlink.com
www.sdc.org/nmwa

**PARTNERSHIP FOR THE
NATIONAL TRAILS SYSTEM**
214 North Henry Street
Suite 203
Madison, WI 53703
(608) 249-7870
E-mail: nattrails@aol.com

SIERRA CLUB
85 2nd Street, Second Floor
San Francisco, CA 94105-3441
(415) 977-5500
E-mail: information@
sierraclub.org
www.sierraclub.org

THE WILDERNESS SOCIETY
1615 M Street, NW
Washington, DC 20036
(800) The-Wild
www.wilderness.org

**THE WILDERNESS SOCIETY-
FOUR CORNERS STATES
REGION**
7475 Dakin Street, Suite 410
Denver, CO 80211
(303) 650-5818
E-mail: co@tws.org

THE WILDLANDS PROJECT
Wildlands CPR
P.O. Box 7516
Missoula, MT 59807
(406) 543-9551
E-mail: WildlandsCPR@
wildlandsCPR.org
www.wildlandsCPR.org

Appendix F: Other Reading and Bibliography

CONTINENTAL DIVIDE TRAIL REFERENCES

Berger, Karen, and Daniel R. Smith. *Where the Waters Divide.* New York: Harmony Books, 1993.

Davis, Lora. *Wyoming's Continental Divide Trail: The Official Guide.* Englewood, Colo.: Westcliffe Publishers, 2000.

Fayhee, M. John. *Along Colorado's Continental Divide Trail.* Englewood, Colo.: Westcliffe Publishers, 1997.

Howard, Lynna. *Along Montana and Idaho's Continental Divide Trail.* Englewood, Colo.: Westcliffe Publishers, 2000.

———. *Montana and Idaho's Continental Divide Trail: The Official Guide.* Englewood, Colo.: Westcliffe Publishers, 2000.

Jones, Tom Lorang. *Colorado's Continental Divide Trail: The Official Guide.* Englewood, Colo.: Westcliffe Publishers, 1997.

Patterson, David. *Along New Mexico's Continental Divide Trail.* Englewood, Colo: Westcliffe Publishers, 2001.

Smith, Scott T. *Along Wyoming's Continental Divide Trail.* Englewood, Colo.: Westcliffe Publishers, 2000.

NEW MEXICO HIKING GUIDES

Evans, Harry. *50 Hikes in New Mexico.* Baldwin Park, Calif.: Gem Guides Book Company, 1995.

Hill, Mike. *Guide to the Hiking Areas of New Mexico.* Albuquerque, N.M.: University of New Mexico Press, 1995.

Julyan, Bob. *Best Hikes with Children in New Mexico.* Seattle, Wash.: The Mountaineers Books, 1994.

———. *New Mexico's Wilderness Areas: The Complete Guide.* Englewood, Colo.: Westcliffe Publishers, 1999.

Martin, Craig. *75 Hikes in New Mexico.* Seattle, Wash.: The Mountaineers Books, 1995.

Parent, Laurence. *The Hiker's Guide to New Mexico.* Helena, Mont.: Falcon Press Publishing Company, 1991.

Pern, Stephen. *The Great Divide: A Walk Through America Along the Continental Divide.* New York: Viking, 1987.

Ungnade, Herbert. *Guide to the New Mexico Mountains.* Albuquerque, N.M.: University of New Mexico Press, 1965.

LOCAL AND REGIONAL HIKING GUIDES
The Santa Fe–Los Alamos–Taos area:

Hoard, Dorothy. *A Guide to Bandelier National Monument.* Los Alamos, N.M.: Los Alamos Historical Society, 1983.

———. *Los Alamos Outdoors,* 2d ed. Los Alamos, N.M.: Los Alamos Historical Society, 1995.

Matthews, Kay. *Hiking the Mountain Trails of Santa Fe.* Chamisal, N.M.: Acequia Madre Press, 1995.

———. *Hiking the Wilderness: A Backpacking Guide to the Wheeler Peak, Pecos, and San Pedro Parks Wilderness Areas.* Chamisal, N.M.: Acequia Madre Press, 1992.

Overhage, Carl. *One-day Walks in the Pecos Wilderness.* Santa Fe, N.M.: Sunstone Press, 1980.

———. *Day Hikes in the Santa Fe Area,* 4th ed. Santa Fe, N.M.: The Santa Fe Group of the Sierra Club.

———. *Pecos Wilderness Trail Guide.* Albuquerque, N.M.: Santa Fe National Forest, Southwest Natural and Cultural Heritage Association, 1991.

The Albuquerque Area:

Hill, Mike. *Hikers and Climbers Guide to the Sandias,* 2d ed. Albuquerque, N.M.: University of New Mexico Press, 1993.

Appendix F: Other Reading and Bibliography (continued)

Matthews, Kay. *Hiking Trails of the Sandia and Manzano Mountains,* 3rd ed., rev. Chamisal, N.M.: Acequia Madre Press, 1995.

———. *The Visitors Guide to the Sandia Mountains.* Albuquerque, N.M.: Southwest Natural and Cultural Heritage Association, 1994.

Southern New Mexico:
Kurtz, Don, and William D. Goran. *Trails of the Guadalupes: A Hiker's Guide to the Trails of Guadalupe Mountains National Park.* Champaign, Ill.: Environmental Associates, 1982.

Magee, Greg S. *A Hiking Guide to Doña Ana County.* Las Cruces, N.M.: Naturescapes, 1989.

Murray, John. *The Gila Wilderness: A Hiking Guide.* Albuquerque, N.M.: University of New Mexico Press, 1988.

Schneider, Bill. *Hiking Carlsbad Caverns and Guadalupe Mountains National Parks.* Helena, Mont.: Falcon Press Publishing Company, 1996.

Western New Mexico:
Robinson, Sherry. *El Malpais, Mount Taylor, and the Zuni Mountains: A Hiking Guide and History.* Albuquerque, N.M.: University of New Mexico Press: 1994.

Northwestern New Mexico:
Hinchman, Sandra. *Chaco Back Country Trails.* Chaco Culture National Historical Park: Southwest Parks and Monuments Association.

———. *Hiking the Southwest's Canyon Country.* Seattle, Wash.: The Mountaineers Books, 1990.

NATURAL HISTORY GUIDES
Chronic, Halka. *The Roadside Geology of New Mexico.* Missoula, Mont.: Mountain Press Publishing Company, 1987.

Fish, Jim, ed. *Wildlands: New Mexico BLM Wilderness Coalition Statewide Proposal,* 1987.

Ivey, Robert DeWitt. *Flowering Plants of New Mexico.* Albuquerque, N.M.: Robert DeWitt Ivey, 1995.

MacCarter, Jane S. *New Mexico Wildlife Viewing Guide.* Helena, Mont.: Falcon Books, 1994.

Mitchell, James R. *Gem Trails of New Mexico.* Baldwin Park, Calif.: Gem Guides Book Company, 1996.

Northrup, Stuart A. *Minerals of New Mexico.* Albuquerque, N.M.: University of New Mexico Press, 1996.

CULTURAL HISTORY GUIDES
Chilton, Lance, et al. *New Mexico: A New Guide to the Colorful State.* Albuquerque, N.M.: University of New Mexico Press, 1984.

Christiansen, Paige, and Frank Kottlowski. *Mosaic of New Mexico's Scenery, Rocks, and History.* Socorro, N.M.: Bureau of Mines and Mineral Resources, 1972.

Fugate, Francis L., and Roberta B. Fugate. *Roadside History of New Mexico.* Missoula, Mont.: Mountain Press Publishing Company, 1989.

Horgan, Paul. *Great River.* Austin, Tex.: Texas Monthly Press, 1984.

Julyan, Robert. *The Place Names of New Mexico.* Albuquerque, N.M.: University of New Mexico Press, 1996.

Sherman, James E., and Barbara H. Sherman. *Ghost Towns and Mining Camps of New Mexico.* Norman, Okla.: University of Oklahoma Press, 1975.

Simmons, Marc. *New Mexico: An Interpretive History.* Albuquerque, N.M.: University of New Mexico Press, 1988.

Williams, Jerry L., ed. *New Mexico in Maps,* 2d ed. Albuquerque, N.M.: University of New Mexico Press, 1986.

Young, John V. *The State Parks of New Mexico.* Albuquerque, N.M.: University of New Mexico Press, 1984.

Appendix F: Other Reading and Bibliography (continued)

MISCELLANEOUS BUT NONETHELESS IMPORTANT REFERENCES

Bryson, Bill. *A Walk in the Woods: Rediscovering America on the Appalachian Trail.* New York: Broadway Books, 1998.

Jardine, Ray. *The Pacific Crest Trail Hiker's Handbook: Innovative Techniques and Trail Tested Instruction for the Long Distance Hiker,* 2d ed. LaPine, Ore.: AdventureLore Press, 1996.

Patterson, David. *Alternative Routes from Mexico to Canada for the Continental Divide Trail.* Redstone, Colo.: White Root Press, 1999.

Ross, Cindy, and Todd Gladfelter. *A Hiker's Companion: 12,000 miles of Trail-tested Wisdom.* Seattle, Wash.: The Mountaineers Books, 1993.

Wilkerson, James, ed. *Medicine for Mountaineering and other Wilderness Activities.* Seattle, Wash.: The Mountaineers Books, 1993.

Appendix G: Glossary of Spanish Words

Azul blue

Agua water

Alamo cottonwood tree

Alto, alta high

Amarillo yellow

Ancho, ancha wide

Angostura narrow

Arroyo eroded, intermittent drainage

Bajada gradual descent, slope

Barranca gorge, ravine, gully, but also hillside

Blanco, blanca white

Boca mouth

Bonita, bonito pretty, attractive

Borrego sheep

Bosque forest, often referring to the thicket of trees bordering a stream or river

Brazo arm, usually referring to branches of a stream or canyon; dim. **brazito**

Caballo horse

Cabra goat

Caja box, often referring to a box or narrow, constricted canyon

Caliente hot, as in a hot spring

Camino road

Canjilon deer antler

Cañada ravine, gulch, canyon

Cañon canyon, gulch; dim. **cañoncito**

Capilla hood, cowl, sometimes a descriptive metaphor for peaks

Capulin chokecherry

Carrizo reed grass

Casa house; dim. **casita**

Cebolla wild onion; dim. **cebolleta**

Cedro juniper

Ceja eyebrow, but usually referring to a fringe, border, or the edge of a cliff or mesa

Cerro hill, but often applied to mountains; dim. **cerrito**

Chamisa a shrub whose English name is rabbitbrush

Chiquito, chiquita small, little

Chivato kid, young goat

Cholla a shrubby, many-branched cactus

Chupadero sinkhole, occasionally a tick

Cobre Copper

Colorado, colorada reddish in color

Conejo rabbit

Corona crown, but also high point or top

Costilla rib, sometimes a metaphor for a ridge or drainage

Crestón hogback

Cuate twin

Cuchillo knife, a descriptive metaphor for a ridge

Cuesta slope, hill, grade

Cueva cave

Cumbre summit

Diablo devil

Diente tooth, spire

Dulce sweet, as in spring water

Embudo funnel, often describing narrow canyons with wide drainage basins; dim. **embudito**

Encina evergreen oak

Escondido, escondida hidden, as in a spring

Florido, florida flowery

Frijoles beans

Frío, fría cold

Gallina chicken, but often referring to gallina de la tierra, or wild turkey

Gigante giant, huge

Gordo, gorda stout, fat

Grande big

Hermano, hermana brother, sister, often referring to closely related landforms

Appendix G: Glossary of Spanish Words (continued)

Hermoso, hermosa handsome, beautiful

Hondo, honda deep, as in a canyon or arroyo

Huerfano orphan, often describing isolated landforms

Indio Indian

Jara scrub willow

Joya basin, valley, hole

Junta junction, confluence

Ladera hillside, slope

Lago lake

Laguna lake; dim. **lagunita**

Largo, larga long

Lindo, linda pretty

Liso, lisa smooth, as of a rock

Llano plain (the noun)

Lobo wolf

Loma hill, typically small; dim. **lomita**

Madera wood

Madre mother

Malpais badland, in New Mexico usually referring to lava flows

Manga sleeve, fringe

Medio, media middle

Mesa table, but also flat-topped landforms; dim. **mesita**

Mina mine

Mogote isolated grove or clump of trees or shrub

Montosa well-wooded, mountainous,

Monte mountain

Morro butte, headland

Nacimiento birth, origin

Negro, negra black

Nogal walnut tree

Norte north

Nuevo, nueva new

Nutria beaver

Ojo spring; dim. **ojito**

Olla earthen water jar, a descriptive metaphor for some landforms

Orilla border, edge, margin

Oro gold

Oscuro, oscura dark, somber

Osha medicinal herb, English name lovage

Oso bear

Padre father, priest

Pajarito little bird

Palo stick

Paloma dove

Pardo, parda gray

Paso pass

Pavo turkey

Pedernal flint

Pedregoso, pedregosa rocky, stony

Pelado bare, hairless

Pelon, pelona bald

Peñasco rocky bluff or spire

Petaca box, metaphor for landforms

Picacho peak

Piedra rock

Pilar pillar

Pinabete spruce

Pino pine

Pintado, pintada painted

Plaza settlement, village; dim. **placita**

Plata silver

Playa beach, dry lake bed

Polvadera dust

Potrero long finger mesa

Potrillo colt

Prieto, prieta dark, black

Pueblo town, in New Mexico used typically for Indian settlements

Puente bridge

Puerco dirty, muddy

Puerta gate

Puerto pass; dim. **puertecito**

Punta point, tip

Quemado, quemada burned

Ratón rodent

Redondo, redonda round

Rincon box canyon, crossroads, corner; adj. **rinconada**

Rio river

Rito stream

Rojo red

Salado salty

Sangre blood

Sarco clear blue

Seco, seca dry

Sierra mountain range, mountain

Sur south

Tecolote owl

Tejón badger

Tetilla small breast, metaphor for landforms

Tierra earth

Truchas trout

Tularosa characterized by reeds

Tusa prairie dog

Uva grape

Vaca cow

Vado ford

Valle valley; dim. **vallecito**

Vega meadow

Venado deer

Verde green

Vermejo brown, auburn

Viejo, vieja old; old man, old woman

Volcán volcano

Yerba herb

Yeso gypsum

Zorro fox

The Continental Divide Trail Alliance
Protecting a Vital National Resource

How can you help?
By becoming a member of the Continental Divide Trail Alliance (CDTA). Your willingness to join thousands of concerned citizens across the country will make the difference. Together, we can provide the financial resources needed to complete the Trail.

CDTA is a nonprofit membership organization formed to help protect, build, maintain, and manage the CDT. CDTA serves a broad-based constituency and includes people who enjoy recreating on public lands, as well as those concerned about overdevelopment.

As a CDTA member, you will:

- Protect a vital and precious natural resource
- Ensure Trail maintenance and completion
- Improve Trail access
- Support informational and educational programs
- Champion volunteer projects
- Advocate for policy issues that support the CDT

What Does It Take to Help Us? Just One Cent a Mile. We realize there are a lot of demands on your time and budget. That's why we're only asking you to give a little—just one cent a mile to support the Trail. For a modest membership fee of $31, you will help us go so very far, and finish what was courageously started so long ago.

For more information
or to send your contribution, write to:
Continental Divide Trail Alliance
P.O. Box 628
Pine, CO 80470
(303) 838-3760
www.cdtrail.org
Please make checks payable to CDTA.

Acknowledgments

I'D LIKE TO THANK THE FOLLOWING PEOPLE FOR THEIR INVALUABLE
CONTRIBUTIONS TO THIS BOOK:

Linda Doyle, Craig Keyzer, Martha Ripley, and Jenna Samelson at Westcliffe Publishers;
Jennifer Blakebrough-Raeburn and Rebecca Finkel; Tom Till, photographer; the AmeriCorps
Program and its volunteers; Lisa Anacleto, former outdoor editor, *Albuquerque Journal,* and
Scott Dunn, outdoor editor, *Albuquerque Journal;* Sandy Baggenstos, Jan Underwood,
and other members of New Mexico Volunteers for the Outdoors; Tom Bombacci of Grants,
NM; Ann Brotman and the other staff members of Recreational Equipment Inc. (REI),
Albuquerque; Emily Drabanski, editor, *New Mexico Magazine;* Bob Gosney of Silver City,
NM; Bob Greenwalt of Mountains and Rivers, Albuquerque; Pat Harris of the Egg Nest,
Hachita, NM; Donald B. Hoffman and Sherry Fairchild, Colorado Springs, CO; Karyn Jilk
and David Patterson, thru-hikers; Joanne Oliver, long-distance hiker, Syracuse, NY; Kathy
Knapp, The Pie-o-Neer, Pie Town, NM; Leave No Trace; Arthur Loy, Patricia Stewart, Allan
Stibora, and Jerrold Widdison, Albuquerque; George Marr, Eldon Reyer, and Sue Steel of
Backcountry Horsemen of New Mexico; Charlie McDonald, Bill and Ruth Stamm, and
the other members of the New Mexico Mountain Club; Kurt Menke of the Earth Data
Analysis Center, University of New Mexico; Mary Wynant, Jessie, Erin, Nate, and the staff
of MAGIC, University of New Mexico; and Mary Stuever and her family, Placitas, NM.

I'M ALSO GRATEFUL TO THE HARDWORKING FOLKS AT GOVERNMENTAL
AND LAND ADMINISTRATIVE AGENCIES: John Barksdale and Brent Botts, U.S. Forest
Service; Martin Frentzel, New Mexico Department of Game and Fish; Ken Mabry, El
Malpais National Monument, and Darwin R. Vallo, National Park Service, El Malpais
National Monument; Roger Payne, Executive Secretary of the U.S. Board on Geographic
Names, Domestic and Foreign Names; Kevin Carson, BLM, Socorro, NM; Mark Hakkila,
BLM, Las Cruces, NM, and Jim Scanlon of Las Cruces, BLM Continental Divide Trail and
wilderness volunteer; Ken Jones, BLM, El Malpais National Monument; Kathy Walter, BLM,
Albuquerque; Mark Catron, formerly of the Cibola National Forest, Mount Taylor Ranger
District, and Arnold Wilson of the Cibola National Forest, Mount Taylor Ranger District;
Jim Christiansen, Gila National Forest, Reserve Ranger District; Dave Harloff, Gila National
Forest, Wilderness Ranger District; Chris Hill and John Pierson, Gila National Forest,
Quemado Ranger Disrict; Jerry Payne, Tim Pohlman, and Dave Warnack, Gila National
Forest, Black Range Ranger District; and Tom Dwyer, Carson National Forest, and Evelyn
Lujan, Carson National Forest, Coyote Ranger District.

SPECIAL THANKS ARE DUE TO: Joseph Gendron, and to his family for sharing him with
me; Carl Smith of Albuquerque; William Stone of Albuquerque; Bruce and Paula Ward and
the Continental Divide Trail Alliance; and finally, my wife, Mary, for her unflagging patience
and understanding.

*A portion of the proceeds from the sale of this book benefits
the Continental Divide Trail Alliance.*

Index

NOTE: Bold citations denote trail descriptions; citations followed by the letter "p" indicate photos; citations followed by the letter "m" indicate maps.

About the Author

Born and raised in Colorado, author and lecturer **BOB JULYAN** has lived in New Mexico for 20 years and hiked every corner of the state. He holds a master's degree in Natural Resources Conservation from Cornell University and is well-known as a writer and conservationist. In addition to writing about hiking and the outdoors for the Albuquerque Journal, Julyan has written *Best Hikes with Children in New Mexico, The Place Names of New Mexico,* and *New Mexico's Wilderness Areas: The Complete Guide.*

About the Photographers

TOM TILL has photographed landscape, nature, history, and travel subjects in all 50 states and on six continents. His images have appeared in many books, including *Along New Mexico's Continental Divide Trail, Utah: Then & Now,* and *New Mexico's Wilderness Areas: The Complete Guide,* all from Westcliffe Publishers. The Tom Till Gallery in Moab, Utah, features his fine art prints. Till lives in Moab with his wife, Marcy, and children, Mikenna and Bryce, near the Behind-the-Rocks Wilderness.

WILLIAM STONE enjoys photographing the landscapes and ancient cultural sites of the Southwest. He recently contributed to *Along New Mexico's Continental Divide Trail* from Westcliffe Publishers. His photographs have been printed in a variety of publications and are available as fine art prints through www.williamstonephoto.com. He supports a number of environmental organizations through his work. Stone and his wife, Carolyn, live in Albuquerque in the shadow of the Sandia Mountains.